THE FATE OF CARMEN

Parallax Re-visions
of Culture and Society

STEPHEN G. NICHOLS

GERALD PRINCE

WENDY STEINER

Series Editors

Evlyn Gould

THE FATE OF CARMEN

The Johns Hopkins University Press
Baltimore & London

05 04 03 02 01 00 99 98 97 96   5 4 3 2 1

The Johns Hopkins University Press
2715 North Charles Street
Baltimore, Maryland 21218-4319
The Johns Hopkins Press Ltd., London

ISBN 0-8018-5366-4
ISBN 0-8018-5367-2 (pbk.)

Library of Congress Cataloging-in-Publication
Data will be found at the end of this book.

A catalog record for this book is available from
the British Library.

To Hap

Contents

Acknowledgments

I WOULD LIKE to acknowledge the National Endowment for the Humanities, the Oregon Council for the Humanities, the University of Oregon Humanities Center, and the Office of Research and Sponsored Programs on the University of Oregon campus for their support for much of the research for this manuscript.

My thanks also extend to Bertrand Augst, Leo Bersani, and Linda Orr for their encouragement of the project during the early stages of its conception; to Marian Smith for her reading of my work on Bizet's *Carmen*, for her superb partnership as a colecturer on Wagner and the "Wagner effect," and for the many helpful discussions about opera in general; to George Sheridan and the students and faculty at the University of Oregon who helped support a collaborative pedagogical project entitled "The Idea of Europe," which has had something to do with shaping this work on *Carmen;* to Elisabeth Lyon and Scott Bryson for their insights and their enthusiasm; to Maria Bertetti for the many conversations; to Marie-Claire Morellec and Craig Wiebe for their help in the preparation of the bibliography and for work editing the manuscript and notes. I am indebted as well to many of my graduate and undergraduate students for participating in discussions relevant to Bohemia and to Carmen's fate;

and to Risa Haberman, Rosemary Dane, and Curtis Salgado and the Stilettos for inviting the "aliveness" at stake in *The Fate of Carmen.*

Finally, I am grateful to my husband, Henry Ponedel, without whom the finishing of any work at all would be unthinkable; to my sons, Benjamin and Jesse, who bring continual new sources of light and energy into our lives; and to my parents, Phyllis and Murray Gould, for giving me the gift of life and the desire to "exceed my grasp." Last, I want to express my warmest regards to Robert Hirsch (one of those high school French teachers most people only dream about) for being the first to inspire visions of *Carmen* in me.

In memory of Jerry Garcia (1942–95), I add only "Vive la bohème!"

THE FATE OF CARMEN

⚜ Introduction

Reading *Carmen*

CARMEN, the tragic story of a fascinating bohemian, continues to lure artists and audiences alike since its original appearance in Prosper Mérimée's novella of 1845. Repeatedly reworked in musical, choreographic, and cinematographic art forms, readings of *Carmen* have produced versions as varied as Georges Bizet's opera (1874); the films of Cecil B. DeMille (1915), Charlie Chaplin (1916), Ernst Lubitsch (1918), and the Marx Brothers (1929); the ballets of Roland Petit and Maya Pliset-skaya (1949); Otto Preminger's film of the musical comedy, *Carmen Jones* (1954); Peter Brook's theater pieces (1981) and subsequent films (1983) titled *La Tragédie de Carmen*; Jean-Luc Godard's film, *Prénom: Carmen* (1983); Francesco Rosi's *Carmen* film (1983); Zeffirelli's sumptuous stage production (1984); Carlos Saura's film version of Antonio Gades's ballet *Carmen* (1983); and, quite recently, the performance art film by Laurie Anderson (1993).

This high-profile-only list avoids mention of the hundreds of *Carmen Fantasies* (on the order of Pablo de Sarasate's) catalogued at the Bibliothèque Nationale, the myriad of very contemporary and original performances of *Carmen* on stage, in jazz and in rock 'n' roll, by the porno industry, lesbian subculture, the Gypsy Folklore Society, and so on.[1] As this ongoing proliferation of new versions of *Carmen* presents an ideal

I

opportunity to study relationships between literature and the performing arts. *The Fate of Carmen* investigates these relationships, exploring in
particular how and why certain literary texts appear to renew their own
textual practices in modes of expression which are not uniquely verbal
and, therefore, not confined to any one national tradition.

Like the *Faust* and the *Don Juan* stories before it, *Carmen* has often
been called a "modern myth," a reverse Don Juan tradition in Western
culture, whose leading character offers a very compelling image of the
kind of fascination her story exerts.[2] That is, there is something essentially self-conscious or self-reflexive about Carmen in that she, the character, is like the story that presents her: ambivalent, fickle, impossible to
pin down, and hard to read. Without minimizing the significance of the
popularity of the modern myth idea, this study focuses on three versions
of *Carmen* and, by placing them in a framework defined by the ambiguities of the "bohemian community," for which Carmen is the most
eloquent of spokeswomen, considers their repeated reappropriation of
Mérimée's self-aware writing strategies into different art forms.

The versions of *Carmen* examined include Mérimée's novella, because
it, after Pushkin's epic poem "The Gypsies," forms the source of all of
the *Carmen*s and presents a highly convoluted and politically ambiguous
narrative structure;[3] Bizet's opera, because it tames Mérimée's story to
render it palatable to bourgeois audiences while reproducing, musically,
verbally, and scenographically the political ambiguities of its writing
strategies; Saura's film, because it openly acknowledges a narrative debt
to Mérimée, readapting his open interrogation into the nature of narrative to the mobile media of film and of dance in its cinematographic presentation of Antonio Gades's flamenco ballet. Each of these versions
shares a self-conscious attention to the question of reading *Carmen*, and
they all juxtapose genres, disciplines, or art forms in order to encourage
a similar self-awareness in their readers, listeners, and spectators. Just as
Mérimée's readers must negotiate a clash between history and literature,
historical chronicle and novel writing, Bizet's must negotiate the disruption of music by dramatic dialogue and Saura's the discrepancies between
the exigencies of film and performance art.

These three versions, taken together, are sufficient to demonstrate the constitution of what I like to call a bohemian community, an "imagined community" created as an effect of reading. Unlike Benedict Anderson's "imagined communities of nations," forged by the overwhelming power of print capitalism to unite peoples, the bohemian community is a community of "readers" (or of "readerly" listeners and performers) ready to be critical of and even to lobby against the unspoken pressures on the formation of identity necessary to Anderson's sense of *thinking* of oneself as part of a larger community.[4] By this I mean not only that Bohemia and its "counterculturalism" supposes a community bent on remaining consciously attentive to the ways that print capitalism or, more recently, pop culture participate in the forging of national and cultural identities and identifications but also that it is a way of dramatizing and performing ambivalence about social identity itself. In this, Bohemia is only a potential and infinitely malleable community, sometimes called an "artistic" community, which functions as both a poetic by-product and an energetic generator of the kinds of textual strategies and self-aware attention to the effects of reading which we see in Mérimée's and in subsequent versions of *Carmen*.

The case of *Carmen* is of course not unique. In fact, by placing *Carmen* in the context of *Faust* or *Don Juan* early on—I might also have suggested the more contemporary example of *The Afternoon of a Faun*—I am already supposing a kind of ongoing give-and-take between forms of literature which program their own renewability and readers who readapt them, creating yet more forms that program their renewability, ad infinitum. In chapter 1 I suggest a model for the kind of balancing of "social" and "literary" effects typical of Bohemia in the prose poems of Charles Baudelaire and Arthur Rimbaud. Following the example of what Ross Chambers has labeled "oppositional narrative," I coin the expression "bohemian narrative" to account both for the possible social effects of those prose poems—namely, the reconstitution of bohemian behaviors, values, and lifestyles—and, more generally, for narrative behaviors whose performance requires the regeneration of idealized future communities through acts of rereading and rewriting. Although readers of Baudelaire or Rimbaud lead us directly into the heart of modern manifestations of Bohemia, their numbers are much too great to circumscribe.

Readers of *Carmen*, on the other hand, can be conjugated in such a way as to constitute an ideal case study of this forming of a "bohemian" readership.

In addition to accounting for the renewability of certain kinds of writing strategies, however, I also coin the expression "bohemian narrative" in order to suggest, after Jerrold Seigel's *Bohemian Paris*, that, as a dramatization of bourgeois social identity, we can locate in Bohemia a nineteenth-century source of current preoccupations with cultural identity growing out of the French Revolution and continuing through the twentieth century to produce both actual and virtual instances of bohemian behavior.[5] By that I mean that, alongside the various "countercultural" lifestyles such as those of the Beats, the Yippies, the Hippies, and the Punks, there is also a variety of contemporary "armchair" manifestations of bourgeois cultural ambivalence which are bohemian in nature: the desire to imagine the diversity of a European *cultural* community, for example, and the "culture wars" of the American academy.[6] By associating the aesthetic history of countercultural sensibility with the larger phenomenon of post-Enlightenment bourgeois cultural identity, my objective is to argue that, because this bohemian sensibility is produced by the very dominant ideology it appears to counter, it reproduces itself in ambivalent and anarchical narratives, such as *Carmen*, which are particularly well suited to appropriation by the performing arts. In this regard it is not the story of *Carmen* which is responsible for its ongoing renewability but, rather, the kinds of narrative behaviors it occasions among readers.

Within the context of Bohemia or outside it, surprisingly few scholars have endeavored to discover what may be responsible for *Carmen*'s renewability, though most believe that it is Carmen herself—"La diablesse aux pieds légers" (Ollier 116) [the light-footed devil], "la Gitane révoltée" (Clément 104) [the Gypsy rebel]. Those who do undertake comparative studies of different versions of *Carmen* continue to describe variations in the adaptation of characters, plots, and themes or to situate the origins of renewability in the opera.[7] To date, no one has traced in them the repeated refashioning of Mérimée's textual strategies by artists working in different art forms; no one has compared them in light of the formal and, indeed, revolutionary reading effects Mérimée's *Carmen* put into practice on the eve of 1848.

To understand fully the revolutionary force of these strategies and effects, I argue in chapter 2 that one must consider Mérimée's *Carmen* to be an exploration into the aesthetic problems confronted by the writer of history, that writer who sets out to relate objective, impersonal facts about the past but whose objectivity is undermined by personal fascinations and choices. As of 1847, the novella presents itself as a historical study whose four chapters conform to what Hayden White has identified, in *Metahistory*, as the four phases of nineteenth-century historiography: research, chronicle, emplotment, and evaluation.[8]

In the first two chapters the narrative voice is that of a historian who travels to Spain to research Caesar's last battle. Though this research forms the narrative frame of the story and establishes the supposed objectivity—and trustworthiness—of the historian, it also takes a detour when the historian begins to chronicle his personal encounters with Don José (chap. 1) and then with Carmen (chap. 2), and becomes fascinated with their bohemian lifestyles. In chapter 3 the historian listens as José takes over the narrative voice to tell his own *Carmen* story. This story repeats and "emplots" the historian's chronicle, though it also precedes it chronologically, suggesting that the historian, far from remaining objective or empirical in his research, has in reality identified with José. In other words, alongside the *Carmen* story there is another story about the novelization of history, a story politically sensitive enough in 1845 to have occasioned the addition of a closing chapter in 1847. That addition, chapter 4, is indeed an afterthought, in which the voice of the historian returns, but in an even more scholarly tone, to present a sociological evaluation that warns against the nefarious effects of Bohemia on the moral fabric of modern society (not to mention, of course, the moral fabric of modern narrative and its readers).

When we consider that *Carmen* is set in 1830 but written in 1845–47, when Bohemia is ambiguously associated both with a contestation of the emergence of bourgeois political power in France and with a reinforcement of bourgeois individuality and freedoms (Seigel 22, 120), its confused chronology and mixture of narrators and identities may be said to be at odds with its apparent sociological "message." Although the historian (the *sujet de l'énoncé*) condemns Bohemia, thereby proffering a reactionary and protectionist view of society, a reinforcement of ancien régime politics resistant to change and to foreign influence, the writer of *Carmen* (the *sujet de l'énonciation*) promulgates a more liberal, even revolutionary view of society by engaging his narrative in a game of aesthetic anarchy. By "aesthetic anarchy" I mean those literary aspects of narrative which openly disrupt the intentions of the writer of history, choices about chronology, point of view, value, language, textuality, rhetoric, fiction, and identity. As a result, the historian, who conforms to the conventions of nineteenth-century historiography, suggests a link between narrative conformity and political conformity. But the writer, who creates an aesthetic anarchy, works within the conventions of historical narrative to unmask or revolutionize the ideological presuppositions that underlie that discourse—primarily, the notion that it can be objective or scientific and, therefore, devoid of ideological or political force.

In his pitting of the historian's conventionality against the anarchy of a writer whose moves transform a search for truth into the ambivalent effects of reading and interpretation, Mérimée also offers a subtle presentation of Bohemia as a phenomenon of bourgeois duplicity and ambiguity. The bohemian lifestyle is, after all, associated with both the stalwart bourgeois, José, a "traveler like me," and the Gypsy Carmen, a "Moorish, or . . . I caught myself, not daring to say: Jewish" woman.[9] In its initially ambiguous designation of the ultimately very separate cultural worlds of the two protagonists of *Carmen*, Mérimée's portrait of Bohemia anticipates the line of thought presented in Seigel's history of Bohemia, as I already suggested, and refines our interpretation of the "Carmen myth" as either a reversal or a passive agent of the values of Western culture and sexuality. Like Seigel's Bohemia, *Carmen* neither reverses nor promotes these values but rather dramatizes their ambivalence.

In his opera *Carmen*, Georges Bizet relies upon a similar aesthetic anarchy to disrupt the conventions of the French comic opera and to restage the bourgeoisie's ambivalence about Bohemia. He does this through the confrontation of a politically tamed libretto (by Meilhac and Halévy) and a revolutionary, or at least oppositional, score. Though there are many

ways in which the Carmen story is tamed, most notable are that Mérimée's thieves and prostitutes have become carefree bohemians and that
the libretto adapts only the third chapter of the novella, José's story,
thereby eliminating its convoluted narrative.

The anarchical force of the composition is sustained, however, in
Bizet's formal innovations in the opera: his particular use of a mixture of
song and dialogue to highlight a conflict between words and music in the
opera (some saw in it the hope of an entirely original French comic-
opera dashed by Bizet's premature demise); his interweaving of popular
Spanish dance rhythms based on overtly sexual cabaret songs such as "El
Arreglito," the model for the "Habañera," into an otherwise conventional comic-opera framework; his use of linguistic, scenographic, and
orchestral cues or motives to create a double or conflicted or, once again,
ambivalent narrative pulled between liberty or abandon (pleasure, or
jouissance) and self-control or self-consciousness (mastery, or *maîtrise*).
In chapter 3 I demonstrate how this operatically self-conscious attention
to the narrative of bourgeois ambivalence is encapsulated in the "Bohemian Song" that opens *Carmen*'s act 2 in which the narrative associated
with the protagonists Carmen and José and with the larger communities
with which they identify (Bohemia and the imperial military establishment) are linked to the affective behaviors of opera listeners. Pleasure
and self-control come to describe the concerns of the Carmen/José narrative as well as the activity of the listener required by Bizet's comic-
opera form.

Within the specific political imperatives of operatic representation in
post-Communard Paris, I put Bizet's self-conscious attention to narrative in opera in context by setting his originally "light," or comic, opera
against the heavy redemptive operatic sound of Wagner, whose effects
on Parisian audiences in the 1860s, and among them Bizet, was so dramatic as to change the course of French lyric poetry and drama in
general. By way of the receptions of Baudelaire and Nietzsche and of
the more recent work of Carolyn Abbate on operatic narrative and
Philippe Lacoue-Labarthe on the "Wagner effect," I argue that the self-
consciousness of Bizet's *Carmen* counters the hypnotic effects of Wagnerian opera and, more generally, of nationalist ideology promulgated
by grand opera as a genre and as an institution. Mimicking the problem-

atic juxtaposition of literature and history in Mérimée's novella, Bizet's opera realizes this counterattack, or what Jane Fulcher has dubbed "operatic opposition politics," through its jarring confrontation of music and dramatic dialogue.[10] Ironically, it is because Bizet is considered a "wagnériste," or "Wagnerite," that his work becomes a meditative oppositional act.

Carlos Saura's reappropriation of both aesthetic anarchy and bourgeois ambivalence in his film *Carmen* rewrites Mérimée's convoluted narrative into the modern-day story of a Spanish choreographer's reconception of *Carmen* in a new flamenco dance version. Therefore, in my final chapter I argue that, just as Mérimée investigates the aesthetic politics of historical narrative by pitting a historian against a writer who unmasks him, and Bizet, those of operatic narrative by creating a jarring contrast between music and spoken dialogue, Saura investigates those of choreographic and film narrative by pitting the story of a choreographer against film and mental moves that intentionally confuse the life of that choreographer with the life of the characters in his ballet. This third reiteration of the double narrative created by a distinction between the life of the choreographer and the life of the characters provides an obvious rereading of Mérimée's novella, in that José's *Carmen* story is appropriated as the subject of the new ballet (as it is in Bizet's opera), while the historian's *Carmen* story becomes a love story played out between the choreographer himself and his lead dancer, Carmen. Since the choreographer identifies with both Don José and the historian of the novella, the two *Carmen* stories become mixed and confused, highlighting an ambivalence about bourgeois identity which bears upon both what Marvin D'Lugo refers to as the "cultural imprints" of Spanish nationalism and the advent of a bohemian "boom" in post-Franco Spain which would enact an ambiguous social reaction to that imprinting of national identity.

As in Bizet's opera, this double narrative is repeated textually at both acoustic and visual levels of the film. Visually, the duplicity is maintained through constant glances into the mirror and by means of a shifting between imaginary and real performance spaces. Acoustically, it is maintained by means of a distinction between, on one hand, voice off and voice on and, on the other, a recorded version of Bizet's score which dramatically confronts the re-Hispanicization of the score by Paco de

Lucia and his classical guitar. Whereas the playing of the recorded version of the opera becomes associated with literature, with the graphic arts of the nineteenth century, and with the choreographer's silent off-screen thoughts, Paco's on-screen guitar playing becomes associated with bodies, with flamenco dancing, and with the characters in the ballet. In this way operatic voice in the film accompanies the movement of creative thought, while the rhythms of the Spanish guitar accompany body movements. And, while the former consciously seeks to engage the mind in a narrative of choreographic creativity, the latter openly dislocates both narrative and psychological logics in a play of aesthetic anarchy.

In addition to reiterating the anarchical textual strategies and self-conscious reading effects of Mérimée's original narrative, Saura's film opens back onto the question of Anderson's imagined communities by suggesting that the intercultural traditions of the contemporary flamenco performance art community in Spain—represented notably in the *Carmen* film by Antonio Gades and Paco de Lucia—may offer a renewed version of Bohemia as a paradigm for modern European cultural identity. This association becomes particularly striking when we consider that the film—more popular in greater Europe than in Spain itself—was made during the height of Spain's negotiations in the 1980s to enter the European Economic Community. As is the case for each of the recent *Carmen* films, the backdrop for Saura's is the still-hard-to-define notion of a greater European identity and of a particularly elusive European cultural community given the progressively more draconian restrictions on immigration to Europe during the 1980s.

In Saura's *Carmen*, however, the film's intermixing of classical European and flamenco performing arts traditions points to the inevitable reconsideration of a "Europe métèque," a patchwork European identity made of "outsiders" and "insiders" and woven together over generations of cross-cultural fertilization. It further suggests that this kind of intermingling of cultural identities may be best reimagined as a performance community, a potentially bohemian audience that European performing artists are actively seeking to form through their theater pieces and festivals. As the theater scholar Antonio Attisani points out, "The theater is no longer a spectacle in our society, for it is the less spectacular, the less informative means of communication that we possess. What we must now try to create is a community, a social audience. . . . now I go to the theater because I understand that I belong to its audience, that by being in that community I lend meaning to the work on stage."[11] Saura's film explores this relationship between audience and community as it records, in film, the ways that spectators lend meaning to works on stage.

This very question of a greater European community is, however, already at the heart of Mérimée's *Carmen*. That *Carmen*'s narrator addresses the chronicle of his travel memoirs to "toute l'Europe savante" (609) [all of educated Europe] recalls that the world of this bohemian narrative caught between two sets of formal, moral, and cultural imperatives is not unlike that of cosmopolitan Europe both now and then. By that I mean both "then," at the time *Carmen* was composed and published, in 1845–47, and "now," during the 1980s, when *Carmen* was so prolifically rewritten. Then, we should recall a Europe caught between, on one hand, the idealistic dreams of a youthful Romantic nationalism, best expressed by Giuseppe Mazzini and best lived in the pan-European youth groups of 1830 and 1848, and, on the other, the stodgy resistance to change of a modern bourgeoisie sympathetic to imperial ideology but also decidedly pan-European in nature. In France these not-so-clearly opposed positions were largely represented by the two bourgeois political groupings that grew out of the compromised government of Louis Philippe's "bourgeois monarchy" in 1830: the Party of Movement and the Party of Resistance (Seigel 7). Yet, despite the fact that the bourgeoisie was more politically powerful in France than in the rest of Europe, the duplicity within the bourgeoisie suggested by these two parties is representative of an equally unclear social division between bohemians and bourgeois which was a general characteristic of a cosmopolitan Europe (22).

Prior to the 1830s, in fact, it seems that the modern middle class was conceived as the solution to the bohemian promise of unrestricted social, psychosexual, and national mobility. In George Sand's *La Dernière Aldini*, for example, it is in the social-utopian space of Bohemia that nobles and peasants, Italian, French, and Eastern Europeans commune.[12] In this light it is noteworthy that the 1 October issue of the rather conservative *La Revue des Deux Mondes*, in which Mérimée's novella first appeared, was decidedly pan-European in flavor, with articles on Belgium, on Germany, on recent political events in France, and on Mérimée's Spain.[13] In fact, the title of the journal, *Review of the Two Worlds*, is itself revealing where the sense of a tension between two cultural landscapes is concerned. With respect to a "second world," the First World felt itself to be more united and more culturally "European" than ever.

Now, by which I mean in a Europe on the eve of 1989, we should sense behind the many remakes of *Carmen* a European culture aligned and "united" because pulled between the tensions of two superpowers and, unable to accept the one or the other, forging a new imaginary community of its own.[14] Indeed, the repeatedly renewed interest in *Carmen* and the resurgence as of 1983 of a plethora of rereadings of the tale on film and on the stage may have less to do with what one critic, representative of a whole generation of critics, has called an "assault against emancipated women" at a time of "renewed feminist activity" (Robinson 147–48 n. 7) and more to do with attempts to envision a new Europe or to further pan-European thinking in direct response to destructive nationalisms and attendant concerns regarding immigrants and their free movement (that bohemian "roving") across national borders. Though the number of immigrants and asylum seekers has more than tripled since 1983, as John Pomfret writes, "many Europeans still think of their countries as the home of a single ethnic group, language, and culture. In Germany, France, and a half-dozen other countries, the mass wave of immigrants has prompted profound debate about national identity and the values of diversity."[15] Clearly, there has been less and less "renewed feminist activity" in France and Spain during the 1980s and 1990s, but, in the period during which Spain sought to negotiate its entrance into the European Economic Community, there were very significant political attempts to pass severe legislation designed to curtail immigration and the movement of foreign nationals as well as a rising mistrust of Gypsies and foreigners.[16]

In *The Community of Europe: A History of European Integration since 1945* Derek W. Urwin notes the importance of the great push forward toward European unity during the early 1980s, thanks to the leadership of the French activist and visionary Jacques Delors (183), and suggests that, during this time in France, Britain, and Spain, the European Community (EC) was the news of the day. He also notes that, whereas in 1981 "there were few dissenters from the view that EC membership would strengthen the young Spanish democracy," by 1983 Giscard d'Estaing had dashed this hope, so that the new Socialist premier of Spain, Felipe González, encouraged Spain's participation in the EC in 1983 despite "an increasing resentment and anti-EC mood among the Spanish electorate" (209–10). It is striking to note that political relations between Spain and France in this context are just as shifting or problematic as the boundaries of the *Carmen* narrative. More important, for Brook, Godard, Gades, and Saura, the *Carmen* compositions parallel turbulent times for Spain's and France's relations to the EC. As for the Italians, Rosi and Zeffirelli, a widespread inquiry, at the time, into the nature of a "Mediterranean," or "Southern," Europe also linked the question of immigrants and of migrant laborers to the national concerns of Spain, Italy, and Greece (180). In general, then, the 1980s represented a period of great hopefulness destined to culminate magnificently in a utopian union of 1992. Yet 1989 ushered in a new mood in Europe which would reshape the cultural, political, economic, and social debates, finally rendering a European cultural community more imaginary than ever.

In relation to this backdrop, an essential distinction must be maintained between the *Carmen*s of the 1980s composed by men during the height of EC hopefulness and controversy—Jean-Luc Godard, Antonio Gades, Carlos Saura, Francesco Rosi, Peter Brook, and Franco Zeffirelli—and the critical analyses of those 1983–84 *Carmen*s undertaken largely by women (with some exceptions noted, of course) who are, on the whole, directly aligned with the revisionist feminist perspectives of American academics. To date, critical analyses of those 1983–84 *Carmen*s are concerned mainly with uncovering the nineteenth-century misogynistic imagination that confuses race, gender, and social class in *Carmen* or, in a parallel gesture, singing the joys of liberty and equality which Carmen can represent.[17] As a result, new comparative studies of Mérimée's, Bizet's, and the 1983–84 *Carmen*s—still only in the works and being produced and printed as I write—tend to focus either on their musical debt to Bizet's brilliant and popular score or on what is often called the "myth of Carmen" herself, the "bad-girl narrative" about a woman who, like the goddess Diana, to whom Mérimée compares her, is so disruptive of phallocentric subjectivity that she must be destroyed.

These discussions do not, as a rule, speculate about the EC nor about the pan-European roots of the original *Carmen* tale. Neither do they attend to the peculiar formal and generic constraints of Mérimée's *Carmen* which work to retrieve the tensions of a greater European cultural identity.[18] Though the feminist critique undoubtedly has a great deal to offer the more general sense of difference and "otherness" accommodated by the idea of a European cultural community, it has not sought to consider this sort of larger cultural context.

Reviving the early, important work of Mina Curtiss and Winton Dean on Georges Bizet, as well as Catherine Clément's discussion of the place of women in opera, Susan McClary's work is the most thorough revisionist scholarship on the *Carmen* phenomenon today.[19] In her endeavor to uncover the heretofore unrecognized aspects of a musical discourse that is culturally and sexually determined and determining, McClary also provides the most noteworthy example of both of the recent tendencies in *Carmen* studies: focus on the musical debt and focus on the bad-girl myth. Defining her perspective in both her Cambridge opera handbook and *Feminine Endings* as one that is designed to study the music and its effects, McClary concentrates most of her energies on the opera and its legacy. For this reason her only passing attention to the literary origins of the *Carmen* phenomenon is evident. Most of the discussion of the opera's literary origins is limited to an opening piece in the handbook by Peter Robinson which underscores the nineteenth-century sexual dynamics of narrative in Mérimée's text.

Any discussion of *Carmen*'s legacy is likewise limited by musical parameters, in that McClary explores only examples of modern *Carmen*s that borrow Bizet's score. As a result, Godard's *Prénom: Carmen* is simply dismissed, despite its formal, rather than thematic, similarity to both the comic-opera and the novella. As McClary puts it, this is because the film is unrelated to the music or because "Godard tries to distance the story from Bizet's music by counterposing Beethoven quartets to the action" (*Bizet*, 155). In my opinion, though Godard's film does not use Bizet's score, its unique counterposing of dramatic dialogue and quartets complements the diegetic splicing of shots of ocean waves into the action of the narrative and can only be explained by its renewal, for the modern spectator, of the formal effects of Bizet's original comic-opera form. But this form is itself a renewal of Mérimée's fundamentally formal antagonisms cast in what Wayne Koestenbaum has called opera's "queer marriage" of music and words.[20] In short, I would argue that some of Bizet's legacy is lost because of an inattentiveness to the effects of its literary model on nineteenth-century readers.

It would be unfair, however, to characterize McClary's study as having given no weight to the formal dimensions of that model. McClary does speak of the importance of the comic-opera form (*Bizet*, 44–47) and of "its extensive restructuring of Mérimée's original narrative strategy," even if she does not concentrate on the lengthy passages from Mérimée's *Carmen* which reappear in the original libretto (*Feminine Endings*, 56). And, in his introduction to McClary's cultural analysis of the music, Robinson's piece does attend to the formal structural pressures created by the addition, in 1847, of *Carmen*'s fourth chapter, even if Robinson uses this detailing of form, predictably if effectively, to serve the "materialist" and anti-phallocentrist-race-class-gender point of view. He points out, for example, that, just as Don José masters and silences Carmen's body, the narrator of the tale must master and silence her language in the tardive fourth chapter (13–14).

As a tale of continual control and manipulation of women by men, Robinson's reading of *Carmen* puts a contemporary twist on the traditional understanding of *Carmen* as a femme fatale, but it also puts a rather more one-sided slant on Nietzsche's sense that *Carmen* is about the battle, indeed, the hatred, between the sexes: "The battle that really interests this text," according to Robinson, "is the battle between the sexes. From the very beginning, Woman is marked as the enemy." This perspective explains why the story opens on what Robinson calls an "uncannily feminine landscape": a "spot of moisture," a "natural space" to be penetrated by the narrator (4). Although the study of the relevance of Mérimée's opening landscapes to the future dynamics of his stories has proven to be a fruitful way of underscoring the skills of the storyteller,[21] this kind of analysis accentuates the unconscious effects of a misogynistic cultural apparatus on Mérimée as a representative nineteenth-century male writer, but it minimizes what I take to be the really potent moral dilemmas and intense identity crises that Mérimée's narrator experiences in his encounter with the disturbing anarchy of Carmen's Bohemia.

Again, I am less interested in being for or against the potentially misogynistic aspect of Mérimée's *Carmen* than in the formal tensions that allow for mutually exclusive readings: Is Carmen a dangerous femme fatale, or is she one of Elaine Showalter's liberated "New Women"?

The tense ambiguities that grow out of the Carmen character herself are taken up by other critics in various ways. Mary Blackwood Collier looks at the mythic proportions of the Carmen character as a figure of rebellion and of Satanism. For Collier it is Carmen as a literary myth which passes from work to work.[22] McClary herself, though almost always coming down understandably on the side of the sexually and racially oppressive, points out that *Carmen* would not have been so enduringly popular had it not played into "some of the most agonizing contradictions of Western culture" (*Feminine Endings*, 63, 65–66). Nelly Furman studies the *Carmen* libretto and deconstructs the internal duplicity of the character, "Carmen ou la Carmencita," compelling us, in the 1990s, to consider from Carmen's point of view a story that has always been told uniquely as José's. In so doing, she draws our attention to the opera libretto as a site not so much of sexual incompatibility but of sexual and psychological undecidedness.[23]

Reading *Carmen* deconstructively, Furman's discussion also opens onto the latent "feminist" aspects of the *Carmen* story and, in this regard, appears to respond, as does McClary's, to Catherine Clément's *L'Opéra ou la défaite des femmes* (*Opera, or the Undoing of Women*), in which we read an effusive ode to "my friend," Carmen. Similarly, Laurie Anderson's recent short video, which fits into the larger performance art event *A Conversation with Laurie Anderson,* muses about what might have happened if Carmen had had her own way.[24] As a kind of response to Clément's nostalgic view of tender words exchanged with that toreador who may have been her first true love (104), Anderson pictures Carmen shackled by marriage and children in the decidedly macho, decidedly unliberated household of the once enthralling toreador. All told, however, even these creative, largely feminist, readings have taken the opera, *Carmen,* as their point of departure. This appears to be due in part to Clément's influence and in part to a more general dismantling of the trend in critical inquiry which has privileged the visual over the auditory (a move equated by recent feminist film scholars with a privileging of male subjectivity over female) but also "absolute music" over music drama. As a result, these readers have considered the Mérimée model only peripherally.

From this peripheral perspective most gestures to the model are designed to tell us either how much like the sinister, voluptuous, and satanic Carmen the music really is (Collier; Comettant; Ollier 115)—this because of its dramatic, chromatic, "hip-swinging" halftone descents—or how different from the story are the opera's libretto (and its cultural raison d'être) because of the changes necessitated by the very public requirements of operatic form (Dean 213; McClary, *Feminine Endings*, 56–57). Only Ollier and Robinson consider briefly the public requirements of a novella appearing in *La Revue des Deux Mondes* in 1845 and 1847. With all of this recent attention to the *Carmen* phenomenon, however, no one seems to account for what appear to me to be Mérimée's own very obvious concerns with genre, with form, and with audience in his *Carmen*—his concern, we might say, with avoiding writing merely another bad-girl narrative that, like Prévost's *Manon Lescaut*, could make a really good opera libretto.

In the context of the bohemian landscape I shall sketch in my first chapter, in fact, Mérimée's *Carmen* is situated at an important point of transition in attitudes about Bohemia and the modern middle class. Between, on one hand, the socialist utopian hopefulness of a society without class distinctions promised by early-nineteenth-century conceptions of the bourgeoisie and, on the other, the image of an oppressive cultural prison from which, by the time of Arthur Rimbaud, there is no escape, *Carmen*'s association with both the crime and exploitation of the urban underworld and the rugged sexual and personal liberties of the fictive Gypsy community represented in it make it an ideal setting in which to figure the ambiguous aliveness of the modern middle class.

In relation to the according of only peripheral value both to Mérimée's model and to literature in general, then, I prefer to read Mérimée's work, the curious formal dimensions of the *Carmen* novella, and the social and political parameters of Bohemia in which it is set as the forceful generators of cultural critique rather than as the passive agents of hidden ideological agendas. Therefore, I shall engage a number of literary figures, cultural critics, social scientists, musicologists, and film critics who argue that narrative is not a neutral discursive form merely filled in by a given content, either real (historical) or imaginary (literary), but that it entails ideological, even political, choices distinct from the content for which it is a vehicle.[25] In so doing, *The Fate of Carmen* will ultimately contend that the ambiguous status of Mérimée's *Carmen*, caught somewhere between history and literature, is a precursor to this modern critical argument—that it is already questioning the ideological content of narrative as a form and that subsequent versions of *Carmen* are similarly intent upon disclosing the ideological power of narrative in their respective art forms as they repeatedly dramatize the cultural ambivalence of the modern bourgeoisie. As always, Carmen's fate depends on her readers.

⋊ 1 ⋉ The Imaginary Scenarios of Bohemia

Il m'a souvent semblé que mon plaisir serait d'aller toujours droit devant moi, sans savoir où, sans que personne s'en inquiète, et de voir toujours des pays nouveaux. Je ne suis jamais bien nulle part, et je crois toujours que je serais mieux ailleurs que là où je suis.

BAUDELAIRE, "Vocations"

[It has always seemed to me that my pleasure would be to go ever straight in front of myself, without knowing where, without anyone worrying, and to always see new countries. I have never been comfortable anywhere, and I always believe that I would be better off there where I am not.]

Truckin'—got my chips cashed in
Keep Truckin'—like the doodah man
Together—more or less in line
Just keep Truckin' on
ROBERT HUNTER, *for the Grateful Dead*

IN THE modern imagination "Bohemia" conjures up an image of counterculturalism, or antisystemic behavior, loosely associated with unconventional dress, mind-expanding drugs, long hair, liberated sexual practices, "Dionysian" or antibourgeois art forms, and various modes of political opposition. It is also a transnational phenomenon in that it has been known to link youth cultures around the globe. As Immanuel Wallerstein points out in *Geopolitics and Geoculture,* from the geocultural perspective of contemporary politics we commonly think of the cultural revolution of 1968 as a symbolic highpoint of Bohemia given that, despite its national particularities, the event took place in several different countries and in several different social milieus simultaneously.[1] The same might be said, however, of the greater European bohemian youth movements of 1830 and of 1848: Young Europe, Young Italy, Young Germany, and a group out of which Karl Marx emerged, the Young Hegelians.[2] The apparent singularity of '68 as a cultural phenomenon notwithstanding, then, our more contemporary Bohemia, the "Woodstock nation," inserts itself into the wider perspective of post-Romantic thought as one more manifestation in the continual reenactment of anarchical and ambivalent agitations that first arose following the crisis in political legitimacy wrought by the French Revolution of 1789.[3]

Today it is useful to rethink these cultural reenactments of what Linda Orr has called Louis's "headless revolution" in light of the creation of a European Economic Community and the proliferation among academic thinkers, on both sides of the Atlantic, of cautious reappraisals of what might constitute a European *cultural* community.[4] Indeed, this cultural community may itself be considered "bohemian" in two ways. First, in relation to the universalizing tendencies of Europe's ministries of culture—or what Gianni Vattimo has recently dubbed a "new Christendom" or what Jacques Derrida has referred to as the "imperial tentacles" of a centralized media brain in Brussels—the elusive notion of a European cultural identity may well be seen as one more in a series of academic responses to the symbolic repression of a symbolic regime that Bohemia seeks, repeatedly, to counter.[5] That is, this new or greater European cultural identity is constructed to underscore diversity in the face of a potentially disturbing move toward universality, transnationality instead of the potentially disturbing energies of national affiliations; it is apolitical (or characterized by a certain political plasticity) and, as yet, largely imaginary (i.e., situated uniquely in the imagination of academic and primarily bourgeois thinkers).

Second, this kind of subtle academic agitation on what Wallerstein characterizes as the "battlefield of culture" (166)—in other words, the phenomenon of culture studies itself and, specifically, of multicultural studies—can be understood at least in part as a modern manifestation of the legacy of Bohemia in a kind of contemporary imitation of what also happened in Paris during the mid-nineteenth century. From this perspective, despite the focus in English departments across the United

States on the British working-class roots of the culture studies phenomenon (itself a legacy of the Victorian bohemians of the early twentieth century), agitated concern with reassessing European cultural identity today undoubtedly grows more immediately out of the bohemian politics of the Tel Quel group in Paris in '68 and its ever-expanding population of readers here on our shores.[6]

In Wallerstein's thinking, because the battlefield of culture is, like Bohemia, a way of coming to terms with changes in the capitalist world economy, it remains at a necessary level of "tactical ambivalence" about ideological values (182). According to Wallerstein, this ambivalence derives from definitions of culture itself, among anthropologists, as both the delimiting of one group's characteristics in contrast to those of another (e.g., Asian Americans vs. Native Americans) and the describing of binary distinctions within groups themselves (black/white; male/female) (158–59). This productive confusion about the nature of culture is deliberate, the probable product of a capitalist world economy—if, for the sake of argument, we follow and accept Wallerstein's line of thought—in that it offers continuity in the face of world change while providing for inequities within the system (166).

More useful to my discussion, however, is the way in which this continual splitting into binary groups also offers an image of the self-generating and energetic movement of postmodernism's "double contradictory binds" that can only develop according to a model of nuclear fission. This image of culture echoes the one Derrida outlines in "L'Autre cap," or "The Other Heading," of an always compromised movement toward an "other" or toward a difference of identity within oneself (29). Later taken up in more properly Lacanian terms by Julia Kristeva's idea that we are, culturally speaking, "étrangers à nous-mêmes" [strangers to ourselves], Derrida refers to cultural identity as an essentially alienated, essentially doubled, essentially mobile state that keeps us constantly in transit toward the other of our own headings. This constant transiting between opposing forces has been associated, in other contexts, with Charles Baudelaire's "bohemian erring and roving" by Margaret Miner, with Napoléon III's "conspiratory customs" by Walter Benjamin, and with the nomadic displacements of reterritorialization by Gilles Deleuze and Félix Guattari, suggesting that the ambiguous antisystemic pressures of "culture" continue to be thought in terms associated with Bohemia. Indeed, Bohemia, like Wallerstein's sense of culture, fulfills the liberal dream of universal equality while opposing, in the name of individual liberties, that dream's universalizing thrust toward assimilation. It accounts socially for the "tactical ambivalence" in our understanding of contemporary culture.

What interests me about Bohemia as an image of modern culture, however, is not its capacity to justify the inevitable inequities of the capitalist world system but, rather, the fact that the modes of behavior associated with Bohemia (and, for that matter, with the terms of Wallerstein's culture as battlefield) have been continually reappropriated from the heart of nineteenth-century Western European culture, from the center of the Paris we think of as Europe's capital during what Walter Benjamin calls the "Era of High Capitalism."[7] Indeed, at the center or the heart of the modern bourgeoisie, symbolic resistance has always been present, even constitutive. Nonetheless, due to its constant contrasting of alternative social identities—be it red coats, black berets, or tie-dyes—to conventional behaviors and those now infamous gray business suits, we persist in believing that Bohemia takes shape in opposition to the rise of modern bourgeois culture in the early nineteenth century and, specifically, in Paris, where the bourgeoisie was so politically powerful. Yet Bohemia is better understood as both produced by and reproductive of the very dominant ideology it appears to counter. As Jerrold Seigel presents it in *Bohemian Paris*, Bohemia is first and foremost an expression of cultural ambivalence by and about the bourgeoisie itself, or, in the present context of Wallerstein's culture as battlefield, a bourgeois duplicity about the very notion of culture.[8]

In this larger provocative context it is intriguing to consider what may be the sources of the renewal of that anarchical expression that is Bohemia in response to a call by artists and writers in nineteenth-century Paris to form, among people whose national expression seemed unfulfilled or marginal, "tactically" or ideologically ambivalent cultural communities that remain, to use Benedict Anderson's term, purely imagined. These communities are at once global, or "geocultural," and local. Locally, however, they remain loosely defined by a variety of urban metaphors— Parisian underworld, migrant worker, *carbonari*, student revolutionary, and the even more general "artist"—which take on a variety of local, and shifting, political meanings.

To insist upon the merely *imagined* nature of Bohemia as a cultural community or upon the duplicity of the nature of culture as both a potentially political battlefield and a product of such imaginary bohemian communities is not to argue, however, that these communities did not or do not exist nor that the antisystemic politics at stake in them are not relevant. Rather, to call Bohemia imagined is to insist that Bohemia, as Seigel observes, is primarily a mental landscape, a merely virtual reality in which to dramatize interpretations of social identity (12). Moreover, in attending to what causes the continual renewal of such imagined communities, I propose, further, that the landscapes of Bohemia are perpetuated through a certain mode of self-conscious narrative fiction—I shall call it bohemian narrative—which continues to reenact a splintering of symbolic effects (or voices) of difference from within that already imaginary opposition of social groups: the bohemians and the bourgeois.

What is imagined about Bohemia, in other words, is that it generates cultural distinctions, such as bohemian/bourgeois, on the basis of purely fictitious, discursive, or narrative borders, borders that appear to be motivated largely through identifications with various literary or dramatic images and representations. But, insofar as these imagined bohemian communities are at least tentatively political, in that within their tactical ideological ambivalence they are potentially capable of shifting alliances among their members or observers—and Wallerstein points out that this is especially true during moments of great cultural upheaval (as was the case in 1848, 1968, or 1989)—it is useful to consider their renewal of cultural distinctiveness within sameness as a response to, or reading of, earlier political euphorias once projected by the "raised consciousness" of writers of previous bohemian fictions. In other words, what interests me in these imaginary bohemian scenarios are the ways in which literary fictions have encouraged the imagining of actual communities.

The Bohemians of Paris

Bohemians took their name from a nineteenth-century fantasy version of the country in Eastern Europe and from an only partially informed sense of the cultural community of Gypsies believed to have originated there (Seigel 5). Travel guides and memoirs, and particularly memoirs of travel to Spain (where Gypsies could be studied and illustrated by nineteenth-century ethnographers in their theoretically "natural habitat"), became increasingly popular during the early part of the century.[9] Those who could not travel eagerly awaited at home the regular appearance in their newspapers of engravings and commentary about such faraway places and lives. The actual travels of, for example, Prosper Mérimée (1830), Théophile Gautier (1840), Alexandre Dumas (1846), Gustave Flaubert (1849–51), and the Englishman George Henry Borrow (1841), whose work would popularize research into Gypsy life and culture, allow us to suppose that some of the traits associated with the lifestyle of the Gypsies were based on observation[10]—albeit across wide cultural gaps, since visiting bohemian communities was not unlike going to the "Orient."[11]

In relation to Edward Said's notion of the construction of the Orient as the other of Europe, however, the Bohemia construct situates that other here at home in opposition to the domesticating social identity of the bourgeoisie—here, within Europe, as an ideally nomadic, transnational, unassimilated community, a domestic community remaining nonetheless "foreign" and able to eschew the restricted definitions of national identity. In this, Bohemia models itself on an image that confuses the Gypsy and the Jew as the infamous wandering others of Europe on European soil; they are not quite assimilable with the barbarian or infidel defined most intently during devout moments of medieval religiosity but are almost equally popular images of domestic otherness in the nineteenth-century European imagination. Witness, for example, the serializing of Eugène Sue's *Le Juif errant* (The Wandering Jew) in *Le Constitutionnel* as an effort to increase readership to forty thousand in 1844–45 (Terdiman 300). Such "literary" Jews anticipate Alain Finkelkraut's notion of the "Imaginary Jew" as a figure detached from its cultural imprints and values as well as Jacques Derrida and his "other headings."

The domesticity, or "at-homeness," of Bohemia as a European otherness here on our shores is easily attested to by the production of a myriad of plays about bohemian life both prior to and following the most celebrated of them, Henry Murger's *La Vie de Bohème,* or *Bohemian*

Life, of 1849.[12] Already in 1844, however, and therefore prior to both Murger's popularity and the revolution of '48, which would put the idea of the bohemian at the center of popular consciousness (Seigel 29), Théophile Gautier reviews one of these plays written in 1843, Adolphe D'Ennery and Eugène Grangé's *The Bohemians of Paris.*[13] In his review of the play Gautier dramatizes the agitated tactical ambivalence characteristic of attitudes toward Europe's "other at home" by enlisting a variety of representations for which bohemians are made to account and by turning his review into a social commentary on his own life in Paris in the 1830s. As one of any number of reviews by Gautier, this review takes on the status of a cultural document representative both of the intense popularity of Bohemia among the bourgeois and of the way in which Bohemia always revitalizes a past moment of nostalgia for revolutionary euphoria. In this case it is by way of a fanciful reference to one bohemian's red coat that Gautier's remarks restage his own participation in romanticism's political and aesthetic revolution of 1830 known as "la bataille d'*Hernani.*"[14]

Having set his remarks in the political and aesthetic landscape of 1830, Gautier immediately decries the play's association of bohemians with the Parisian underworld of petty thieves and criminals (a group that, like the Gypsies, had become an urban other and that, also like the Gypsies, was made popular largely because of literary images in the weekly installments of Eugène Sue's *Les Mystères de Paris* which helped to inspire the sets for this play [107]). Then, invoking his own travels in Spain, Gautier sets up a countersuggestive association of bohemians and artists which gives us a clear sense of the wide-ranging and loosely defined nature of the bohemian community of 1844. He distinguishes the characters in the play from the true Gypsies he has seen on his travels before defining the Parisian variety:

> Avez-vous jamais vu les véritables bohémiens? —Nous en avons vu, par douzaines, et nous pouvons vous assurer qu'ils ne ressemblent guère aux vôtres. . . . Decamps les eût suivi, le crayon à la main, avec une respectueuse admiration. Dans leur oeil de diamant noir respire l'antique et mystérieuse mélancolie de l'Orient. . . . Les enfants de la bohème ont leur hiérarchie, leur religion, leurs rites;

leur origine se perd dans la nuit des temps; un intérêt poétique se rattache à leurs migrations.

Il est aussi une autre espèce de bohémiens non moins charmants, non moins poétiques; c'est cette jeunesse folle qui vit de son intelligence un peu au hasard et au jour le jour: peintres, musiciens, acteurs, poêtes, journalistes, qui aime mieux le plaisir que l'argent, et qui préfère à tout, même à la gloire, la paresse et la liberté, race aimable et facile, pleine de bonnes instincts, prompte à l'admiration, qu'un rien enlève et détourne, et qui oublie le pain du lendemain pour la causerie du soir.—De cette bohème, nous en sommes un peu tous, plus ou moins, ou nous en avons été. . . . —Avec les gitanos d'Espagne, les gypsies d'Ecosse, les zigeuners d'Allemagne, voilà les seuls bohémiens que nous reconnaissions, et . . . comme le comédien Lélio dans *la Dernière Aldini* de madame Sand, nous chantons d'une voie ferme et pure: "Vive la bohème!" (106–7)

[Have you ever seen real bohemians? —We have seen some, dozens of them, and we can assure you that they hardly resemble yours. Descamps followed them, pencil in hand, with respectful admiration. In their eyes of black diamond breathes the ancient and mysterious melancholy of the Orient. . . . The children of Bohemia have their own hierarchy, their religion, their rites; their origins are lost in the night of time; a poetic interest is drawn to their migrations.

There is also another species of bohemians no less charming, no less poetic; it is that fanciful youth that lives by its own wits, and a bit by luck, from one day to the next: painters, musicians, actors, poets, journalists, who like pleasure more than money and who prefer, above all, even more than glory, laziness and liberty, an amiable and easy race, full of good instincts, ready to admire, whom a mere trifle can uplift and reroute and who forgets tomorrow's bread for this evening's conversation.—To this Bohemia we all belong just a little, more or less, or we once did. . . . With the *gitanos* of Spain, the Gypsies of Scotland, the *Zigeuners* of Germany, these are the only bohemians we recognize, and, . . . like the player Lélio in *The Last Aldini* of Madam Sand, we sing with a pure and firm voice: "Long live Bohemia!" (My trans.)]

Insisting that Parisian bohemians are more like real bohemians than the characters of the play at the Ambigu, Gautier decries the play's association of those "painters, musicians, actors, poets, journalists" with the Parisian underworld. Indeed, if they are criminals, it is only insofar as they refuse to conform to bourgeois values, preferring pleasure to money and prizing laziness, liberty, and good conversation over glory and tomorrow's bread.

In this already oppositional and transnational, or pan-European, stance associating the Gypsies of Spain, Scotland, and Germany with the artists of Paris, Gautier further opposes the obvious bourgeois values of the West to the bohemian values of a poetic and mysterious Orient. This opposition is spurious, however, since this Orient, like the Spain Gautier visited, is contained within the stronghold both of Western Europe and of Western European revolutionary values as they were rearticulated in 1830 to recall the first French Revolution in 1789. Moreover, like those bourgeois values (money and glory) which oppose other apparent bourgeois values (laziness and liberty), imaginary social distinctions like *nous* and *vous* (*we* and *you*), "our bohemians and yours," are drawn between readers of reviews who can all only be French and bourgeois.

In the context of these imaginary distinctions it is important to recall that part of the legacy of the Revolution of 1789 and of the subsequent rapid rise of the bourgeoisie was a surplus of time and resources which would make Gautier's "pleasure, laziness, and freedoms" available to the greater ranks of the bourgeoisie. Charles Baudelaire, for example, would address his writings to that armchair reader who has the leisure time to read and to dream of Orients. Likewise, the regime produced by the Revolution of 1830 was a monarchy that encouraged the "democratic" defusing of conventional bourgeois versus bohemian energies in major political groupings that formed, according to Seigel, in the aftermath of 1830. The representative opposition of the Party of Movement and the Party of Resistance (Seigel 7) is a good example. As these names suggest, the Resistance party was allied with the representatives of the pre-revolutionary ancien régime, hence its monarchist values: resistance to change, restrictions on political debate, and protectionism, or "glory and bread." The Party of Movement, as its association with "the Movement" of the sixties might suggest, was allied with the political Left, valuing

freedom of speech and of the press (an accepted idea but a radical practice) and interventionist foreign policy, or "pleasure and freedom." Although bohemians best resembled members of the Party of Movement,
as both wanted to retain a society open to new elements and energies, or
to what we could call "nomadic slippages" between national entities,
they were not all members of this party. Moreover, the successes of the
Resistance party would lead to the workers' revolution of 1848, creating
a new association for Bohemia as the setting for revolution (Seigel 7–8).
In 1844, then, Gautier appears to be recalling that within the conflictive
values of the bourgeoisie itself there existed a bohemian conscience that,
although suggestive of a multiplicity of possible identities and political
affiliations within the bourgeoisie, also managed to contain the splintering energies of this multiplicity within an imagined social community (a
particular "race")—"nous en sommes un peu tous" [we all belong just a
little]—whose political or oppositional force was merely "charming."[15]

If, according to Seigel, it really was the defeat of the revolution in '48
and then of the Commune in '71 which repopularized Bohemia, rendering any further definitions of it unnecessary (61), it would seem that
Bohemia best nurtures its followers in moments of disappointment over
hoped-for social transformation, moments traditionally associated also
with a plethora of social utopias. In this context a growing disillusionment in 1844 with the "bourgeois" and falsely "democratic" aspects of
the bourgeois monarchy (as well as speculation about future agitation
due to economic difficulties [64]) might explain the euphoric quality of
Gautier's own reminiscence of 1830. Like other nostalgic bohemians,
Gautier seems less interested in political revolution than in sustaining
revolutionary enthusiasms in the service of art. This stance is suggested
most emphatically by his closing gesture to the fictional bohemian Lélio,
from George Sand's novel. It is significant, moreover, that the principal
character in the once popular novel by Sand is a traveling bohemian
actor who looks back on a life of only tentative social transgression as he
settles, nostalgically, into his middle-class comfort. In this way Lélio is a
likely candidate for the imaginary dramatization of Gautier's own bohemian social identity.

From Gautier's portrait of Bohemia in mid-nineteenth-century Paris
there are three points to retain. First, as my brief exposé of Jerrold Sei-

gel's work demonstrates, Bohemia exists within the malleable boundaries of the bourgeoisie, despite its continual claims to the contrary. Both were formed at the same time, and, as it was commonly heard in the 1830s, "scratch a bohemian, find a bourgeois" (Seigel 5). Moreover, despite both Seigel's and our own clear-cut contemporary sense that bohemians flatly reject the bourgeois values of their parents (while unknowingly adopting them later in life), George Sand's bohemians—Lélio but also la Checchina and the others in her novel *Aldini* (1837–38)—understand Bohemia as a social space that erases race-class-gender confines in a utopian vision of the modern middle class.

Bohemia and the plasticity of its changing attributes are best understood, therefore, not as a reaction to so much as a feeling of ambivalence toward the values of the bourgeoisie. To consider a contemporary version of the same social ambivalence, one that highlights the enterprising capitalism employed so effectively by New Age hippies: Of what contentious social or political value is a tie-dyed shirt if "they're not just for hippies anymore"?[16] But what these examples of malleable boundaries suppose is a potentially dangerous force related less to Bohemia's political or social affiliations than to the political fluidity of its countercultural energies, its production of what Said has called "amoral dissenters," or "amateurs," its capacity to power utopian visions and political enthusiasms that do not necessarily reflect clear ideological positions.

Second, the relation of Gautier's "melancholy Orient" to the West assumes a similarly ambivalent status in that this Orient is perceived as both opposite to and contained within the bourgeois values of Western Europe. That is, though this appropriation of the Orient into European society clearly participates in Said's "Orientalism," as I already suggested, it also shifts the scene of the European-Oriental opposition onto the theater of daily bourgeois life and identity in Paris. This shift may be best conceived in terms of what Ross Chambers understands, in Baudelaire's Oriental landscapes, to be a movement away from Said's Orientalism toward Marx's "Oriental despotism"—a "figure for the relationships, whether political, psychosocial or poetic, that are bred in the West by the conditions of contemporary existence: the death of God, the experience of revolution and repression, the many alienations inherent in the growth of capitalist society, industrialized and urban" ("Asiatic

Mode," 115–16). More than its location "here" rather than "there," in other words, this Orient represented by Bohemia is significant as an internalized response to the perceived despotism of hypocritical political repression, to the conventions of an organized bourgeois social life, to what Gautier would later call "la civilisation envahissante" and what Goethe understood as a profound moral order missing under the empire (Füglister 120).[17]

Gautier's situating of Bohemia as an Orient "here at home" allows him to think of Bohemia domestically and subjectively as an alterity within himself: "De cette bohème, nous en sommes un peu tous ou nous en avons été" [To this Bohemia, we all belong a little, or we once did]. This reference to Gautier's own sense of himself as a bohemian must be understood either as a gesture to his own youthful practices (such as the red coat worn to the premiere of *Hernani*) or as that identity he inhabits when he is not writing reviews: *vous* versus *nous*. In this light Lélio is once again instructive insofar as he is a figure who both blends art and politics on the stage and narrates moments of exceptional commitment to bohemian ideals as he watches himself perform. Because of his duplicity, Sand gives him two names, Lélio and Nello, which anticipate this breach of identity—or breach within identity—which Gautier himself inhabits.

This doubled bohemian identity not only echoes Kristeva's sense that we are "étrangers à nous-mêmes"; it also leads eventually to the conception of both an "Orient of my thoughts" (in the work of Gustave Flaubert, Stéphane Mallarmé, Arthur Rimbaud, and Marcel Proust) and to what Beryl Schlossman has called an "Orient of style." Whereas the first supposes a way of evoking the repressed part of thinking or writing which refuses the limits of conscious logic, of philosophical rationalism, of scientific positivism, and of Romantic and "domesticating" narratives, the second provides an image of modernism's ideal textual materiality designed to correspond to the figures produced from out of the Orient of thought and symbolized by a land of style "made real."[18]

Recourse to the bohemian as a symbol for this breach in identity and in literary style is perhaps best rendered, as we shall see, in the work of Charles Baudelaire and of Arthur Rimbaud, whose staging of an "Orient of my thoughts," of a "Bohemia within myself," takes place primarily in a tense shifting between the exigencies of narrative and of textuality characteristic of both their lyric poetry and their poetic prose.[19] In the prose of the *Petits Poèmes en prose* and *Une Saison en enfer* this shifting manifests itself in a series of disrupted and orchestrated encounters among an array of other discursive voices. Questions of style, music, and shifting identities are intimately linked by way of their common association with what Margaret Miner has called the "errances dionysiaques," "vagabondages," or "une certaine énergie transgressive" [Dionysian erring and roving, vagabonding, or a certain transgressive energy] of bohemian behavior.[20] Put otherwise, Miner is highlighting a stylistic rendering of the nomadic agitations and tactical ideological ambivalences of Wallerstein's Bohemia.

In Baudelaire's prose these nomadic agitations are realized primarily through shifts in modes of address which complicate relations between interlocutors, as we shall see. They are subsequently taken up more overtly by Rimbaud, who saw himself as the inevitable instrument of other voices. "I is an other," he wrote to justify his literary dismantling of Western European values while at the same time locating this dismantling at the very core of his inescapably barbaric European formation. An openly "breached" bohemian, Rimbaud's use of various violent resources—drugs or absinthe and unconventional sexual practices—to favor a "dérèglement de tous les sens" [derangement of all senses, meanings, and directions] ultimately gives voice not to the unconscious visions of a euphoric self-destruction but, instead, to those bohemian impulses from the "Orient of thought" determined, finally, by "Europeanness" itself.[21]

In the cases of Baudelaire and Rimbaud this stylistic staging of the textual sounds of a breached bohemian identity, these "voices of the Orient" (or reorientations of voice), might be best understood in the terms I associated earlier with Jacques Derrida's representation of the alienated status of cultural identity itself: "a culture of oneself *as* a culture *of* the other, a culture of the double genetive and of the *difference to oneself*" (10). These voices make cultural identity into an exercise in ventriloquism and mark Bohemia as a privileged location in which to think about cultural identity. Moreover, this shifting and derangement of the voices contained in what I have characterized as the agitations of bohemian style have been remarkably successful in perpetuating an imagined Bohemia beyond the political and social setting of the mid-nineteenth century. This Bohemia can be traced quite directly, in fact, to artists as varied as Albert Glatigny, Paul Verlaine, Guillaume Apollinaire, Paul Hindemith, and the Beatles but also across the Atlantic to the work of Allen Ginsberg, Jack Cassidy, Jack Kerouac, Bob Dylan, and the Grateful Dead and, by way of their astonishing popularity, to mass culture and to my own local community in Eugene, Oregon.[22]

Finally, however, there is a third of three points to retain from Gautier's portrait of Bohemia. Like the Gypsies, at least as they were portrayed by artists such as Gautier, Victor Hugo, Johann Wolfgang von Goethe, Heinrich Heine, Alexander Pushkin, Baudelaire, Apollinaire, Mérimée, and Bizet; by Fanny Elssler in character dance; in the "café-concerts" performances of popular bohemian songs by Béranger (Füglister 122); in those even more popular engravings to illustrate travelogues by Alexandre Gabriel Decamps (Gautier, *Histoire*, 106), Charles Davillier and Gustave Doré (Martinoty 100); or in the paintings of Dehodoncq, Honoré Daumier, and Delacroix (Füglister 133–41), Parisian bohemians wanted to think of themselves as part of an international community untethered by restraints of a social, political, national, or class order. To use a formulation by Fredrich von Hagedorn, later echoed by Bizet: "le monde est notre patrie" (Füglister 115) [the world is our homeland]. As a result, cosmopolitan bohemians liked to imagine themselves as sharing a marginal existence with Gypsies and members of the urban underworld because of their unwillingness to assimilate into the boundaries of acceptable social comportment. On this imagined model of the Gypsies they wanted to define a cultural identity, a "pureté de race," which would extend nomadically, at least theoretically, beyond spatial, psychological, and temporal boundaries into community. As Béranger's most popular song put it, this would be a community "sans pays, sans prince et sans lois" (Füglister 122) [without country, without prince, and without laws], or, as Lélio describes it, "un monde sans patrie" [a world without homelands].

The legacy of this Parisian Bohemia proves that, like the bourgeois and capitalist culture it enlisted the image of the Gypsies to confront, Bohemia may ultimately have accomplished its ironically imperial goal. For Bohemia has expanded its frontiers through the continual recreation

of "artistic" communities defined not by traditional group and class formations but, rather, by their political plasticity and their slippery and
mobile social identities, which celebrate contradictory notions of culture
and of cultural identity. As the performance culture of Gypsy communities suggests, moreover, Bohemia continues to be conceived still today
as a social performance that both dramatizes ambivalence about cultural
identity and legitimizes ambivalent cultural response. This culture may
also point to the notion that performance communities—communities
shared by performers and spectators, or in which, on the model of Bakhtin's carnival, performers and spectators become intermittently indistin-
guishable—are a potentially ideal setting in which to renew capacities to
forge ideal cultural communities. In the case of today's Europe, in fact,
the intercultural performances of popular music gatherings and theater
festivals throughout Europe attest to this very possibility and begin to
make the eventuality of a European cultural community thinkable (Dasgupta 63–70). Moreover, as Derrida dreams of a "newly new" Europe, a
certain Bohemia appears figured in the fascinating performance of the
deconstructive critical imagination.

In "The Other Heading" Derrida writes:

> And what if Europe were this: the opening onto a history for which
> the changing of the heading, the relation to the other heading or to
> the other of the heading, were experienced as always possible? an
> opening and a non-exclusion for which Europe would in some way
> be responsible? for which Europe *would be*, in a constitutive way, this
> very responsibility? as if the very concept of responsibility were
> responsible, right up to its emancipation, for a European birth
> certificate? (17)

This newly new Europe would be oppositionally open, according to Derrida, a utopian social space of syncretic yet unassimilated and diverse
cultural identities, a tentatively mobile and expanding community of nomadic "reterritorialized" individuals, an ever-imaginary setting in which
to dramatize visions of Bohemia.

In defining Bohemia as a kind of performance community—both one
that, like that of the Gypsies, performs a simulacrum of its own cultural
identity and one that is most often celebrated in or at performances (fes-

tivals, fairs, concerts, radio broadcasts, dramas, but also the histrionics of critical writing)—I am suggesting a relationship between imaginary performances of cultural identity, such as we see in Gautier's review of the "Bohémiens de Paris" (or in Derrida's idealized Europe), and the production of actual lived communities, such as that of the Parisian bohemians to whom Gautier refers. This question of the role of literary and artistic performance in the projection, but also the production, of various modes of political and social behavior is central, in fact, to my understanding of what renews manifestations of bohemian communities.

Tracking the Bohemian in Baudelaire and Rimbaud

The aesthetic and cultural legacy of Gautier's imaginary bohemian scenario of 1844 encourages us to move forward from what Walter Benjamin characterizes as the "bohème dorée" of Gautier and Nerval to the more ambiguous Bohemia of the generation of Baudelaire (11). The usefulness of this move forward is ultimately that the *Carmen* story, written in 1845, finds itself at a critical juncture within this movement from a golden age of bohemian ideals to the more politically surreptitious representations of bohemian tendencies (a critical juncture within what Richard Terdiman refers to as a movement from thematic to formal representations of opposition to power [71]). Moreover, in their repeated confrontations of two genres, *Carmen* and its contemporary avatars insert themselves into the larger framework supposed by bohemian narrative, the ideal model for which, during the generation of Baudelaire, may well be Baudelaire himself and the many examples of prose poetry or poeticized prose in which strategies of tactical ambivalence proliferate.

In his celebrated portrait of Baudelaire as a bohemian Walter Benjamin conjures an image of the poet's complicity with the politics of duplicity associated with Napoléon III's rapid rise to power. In this context Baudelaire's Bohemia not only supposes a milieu from which, according to Marx, Napoléon III would derive his cadres and his "conspiratory customs"; it also constitutes those customs themselves: abrupt shifts in political affinities which occurred behind the backs of the French parliament (12–13). According to Benjamin, these very customs, or shifts in affinities, become writing strategies in Baudelaire's theoretical prose

(12). While he begins in this manner, however, by drawing associations between the poet's writing strategies and the politics of Napoléon III's power, Benjamin finishes his portrait by acknowledging Baudelaire's self-conscious awareness of that association. "Whether he bestows his sympathies upon clerical reaction or upon the revolution of 1848, their expression remains abrupt and their foundation fragile," writes Benjamin (13). That is, Baudelaire's self-conscious distance from his own prostituted participation in a political maneuvering that resembles that of Napoléon III serves Benjamin less as a way of condemning the poet's "conspiratory customs" than as a way of marking the space of representation in Baudelaire's writing as the container for an often ill-perceived "theoretical energy," a shifting or shuttling between positions as both the advocate for the bourgeoisie (in the *Salon de 1846*) and their primary detractor (12–13). In this way expressions such as "theoretical energy" and "fragile foundations" come to define the bohemian in this study and in Baudelaire's writing less as a sphere of economically unstable "professional conspirators" than as a fertile ground for hypocritical political dissension, or stylistic maneuvering.

What interests me in this portrait of Baudelaire's politically fluctuating bohemian tendencies is less the history of the changing definitions of the term which Seigel traces, or the cultural communities associated with it, than the only potentially politicized and primarily imaginary effects that such writing may produce in readers. I am less concerned with condemning the poet's "politically unconscious" complicity with the duplicity of the Second Empire than with his capacity to induce, among readers, reiterations of his own "theoretical energy," his own "fragile foundations." In other words, I am captivated by Baudelaire as a writer— and, more specifically, as a reader and purveyor—of his own anarchical shuttling among possible political affinities and social roles.

It is a commonplace to note that in *Les Fleurs du mal* Gautier's doubles, among others, reappear in several manifestations and are continually thrown up against the constraints of poetic form. But what is most striking, in the context of the agitation of bohemian style, is Baudelaire's rereading of his own poetic duplicities. By his "rereadings," I refer to Baudelaire's poems that find themselves doubled in prose and verse, lyric poems renewed in the narratives of the *Petits Poèmes en prose* and vice versa. These poems include "Un Hémisphère dans une chevelure" (A Hemisphere in a Head of Hair), which becomes "La Chevelure" (The Head of Hair); "Le Crépuscule du soir" (Evening Sunset), which repeats both its verse homonym and the celebrated "Recueillement" (Meditation); "La Belle Dorothée" (The Beautiful Dorothea), which echoes both "Bien loin d'ici" (A Long Way from Here) and "A une Malabaraise" (To a Malabar Girl); and the two versions of "L'Invitation au voyage" (Invitation to Travel).[23] In the prose setting these poems are accompanied by intuitive critical remarks reminiscent of the essays in *Le Peintre de la vie moderne*, thoughts about artists, music, and the city which work to analyze the processes at stake in those narrativized translations.

Though much has been said about Baudelaire's double versions of lyric and prose poems, what intrigues me about them is Baudelaire's capacity to render the discursive force of his poems subordinate to the exposition of their own formal vehicles because of the demand put on modern readers to shuttle between the two versions. As Barbara Johnson has demonstrated magnificently, modern readers must continually question how lyric verse relates to prose narrative and vice versa: "Entre le poème en prose et le poème en vers, le travail de mutilation et de correction s'engage donc indéfiniment, dans les deux sens. Chacun des textes sert de pré-texte à l'autre" (159) [Between the prose poem and the verse poem, the work of mutilation and correction is engaged then infinitely, in both directions. Each of the texts serves as a pretext to the other (my trans.)].[24]

Among the many readers who have undertaken this shuttling, following the advice of Johnson, Marie Maclean and Richard Terdiman are recent examples of readers who, in shuttling, discover that, whereas the world of lyric verse addresses an audience of bourgeois cultural elitists (primarily in intimate dialogues between *I* and *you*), the poeticized prose counters and complicates that address through its association with the "one" of mass communication.[25] In this way privileged readers, such as the "hypocritical brother," whom Marie Maclean characterizes as one of the "happy few" because he can grasp the textual strategies of the *sujet de l'énonciation* (49), are thrown up against figures of what Maclean calls the "average self-satisfied bourgeois," an image of the general public

(48–49). For Maclean the result is a performance of alternating addresses in the prose poem which encourages the actual reader to feel both
identified and estranged from the world of the narrative *énoncé*, as would
the spectator to a performance (34). For Terdiman the pairing allows the
prose poem to "become more conscious of its capacity to express tensions within the social formation itself."[26] For Johnson the result is that
the prose poem subverts the intimacy of the I/you relationship and compromises the rarefied exclusiveness of poetry by revealing its own social
mediation in the triangularity of I/you/one (121). But, insofar as the
I/you dialogue characteristic of most of the lyric verse may be a representation not of public communication, not of an actual address to an
intimate reader, but rather one intended to stage the inner dialogues of
thought, the prose also figures the capacity of social discourses to mediate—or, better, to contaminate—the very movement of thought itself.

The agitated shuttling provoked for Johnson, Terdiman, and Maclean
by Baudelaire's prose poems recalls Benjamin's notion of conspiratory
customs, Miner's "Dionysian erring and roving," and Baudelaire's own
image for modernity in both *Le Peintre de la vie moderne* (The Painter of
Modern Life) and *Le Spleen de Paris* (Parisian Spleen). It is undoubtedly
this shuttling that is at the root of the ongoing legacy, among leisurely
bourgeois readers, of the aesthetic politics of this poetry's "bohemian
behavior" (as the work of these three readers leads us to suppose). Like
the relationship between the *Parisian Spleen* prose poems and the modern city from which they have emerged, what is striking about the
aesthetic politics of Baudelaire's shuttling effect is not their capacity to
represent political or social reality but, rather, to *repeat*, and in turn solicit
further repetitions of, figures from that reality.[27]

This repeating of figures from social reality is best exemplified by the
dual oppositional social identities that Baudelaire played intermittently
in his personal journals: the dandy and the bohemian.[28] The dandy dramatizes the stoic and narcissistic image of art for art's sake as a closed
autonomous system: "toujours devant un miroir" [always in front of a
mirror], he is thoroughly engaged in private dialogues with himself—
this, even in the public domain of the *flâneur* (saunterer). In the essay
titled "Le Dandy" we encounter a self-contained and self-consciously,
rather than overtly, oppositional figure who sets out to "étonner sans être

étonné" [to astonish without being astonished]. His opposition is subtle
and restrained. The bohemian supposes, on the other hand, a "culte de la
sensation multipliée" (*Mon Coeur mis à nu*) [cult of the multiplied sensation (My Heart Bared)] which seeks to renew the agitation of everyday
modern life as a rhythmic reverberation both within his own person and
in modern art forms "doué[s] d'enthusiasme" [shot through with enthu-
siasm]. This duality foregrounds Baudelaire's (and, for that matter, Benjamin's) reading of the artist as a "man of the crowd," a convalescent
lost in the kaleidoscopic undulations of city life in *Le Peintre de la vie
moderne;* a being attracted to adventure and solitude by vocation in "Vocations" (OC 335); a participant in a community or cult of the Gypsy
rebel in *Du Vin et du hachisch* (Of Wine and Hashish) (OC 383–86). In
real life Baudelaire did oscillate between these roles, and, as Benjamin
suggests, this shifting was directly related to Baudelaire's highly mercurial economic resources. It is, however, the imaginary scenarios surrounding them which are useful in the context of bohemian style.

If we associate these two social roles with stylistic phenomena, the
dandy's elitist stoicism evokes the I/you dialogues of lyric verse as well
as the intimacy of an address to a "semblable" [a similar type individual],
whereas the bohemian evokes the appeal of prose to the larger community, the social discourse of the one/we designed for public consumption.
But just as the prescribed shuttling between forms splices the other into
the one, so too does the prose poem manage, in its hybridity, to figure,
stylistically, something akin to Gautier's breached bohemian identity. In
the prose poem, in other words, one could be both sufficient unto oneself
and yet able to "élire domicile dans le nombre," to "take up residency in
the plural." This situating of the dandy's narcissistic self-sufficiency
(I/you) within the bohemian's marvelously fluid and multiplied public
domicile (one/we) allows the prose poem to take on a specifically oppositional literary character by contesting, in this confrontation, assumptions about the two forms of address which poetic and prose narrative
communicate. The resulting effect of the critical stance of the prose poem
is a world "endowed with the enthusiasm of the artist's soul," as if the
agitation of Baudelaire's modern social identities inspired a form of lyric
prose which in turn energized a modern agitation in readers who were
provoked to inhabit similarly ambiguous imaginary social identifications.

The prose poem's energizing of modern agitations helps reconsider what Terdiman, Benjamin, and Sartre see as Baudelaire's apparently unconscious complicity with dominant social discourses.[29] In "L'Invitation au voyage," for example, Baudelaire's portrait of a land "là-bas," of an Orient full of commodities designed to satisfy consumer instincts in the West, seems to reiterate the dominant ideology of "free market" imperial expansion and colonial extraction—a "discourse of power" which has inevitably commodified the poet's voice in the lyric poem. Invitations "over there" do indeed help justify adventurous voyages overseas, the excitement of travel and of the foreignness of other places, and, because those places are located within the private sphere of our own desires, they also help justify the opium trade to which seekers of undulating and multiplied sensations were also inevitably drawn: "c'est pour assouvir *ton moindre desire* qu'ils viennent du bout du monde" (my emph.) [it is to satisfy *your every desire* that they arrive from the ends of the earth]. This circumscribing of a space of private consciousness to which all products flow may well aid and abet a colonial discourse of power while hiding, or rather poeticizing, the exploitative realities behind the exchange of those commodities. From this perspective Baudelaire's lyric poem does construct a private space of pleasure for privileged readers— an "oriental splendor" right here at home—which enables the larger political and economic project, unwittingly.

If this lyric invitation to dream participates in the perpetuating of the dominant culture, however, the prose invitation discloses this complicity by uncovering and making available to our scrutiny relations between private desires and the colonialist ideology of the West. It does this by bringing economic concerns into the world of poetry and by eliminating all signs of seduction, as Johnson demonstrates quite dramatically (135–39, 153). In the prose, for example, the Oriental room is transformed into an image of an "hôtel bourgeois," the home of an "honnête homme" [working man] who makes a living: "Les trésors du monde y affluent, comme dans la maison d'un homme laborieux et qui a bien mérité du monde entier" (OC 89) [The treasures of the world accumulate there, as in the house of a man who works and who deserves the riches of the entire world]. Instead of an expansionism enabled by the circumscribing of consciousness as a private space, then, the prose links our desire for private possessions, and, for that matter, for the private reading of poetry, to the domestication of "worldly treasures" through hard work. Rather than reinscribing the exceptional status of poetry, then, its surplus value and its capacity to exist beyond or outside of the world of banal bourgeois concerns,[30] the prose poem stages the complicity between poetry and the dominant bourgeois culture, the commodification of art as a kind of unconscious ideological support system, and makes it available to our critical consideration.[31]

This subversion of an ideology of poetic purity is accomplished formally, as I have already suggested, through the intermixing, rather than the synthesizing, of the generic exigencies of lyric poetry and prose narrative. In this intermixing the prose poem does not do away with lyric voice but, as Dominique Combe points out, looks at it and refers to it with a certain critical distance (103–5). So, for example, the poet's imaginary voyage is addressed, in the third person, to any and all readers who share the dream of "la Cocagne," a "land of plenty" (of milk and honey, of streets of gold), which "goes without saying": "Il est un pays superbe, un pays de Cocagne, dit-on, que je rêve de visiter avec une vieille amie" (OC 301) [There is a superb land, a land of plenty, as we say, that I dream of visiting with an old friend]. The unacknowledged knowledge presupposed by the "dit-on" (as we say) in this opening not only identifies this land as a product of social discourse—one, indeed, which only exists in social discourse—it also identifies it as a by-product of an unconscious collective dreaming about the "better life."

This attention to the unconscious nature of ideological persuasion provides a new context for the space of desire to which all things flow in the lyric poem by making it into a decidedly public, or social, space. The intimacy of the private dialogue between the poet and his new old friend is subverted by social mediation (Johnson 120). In lieu of a private tête-à-tête Baudelaire's prose poem now reveals a subject locked in an ideological exchange system according to which "ces choses pensent par moi, ou je pense par elles" ("Le *Confiteor*," OC 278) [things think through me, or I think through them]. In this way it whittles away at the unconscious force of the discursive clichés, those "voices of the Orient" lodged here inside me, and maps out parallels between the hidden pressures of psychic repression and those of ideologically repressive social discourses.

From this perspective it is not surprising that the ideal country depicted in the prose version is explicitly defined as an Orient transplanted into Europe by way of the work of fantasy:

> Pays singulier, noyé dans les brumes de notre Nord, et qu'on pourrait appeler l'Orient de l'Occident, la Chine de l'Europe, tant la chaude et capricieuse fantaisie s'y est donné carrière, tant elle l'a patiemment et opiniâtrement illustré de ses savantes et délicates végétations. (OC 301)

> [A singular country, drowned in our foggy North, and that we could call the Orient of the Occident, the China of Europe, so productive has the warm and capricious work of fantasy been, so patiently and opinionatedly has it illustrated this land with wise and delicate vegetation.]

In associating the illustrative work of fantasy with horticulture, or the growing of vegetation, we could say that, whereas the lyric version of this poem merely gives free reign to that illustrative work (*"songe* à la douceur d'aller là-bas" (my emph.) [*dream* of the sweetness of going over there]), the prose demonstrates how this work also obfuscates the raison d'être behind our capacity to think up an Orient here at home—namely, the way in which fantasy taps into an unconscious ideological support system that allows our collective dreaming to *seem* intimate. In so doing, "L'Invitation au voyage" acknowledges both Baudelaire's and our own complicity with what Benjamin calls conspiratory customs.

As the example of the ideal (discursive) land supposes, "L'Invitation au voyage" also conspires to repeat insistently in formal terms what it only suggests in thematic terms. That is, the image of an Orient in the Occident, a China in Europe, a warm and southern tropical locale in our foggy North, parallels the undermining of private dialogue by public discourse. Yet the subsequent interaction of a progressive narrative (implicitly addressed in the third-person *on* to *us* [*nous*]) and a lyric turbulence (the *I/you* that forms another implicit *us*) further dramatizes this undermining. The lyric turbulence is figured through the infinitely substituted *tu* (familiar *you*), as Johnson has also suggested (118). No longer an incestuous sister or child, *tu* has become rather more unwieldy, as it signals an empty subjectivity defined only by mobile and shifting promises of an ever-expanding intimacy.

Tu is indeed a curiously subdivided friend ("tout *vous* ressemble," "*Tu* connais" [301–2] [All resembles *you*, *You* know]). It becomes the infamous flower (of evil) ("Fleur incomparable . . . c'est là, n'est-ce pas" [303] ["Incomparable flower . . . it is there, is it not"]) as well as the luxuriant objects of exchange themselves ("Ces trésors, ces meubles, ce luxe, cet ordre, ces parfums, ces fleurs miraculeuses, c'est toi" [These treasures, this furniture, this luxury, this order, these perfumes, these miraculous flowers, they are you]). Even the flow of the waterways that direct my thoughts ("C'est encore toi" [303] [It's you again]). Most striking, however, is the silent and absent locution that forces the narrator to engage in an intimate dialogue almost despite himself: "Oui, c'est là qu'il faut aller" [Yes, it is there that we need to go]. And "Oui, c'est dans cette atmosphère qu'il ferait bon vivre" [Yes, it is in this atmosphere that it would be good to live]. In this silent dialogue the poet acknowledges the voice of a fantasy interlocutor (one only he hears) as if he were the flower to whom the poet thinks his invitation. "Yes," he answers, as if a question had been posed. Although these are responses to thoughts that originate elsewhere, these thoughts, like the China in Europe, are already internalized and defining his own subjective space of desire.

The expansive designs of the lyric turbulence created by these shifting addresses are contained only by the promise of narrative continuity and of a forward-moving "plot" based loosely on the three progressively larger settings of the lyric poem: the landscape in a lover's eye, the chamber, and the ocean port. This promise of narrative continuity, combined with the variable tonality of lyric repetitions similar to those occasioned by operatic arias ("Tu connais . . . oui, oui. . . . Fleur incomparable"), finish by creating unresolvable double binds by inscribing two kinds of reading strategies: that of the private dialogue with the poet or with his persona and that of public communiqués. These two reading strategies force us into a state of mental (moral) agitation, or shuttling, because, like the two implicit *nous* we are led to inhabit, we are both third-party observers and an intimate first-person interlocutor.

Vincent Kaufmann describes a similar kind of bind in the context of Mallarmé's address quatrains, *Les Loisirs de la poste:* "Non seulement le lecteur occupe une double place (celle d'un destinataire et celle d'un témoin de la règle propre à la transmission qui fait de lui un destinataire), mais ces deux places s'avèrent contradictoires (et le lecteur ne sera en fait témoin que de sa disparition en tant que destinataire antérieur)" (*Le Livre et ses adresses,* 51–52) [Not only does the reader occupy a double place (that of addressee and that of witness to the rule that governs the transmission that makes of him an addressee), but these two places prove themselves to be contradictory (and the reader will be witness, in fact, only to his own disappearance as an anterior addressee) (my trans.)]. In the case of Baudelaire, by drawing attention to itself as a hybrid genre that can neither confine itself to the structured regularity of lyric form nor quite make narrative sense, the prose poem also creates a double place: that of the addressee, which is also that of the witness. In so doing, it forces us to attend to the kinds of messages purveyed by both of the genres that it includes: the private but ideologically persuasive intimacy of lyric poetry and the public, potentially illustrative morals of prose narrative.

Rimbaldian Revisions

To the extent that Rimbaud accepts Baudelaire's invitation to travel, his work confirms that the prose poem of the late nineteenth century examines relationships between private enthusiasms and social ideologies. It confirms this hypothesis by repeating the effect of "vagabondages bohémiens," that is, of narrativized poetry that shuttles between the exigencies of two genres or two textual pressures: lyric intimacy and prosaic sociability. This effect is particularly apparent in the writing of *Une Saison en enfer,* but it is already present in "Le Bateau ivre" (The Drunken Boat) and "Le Coeur volé" (The Stolen Heart), in which a constant unresolved tension is maintained between narrative continuity and the variability of lyric tonality. Like Baudelaire's, Rimbaud's voyage in "Le Bateau ivre" also stages a project of discovery, colonization, and free trade. It, too, discovers or discloses a complicity between the poet's "Asiatic despotism" and the louder or more powerful discourses of a European ideology which form his own revolt against them. And, like Baudelaire's China in Europe, what might be called bohemian, or Oriental, dissonances in "Le Bateau ivre" map a properly European landscape.[32]

To read Rimbaud's "Le Bateau ivre" we must follow both a narrative of continuity, or progression—a story someone tells to someone else—and an exercise in tonal variety which revels in the pleasure of a repetitive lyric performance. As the story goes, the drunken boat leaves the shore and all that would limit or define a search for authenticity in order to descend "où je voulais" [where I wanted]. Then, dispersed by the purifying vomitus of inebriating waters, the boat's fragments enter into the "Poem of the Sea" and, becoming "voyant," but only intermittently, or "par instants," finds itself disillusioned, deceived, and exhausted by the effort, as it regrets having left "l'Europe aux anciens parapets" [Europe with its ancient parapets]. The poem closes by underscoring a project that is both impossible, or failed, because it requires an output of vigor too difficult to sustain, and inevitably renewable—an example of what Georges Poulet characterizes as one more in an endless series of "éveils," or awakenings.[33]

Against this narrative of progressive success and disillusionment, however, the poem also rereads itself by staging three renewals, or versions, three ways of telling the same story from three different perspectives. (As an exercise in rereading, the poem anticipates a similar effect produced three years later in Mallarmé's "L'Après-midi d'un faune," in which the faun continues to retell the same "story" three times.) In "Le Bateau ivre" the superbly difficult images of true sight spewing forth from the second section of the poem—"Je sais, . . . j'ai vu, . . . j'ai rêvé" (OC 101) [I know, . . . I have seen, . . . I have dreamed]—liquefy the story of the boat's descent which opens the poem. It follows that from a dispersed subjectivity "voyance" will ensue. This second section, however, may also be said to repeat the sensual effects of the first part in visual terms. Likewise, the third section of the poem continues the story of the boat's return to European shores while reiterating, or restaging, the voyage in new terms.

In each case, or part, the poem relates the boat's descent toward the bottom of the ocean, its concomitant awakenings, its violent waters, its explicit time markers ("l'autre hiver, des mois pleins, dix nuits" or, later, "les juillets" [OC 100, 101, 102] [the other winter, whole months, ten nights or, later, Julys]), its situating of "Europeanness" at the center of a private imagination, and its childlike version of a New World Order that would reverse values (the "redskins" that nail hailers to totems, the human-skinned panthers, the vigor of golden birds or singing dolphins [ibid.]). In other words, the textual and tonal variety of the three parts puts into relief the contours of an essentially repetitive scenario and the variety of poetic textures and tones which may be employed to present that obsessive scenario.

As it closes, the poem's final stanzas comment upon the ambiguity of a poetic project of progress and repetition, of narrative force and textual, tonal variety. While "J'ai trop pleuré" [I have wept too much!] supposes the end of the voyage and the defeat of the insightful poetics, the exclamation at the end, "O que ma quille éclate, o que j'aille à la mer!" (OC 103) [O let my keel burst! O let me go into the sea!], sets the course for yet another voyage, another awakening, another version. Then, at the very end of the poem, while the prison ships of slave runners and the forces of national pride and free market enterprise are understandably too severe for the poet to confront—they make the path too exhausting—the image of the sad boy releasing his play boat calls to mind the deaf origins of fantasy, the infinite energy of a childlike imagination, the constantly renewable fictions formed of deflected desires, and the capacity to rethink the same voyage again and again (ibid.). The end of the poem thus calls to a new beginning as it both promises and pulls against the satisfying conclusion of plot.

By figuring an ambiguous encounter of narrative and textual writing strategies, "Le Bateau" anticipates the "oppositionality" of bohemian shuttling characteristic of Rimbaud's prose. Although, as Jean-Luc Steinmetz has shown, the prose narratives of the *Illuminations* also present a very rich landscape in which to investigate questions of narrative presentation and representation, the most self-conscious example of Rimbaud's own shuttling, or rereading of his own lyric project in prose remains the texts in *Une Saison en enfer* which Maurice Blanchot has referred to as *récits*. Kristin Ross has pointed out that the term *récit* is used by Blanchot to lend to the prose of *Une Saison* a measure of its stylistic and generic ambiguity relative to the "realist" mode of development of the bildungsroman.[34] While the *récit* is not a genre, it does suppose a narrative, or telling.[35]

In Rimbaud's *Saison,* as in Baudelaire's "Invitation," the self-conscious situating of the concerns of lyric poetry at the center of a prose narrative displays and forces recognition of a relationship of complicity between the poet's personal confession of a poetic project gone awry and the dominant discourses of ideology which may themselves be "responsible" for the terms of the project. More precisely, the project is no longer opposed to the values of a bourgeois and Catholic culture that Rimbaud would overturn or replace according to a "revolutionary" model; these values are presently depicted as the source of the project itself. This is particularly true of "L'Alchimie du verbe," in which, as Dominique Combe argues, the placing of completed lyric poems within the prose narrative turns the prose into an ironic and critical evaluation that depreciates the earlier verse in relation to the current prose (104). Yet the whole of the *Saison* may be said to offer a more general looking back at the reasons why the project failed. In fact, the project announced jubilantly in the 1871 "Lettre du voyant" to render himself *voyant* through acts of violence and "the derangement of all senses," to seek the unknown, and to express a debt to society in his capacity as poet are clearly seen, by 1873, as the result of cultural voices louder than the poet's alone.[36] Violence is French and Christian, Rimbaud points out in his confession; to seek the unknown is to participate though one's imagination in the colonial project of the West (it is to repeat the pitfalls of Baudelaire's imaginary travels); and to understand the poet's work as the expression of a debt to society is a humanist and perhaps even positivist ideal. In other words, if Rimbaud's is the confession of the failure of his project, it is also a confession of innocence relative to the unconscious formation of a greater European identity.

It is the paradoxical relationship between a confession of innocence and a confession of guilt that results in the operatic pressures of the *Saison en enfer,* whose reader is constantly torn between the forward-moving progress of a personal, confessional narrative and the aria-like interludes, or "numbers," which both thwart and encapsulate the larger whole of the narrative, in repetitive moments that retell the same confession. Indeed, it can be argued that each of the prose-poem-essays which make up *Une Saison* repeats, in changing thematic terms, four or five essential components: the evocation of an idealized childhood; the rejection or stripping away of all that would have formed the poet in a project of violence which is too physically demanding; the search for a "clef du festin ancien" [key to the ancient banquet] in variously Christian or social modes of charity; a hoped-for salvation in a community of friends; and while waiting for that salvation or that charity, the waiting—most often, the writing—the dedication of hideous pages, "cet horrible arbrisseau" [that horrible tree] which is the *Saison* itself.

Seen from this perspective, the confession is both the development of a plot that is the "story" of the *Saison*—the autobiographic unfolding of the identity of a poet moving toward a hoped-for redemption in poetry or in the world—and, at the same time, an orchestrated or theatricalized staging of an identity that has become an "opéra fabuleux" [fabulous opera].[37] This orchestrated biography is pulled, as we shall see, into a play of elided phrases, thwarted cadences, and repetitive themes or motives that disrupt, or "deregulate," our attention to the forward progress of narrative. The *Saison* moves from "Bad Blood" to "Hell" to the "Delirium" provoked by the project to the "Impossibility" of the task but, then, to the "Flash" of insight, to the "Morning" of hope, and to an "Adieu" to God or to poetry. But, at the same time, the *Saison* features the repetitive retelling of this obsessive confession within each single prose-poem-essay.

In the example of "Mauvais Sang" (Bad Blood) Rimbaud's obsessive retelling confesses the impossibility of a project designed to resist the values of the West.[38] The problem, in this piece, is that these values have been woven into the very fabric of his subjectivity. In fact, the woven fabric of subjectivity occasions a manner of self-expression or confession comparable to a Wagnerian web of places, memories, voices, and fantasy identities held together by catchphrases of popular culture, historical moments, and intermittent personal experiences. The result is a form of writing that literally effaces any single, rational, or logical biographical speaking subject and a poet who seeks furtively to locate his own being: "I have lived everywhere. I know every family in Europe" (175); "What was I in the last century? I recognize myself only today?" (177); "In whose blood shall I walk?" (179); "Do I know nature yet? Do I know myself? *No more words.* . . . Quick! Are there other lives?" (181);

"My life does not weigh enough" (183). And, at the end, the poet becomes a collection of mere body parts: "Ah! my lungs are burning, my
temples pound! I see black in this sunlight! My heart . . . My limbs . . ."
(183 [Rimbaud's elisions]). This slow effacement of the very person of
the writer also explains why he cannot determine who guides him. His
voice seems to belong to or to be guided by someone or something else.
It is as much the product of a cultural identity formed for him, we are
led to believe, as it is of his own making: "But who made my tongue so
perfidious that it has guided and preserved my sloth up until now?"
(175).

This orchestrated identity or subjectivity is also specifically operatic
in that it obscures narrative intelligibility and continuity while retaining
the forward impulse of a narrative about a life. This poetry is after all
a kind of poetic narration in prose about the formation of identity in a
line of confessions indebted to Saint Augustine, Giambattista Vico, and
Rousseau. Recalling Blanchot's reference to intimate relations between
the *récit* and the bildungsroman, in fact, the story goes something like
this: "I was born in France. I had a privileged bourgeois and Catholic
education. I was not interested in women and marriage or in the oppor-
tunities open to me. Becoming a writer, I fell in love with boredom, rage,
debauchery, madness and frivolity. Now, I should get a job but I'd rather
face a firing-line as a deserter. Ah, but . . . I will get used to it. It will be
the French way of life, the path of honor!" (183). Like the bildungsroman, this *récit* tells of coming to age and of coming to terms with middle
age, and it is recounted in the past tense as a story about the poet's life.
According to this story, all of the exuberance of youth and history end
in the ironic conclusion of body parts molded into a national French
identity.

On the other hand, the forward impulse of this story is arrested or
blurred, as I suggested earlier, by an orchestrated—indeed, specifically
Wagnerian—textuality made of "endless music," recurring themes, and
repeating motives. Each time we get a space in which to pause or breathe
at the suggested ending of a phrase, more music wells up from inside,
often interrupting the story of the past life in the present tense. For
example:

Nous allons à l'*Esprit*. C'est très certain, c'est oracle, ce que je dis. Je comprends, et ne sachant m'expliquer sans paroles païennes, je voudrais me taire.

Le sang païen revient! L'Esprit est proche, pourquoi Christ ne m'aide-t-il pas, en donnant à mon âme noblesse et liberté. (176)

[We are moving toward the *Spirit*. I tell you it is very certain, oracular. I understand, and not knowing how to explain this without using pagan words, I prefer to be silent.

The pagan blood comes back. The Spirit is near. Why doesn't Christ help me by giving my soul nobility and freedom? (177)]

In this example, the silence projected at the end of the first paragraph and marked by the space between "sections" of the narrative is thwarted or elided to the continuing saga by way of repetitions ("Spirit, pagan") and the sense of continued movement ("moving toward, near"). A shift from an active insistent voice ("I tell you . . .") to a passive recipient of other voices ("The pagan blood is coming back [*revient*]") also underscores the urgency of an elision created almost despite the conscious choice of the speaker. This active thwarting of endings means that there are no finishes to scenes, acts, or parts, in the same way the obsessive concerns of this single essay, "Mauvais Sang," are as if repeated in the other essays, all of which are contained in the larger, cyclical structure of *Une Saison*.

This last example also shows there is a play of repeating motives that both highlight essential concerns in and create a logic outside of the narrative story of the life of the poet. One such motive is that of this barbarian, or pagan, ancestry reminding us that the *Saison* was initially titled *Livre païen*. At the outset the poet is as barbaric, "aussi barbare," as his Gallic ancestors (174); then, in rhythmic waves of remembrance, the associations with barbarism recur: "I have always belonged to an inferior race" (175); "The inferior race has covered everything: the people, as they say [*comme on dit*]; reason, nation, and science. . . . I am of an inferior race from all eternity" (177); "I am a beast, a savage [*une bête, un nègre*]. But I can be saved. You are false savages [*de faux nègres*]. . . .

Merchant. . . . Magistrate. . . . General. . . . Emperor, old mange, you are a savage" (179). This series of associations among paganism, inferiority, and savages is designed, of course, to justify colonial exploitation to the popular imagination. But in "Mauvais Sang" it has been turned around to describe the barbaric nature of Europeans themselves. It is followed by the most dramatic moment in the essay, in which, having lived through the perspective of the colonizer, the poet now takes on that of the colonized: "The white men are landing. The cannon! We will have to be baptized and put on clothes and work" (181).

As this last example demonstrates so strikingly, the logic of narrative continuity is not only disrupted by orchestrated effects of writing; it is also disrupted by what we might call orchestrated effects of identity, a series of fantasy identifications that make the speaking subject into something of an Emma Bovary or of a Saint Antoine, if in a more dispersed manner:

As a serf, I would have made the journey to the Holy Land. . . . —I, a leper, am seated on shards and nettles. . . . —Later as a mercenary, I would have bivouacked under German nights (175). I am dancing the witches' sabbath. . . . Here I am on the shore of Brittany. . . . Now I am an outcast (176). I am a beast, a savage (179). The white men are landing. . . . I have been shot in the heart by grace. . . . Quick! Are there other lives? (181). What an old maid I am becoming. . . . Fire! Fire at me ! Stop! or I'll surrender.—Cowards!—I'll kill myself! . . . Ah! . . . —I will get used to it. It will be the French way of life, the path of honor! (183).

In this series of possible lives, we see the same story of the *Saison:* the evocation of childhood; the rejection of all that has formed the poet in a project of violence which is too physically demanding; the search for a hoped-for salvation in a community; and the waiting. More important, however, we also see that, as the poet casts himself as one of several infamous others of Europe, one of the outcasts—the serf, the leper, the mercenary, the criminal, the colonial subject, the deserter, and, we are to assume, the poet—it is clear that these roles of social pariahs are also determined by his very Europeanness. For woven into the story of an individual life are the popular catchphrases of French nationalism which clothe an ordinary human existence in legendary robes.

Through a magnified orchestration of one individual's tendencies, Rimbaud shows us how the forging of popular national legends can be accomplished in such a way as to leave individuals by the wayside, or literally to efface them. We could say that the poet's voice becomes one instrument in the "democratic" fabric, while any sense of real history is erased: "I don't remember farther back than this land and Christianity"; "What was I in the last century?" (177). In a gesture akin to the forging of a legendary history of German national identity in Wagner's operas, a history of France based on the popular catchphrases, or "sound bites," of dominant discourse replaces or fills in the gaps of individual memory: "It will be the French way of life, the path of honor!" "the Rights of Man," "the Age of Reason," "life flourishes through work," or "the people, as they say; reason, the nation, and science." We could say that, as Rimbaud interweaves both the discourses of dominant culture and his own contestation of it, he repudiates both. His is not a call to revolution, a desire to overthrow a given system of power and replace it with a new order somehow forged by the outcasts, but a version of aesthetic anarchy designed to shuttle between possible systems and beliefs: "Yells, drum, dance, dance, dance, dance!" (181).

What does it mean, however, to shuttle among possible readings or to remake the sense of this "autobiography" by reading over and over, through again and again, according to different schemata of intelligibility? As the unique experience of readers, rather than opera spectators, the renewability of "Bad Blood" contests the dulling of mental labor and of the senses associated with narrative intelligibility. And as the poet oscillates between self-analysis and fantasy identifications, dominant discourses and their contestation, the reader feels both estranged by this odd life and the lack of logic which defines it and, at the same time, oddly identified with it. For although "Bad Blood," like the rest of the *Saison*, exposes the programming of national, cultural, or European identities through the official institutions of culture—the church, the military, the public schools—and through the popular discourses of those institutions, it also situates these voices of culture within both the poet and us. Before facing Europe's others, it is suggested, we must contend with the others within ourselves. Is this not, then, "an opening and a non-exclusion for which Europe would in some way be responsible?" (Derrida 17).

Though the *Saison* does not directly imitate Baudelaire's social concerns in the *Petits poèmes en prose*, Rimbaud saw himself as continuing an exercise in seeing (in "voyance") of which Baudelaire was the master. In 1871 he wrote: "Baudelaire est le premier voyant, roi des poètes, *un vrai Dieu*. Encore a-t-il vécu dans un milieu trop artiste; et la forme si vantée en lui est mesquine. Les inventions d'inconnu réclament des formes nouvelles" (OC 257) [Baudelaire is the first seer, king of poets, *a real god!* And yet he lived in too artistic a world; and the form so highly praised in him is trivial. Inventions of the unknown call for new forms (Rimbaud 311)]. While seeking to further develop Baudelaire's poetic project, Rimbaud clearly hoped to do so outside of the autonomous and ultimately self-serving "artistic milieu" Baudelaire had inherited from Gautier and the Romantics. Like Baudelaire's, his work does explore the agitation of modern life and the mutability of identity under the pressures of the voices of dominant social discourses. And, like Baudelaire's, it does take up, in its effort to represent the noise of these voices, the kind of "musicality" which Baudelaire describes as an ideal "poetic prose": "musicale sans rhythme et sans rime, assez souple et assez heurtée pour s'adapter aux movements lyriques de l'âme, aux ondulations de la rêverie, aux soubresauts de la conscience" (OC 229) [musical with neither rhythm nor rhyme, supple enough and agitated enough to adapt to the lyrical movements of the soul, the undulations of daydreams, the somersaults of consciousness].[39] In other words, it repeats, in its orchestrated textual effects, the conspiratory customs of Baudelaire's bohemian literary behavior.

At the end of *Une Saison en enfer* Rimbaud seems uncertain about the possibility of creating an exercise in "seeing" which would extend beyond the requirements of aestheticism into the realm of an actual social community. "Suis-je trompé? la charité serait-elle soeur de la mort, pour moi?" [Was I wrong? Could charity be the sister of death for me?], he asks near the end of the *Saison*. "Mais pas une main amie! et où puiser le secours?" (OC 229) [But not a friendly hand! Where can I find help? (Rimbaud 209)]. Although Rimbaud both sought this community and felt discouraged about ever finding it, the uncertainty marked by this proliferation of questions about charity anticipates the effect of futurity inscribed in the poet's conspiratory customs. Indeed, others have sought to answer these questions, and the community has continued to expand as an effect of reading Rimbaud. Similar conspiratory customs and a similar "musicality" of formal effects find themselves renewed in Jack Kerouac's jazzy "wild writing," in the jazzed-up cosmosocial poetry recordings of Allen Ginsberg's "spontaneous mind" (Knight 240), in the expanded tonal harmonies of Hindemith's tone poems, and in Dylan's cynical soul-searching vocal slides across the constraints or the very phrasing of intelligibility; it is no doubt prolonged as well in the ballads of Robert Hunter resonating through the mile-high speakers of the Grateful Dead.[40] And, in this apparently final destination of the high-tech, mass-culture, rock concert forum, these effects conspire to produce meditative enthusiasms that engage people individually but from within a bourgeois community united by analogous responses to the idea of political and social opposition.

Ultimately, shared by each of these new ways of rereading Rimbaud is the desire of these artists to seek solutions to social ills through the formation of future communities brought together through art and to do so by repeating Rimbaud's drunken voyages in new art forms: novels, poems, tone poems, popular ballads. Though this phenomenon of formal reiterations is certainly not exclusive to Rimbaud, who nonetheless furnishes the most dramatic example, nor to Baudelaire, whose readers are too numerous to study (*Europe*, 3), it does suggest a mode of narrative behavior which parallels, provokes, or reiterates certain modes of social behavior and which, in so doing, produces idealized communities through acts of rereading and rewriting. I call this narrative behavior "bohemian narrative."

Bohemian Narrative

By assigning the label "bohemian narrative" to the particular mode of literary behavior which results in this kind of social potential for community, I am less interested in who actually listens or reads or what actual political or social inequity may or may not be resolved than I am in the ways in which these narratives represent the acts of listening and reading and, in so doing, solicit renewed and potentially politicized performances of themselves. In this light it is important to consider that much attention has been accorded recently, among literary and cultural critics, to the question of how literature, performance art, and other aesthetic practices may actually program new social or political behaviors and communities. Although it is not my intention to review this discussion in its entirety, some sense of it is useful to an understanding of relations of art and community in Bohemia.

In *Desire and Domestic Fiction,* for example, Nancy Armstrong has argued that literature is both the document and the agency of cultural history and that eighteenth-century "written representations of self allowed the modern individual to become an economic and psychological reality."[41] For Armstrong, then, eighteenth-century novels become the place in which dominant cultural behaviors are programmed to take precedence over marginal or oppositional behaviors. These novels "domesticate" the dissonant voices of public opinion (while at the same time making them available to modern critics) and mold them into narratives by which we live our lives. Similarly, but in a different context, Hayden White supports continued attention to structural and textual analyses of historical narratives to understand the ways in which histories create "desires for the Real," or desires to create actual realities that mimic the coherencies such narratives encourage. For this reason, by questioning the moral imperatives, ideological presuppositions, or "metahistories" channeled by the specific formal means of expression which characterize specific genres, certain modes of narrative, and the study of such narratives, we open directly onto questions of a political, social, or cultural nature.[42] Furthermore, as Susan Stewart points out, decrying the recent emphasis in cultural studies on narrative and realism and a concomitant inattention to lyric in American universities, "aesthetic modalities correspond to the situations of subjects under the historical pressure of cultural processes. They bring forth the intersubjective work of evaluation by which culture is thought and made."[43]

Bohemian images and modes of presentation in literature and performance tend to respond to each of these suggestions. They foreground "aesthetic modalities" through attention to the limits or conventions of genre, and they question the ideological presuppositions channeled by narrative. Yet, whereas the eighteenth-century novel provides, for Armstrong, a form of fiction which appropriates and domesticates political resistance to the advantage of a middle-class struggle for dominance (24, 35), I would argue that nineteenth-century narratives about Bohemia containing what I have characterized as the agitations of bohemian style appear to question that very process of narrative domestication. On the contrary, they emphasize their own internal dissonances—tensions between linear continuities and textual or tonal ambiguities—and provide the reader with unresolvable contradictions, questions, or moral double binds. In these literary fictions Bohemia becomes a way of representing both a *social behavior* based in oppositional politics, an imagined or performed cultural community, and a form of artistic influence, or *narrative behavior*—fictions openly critical of the ideological component of their own formal mechanisms. Rather than domesticating, they appear to reproduce resistance to both social and narrative domestication by renewing their own modes of self-conscious behavior among their readers.

I have coined the term *bohemian narrative* for this oppositional literary phenomenon, then, to characterize a form of narrative fiction which tells a story about bohemian social or moral behavior and one that, in so doing, employs tactical ambivalence and self-conscious critique with a view to producing moral—and only potentially political—agitation among readers. Like the social behavior from which it takes its name, *bohemian narrative* indicates forms of narrative fiction which, as the examples of Baudelaire and Rimbaud demonstrate, maintain both generic and disciplinary boundaries only to cross those boundaries and to render them problematic. As a consequence, the modalities of this fiction are as, or more, available in the tendency of operatic, choreographic, and jazz compositions to rearrange their narratives continually as they are in literature. These are also forms of narrative fiction which rely upon the idea that politics can be enacted aesthetically without necessarily representing any precise political issues. That is, any political maneuvering in such narratives remains purely aesthetic, its goal being, like Gautier's, to "fuel private enthusiasms," whether or not these enthusiasms actually serve as a source for political change.

Such aesthetically politicized effects of bohemian narrative spring from the fact that these narratives translate into formal and moral concerns the kinds of thematic doubles we have seen in Gautier's review but which are observable as well in most nineteenth-century fiction. The bourgeois/bohemian theme appears in the form of ambiguous models for reader, listener, or spectator participation embedded in the modes of address of the narrative itself and which allow mutually exclusive but fully closed readings; the theme of the "Orient at home" appears in the form of voices that disrupt the expressive packaging of narrative communication through representations of multiplied identities or doubled subjectivities; and the image of Gypsies is taken up in the projecting of imaginary cultural communities to which future readers may already belong. It is in this final projection of the nomadic or transnational image of Gypsies that the idea of an as yet imaginary conception of a modern European cultural community begins to take shape.

Among the many examples of self-conscious fiction so prevalent in the latter half of the nineteenth century in France, bohemian narrative may be characterized as one particular type of narrative fiction in which symbolic gestures of opposition to dominant cultural values become increasingly surreptitious. In this respect bohemian narrative participates in the larger phenomenon of counterdiscursive, or oppositional, narrative at stake, in particular, in the recent work of Richard Terdiman and Ross Chambers.

In *Discourse/Counter-Discourse* Terdiman characterizes bourgeois art by referring to strategies of tactical ambivalence characteristic of late-nineteenth-century French fiction as the "discourses and counter-discourses" of narrative. Like the bourgeois and the bohemians who only symbolically oppose them, discourses align themselves with dominant forms of social behavior and are best defined, according to Terdiman, by counter-discourses that oppose them. That is, while counter-discourses define the dominant values of cultural ideologies in order to challenge them, Terdiman argues that they inevitably demonstrate a complicity with the sources of power they would decry. For example, Honoré Daumier's cartoons as well as the oppositional journal *Charivari* in which they often appeared attack the politics of the Second Empire, but they also rely upon the power of the newspaper industry in the very diffusion of their theoretically subversive messages. Likewise, Flaubert goes to the Orient to oppose bourgeois values but ends up seeing the West over there (232). In relation to this necessarily self-defeating system of resistance whereby any opposition inevitably serves dominant ideology, if despite itself, bohemian narrative encourages a multiplicity of subjective legitimacies—that "do your own thing" characteristic of bohemian communities—by reiterating the binary distinctions on which counterdiscursivity relies in unresolved formal and moral tensions.[44]

Whereas Terdiman, wishing for a literature productive of revolutionary change but locked into a Marxist model of the inevitably closed system of power, sees the oppositional force of any counter-discourse as essentially silenced, or domesticated, because of its inevitable complicity with the modes of capitalist production it would both counter and thereby define, I posit bohemian narrative as an attempt to rearrange the "system"—or, at least, to re-present it—by encouraging reappropriations of its own disruptive strategies and voices. In other words, I solicit the self-regenerating quality of bohemian narratives as proof of the fact that future readers do read, if not "outside the system," then as self-consciously aware of it, making any counterdiscursivity, or oppositionality, into an effect of reading.

Bohemian narratives turn counterdiscursive strategies into reading effects by figuring within themselves what happens to the discourses and counter-discourses of bourgeois art when they are performed (either staged or simply read). That is, they inscribe the complicity of Terdiman's discursive and counterdiscursive strategies self-consciously, largely by pitting two genres against each other. As a result, in a reading or performance a space of choice opens up between the two discourses, a space comparable to the social space occupied by Bohemia, in which readers or listeners are compelled to shift back and forth between possible ideological or moral intentions. Bohemian narratives do not, as such, *reflect* social or political realities in their double discourses; rather, they *repeat* figures from that dissonant reality. In addition, although they may be politically irrelevant in the moment of their most intense anarchical expressions, they nonetheless persist at the center of bourgeois popular art and life as a way of literally diffusing a surcharge of oppositional energy and of giving voice to desires for movement or agitation which find no place in a properly political arena.

Like the oppositionality that Ross Chambers describes in *Room for Maneuver: Reading (the) Oppositional (in) Narrative*, the politically, socially, or morally subversive effects of bohemian narrative are only a potential event that both readers and texts create.[45] Following a line of thought which echoes Terdiman's and defines itself as indebted to Michel de Certeau and Michel Foucault, Chambers explains his notion of oppositionality in relation to what it is not: resistance, counterforce, or revolution. Whereas the latter suppose modes of counterdiscursivity in literature which seek to reverse a system of power and authority, to fill in the shoes of the deposed monarch, as he puts it, and to establish a new authority in its place, Chambers's oppositionality is a phenomenon born of repeated disillusionment with revolutionary reversals. To fuel subversive enthusiasms, therefore, the oppositional works within a system and within the space tentatively carved out by certain narratives between a discourse of repression and another of revolution, or between what Terdiman calls the discourses and counter-discourses of nineteenth-century bourgeois art.

Chambers is interested, in fact, in moving beyond Terdiman's argument, which, on the model of Michel Foucault's thinking, supposes that any counter-discourse necessarily demonstrates a complicity with the voice of the power system it challenges, as if generating its power from the very source it would bemoan (xviii). Because Chambers agrees, he poses oppositionality as a "way out," or, more precisely, as a way of shifting patterns of desire between the two discourses (xvii). This shifting or deflecting of desire can result, according to Chambers's argument, in the hoped-for political or social change revolution or counterforce would only reverse, precisely because oppositionality can influence the desires and views of readers. The way out (though the term is admittedly inexact, as Chambers points out, since there is no outside of power) lies in the fact that certain narratives address or appeal to readers outside of the culture and time period in which they are written. They "transcend the context of their production" (12) by inscribing reading as a mode of reception without historical closure and, in this way, making their oppositionality available at a later time (2–3). Ultimately, future reading is the maneuvering for which certain narratives create "room."

Bohemian narratives may be understood as one manifestation of this kind of oppositionality and its potential to deflect desires, in that they solicit the kind of maneuvering Chambers proposes by staging this very capacity to "deflect desire." The term *bohemian narrative* is designed, however, to further suggest a suprageneric phenomenon composed of narratives that move between the boundaries of signifying practices in various art forms, including those of literature, music, dance, and film.

The *Carmen* story, which will be the main focus of my attention in the remainder of this book, provides an ideal example of this suprageneric narrative phenomenon. Continually rejuvenating itself in new modes of expression, *Carmen* reuses the story of a certain Bohemia as the foil against which to unmask the ideological presuppositions inherent in any of the narrative forms the story takes. Read in this manner, the *Carmen* story will tell us more about the forms used to relate the story, and the power of those forms, than about the values or psychology of the *Carmen* characters. Furthermore, the constant relaying of altered versions of the same *Carmen* story in new art forms does suggest the capacity of certain kinds of narratives to enlist communities of future readers and perhaps, even, to forge future communities. The aesthetic history of the *Carmen* narrative—remakes in music, dance, and film each concerned quite pointedly with the ideological underpinnings of the potential intensity of deflected desires—ultimately attests to the regenerative capacity of bohemian narratives.

The always tentative social and political setting for my remarks about Bohemia and about bohemian narrative underscores what we assume since 1968 to be the political nature of this community's countercultural-ism. In reality, however, the individualism of Bohemia undermines political positions. In 1843 Marx saw it as the enemy of the revolution, since its political style is one of ambivalence toward the bourgeoisie (Seigel 212). Its persistence through and beyond the political milieus of nineteenth-century Paris further underscores its politically nonspecific or malleable boundaries. In the final analysis its only cogent descriptive characteristic is its tendency to be oppositional, and by that I mean, after Chambers, its tendency to dissent by moving between, rather than staking out, positions.

For the Parisian bohemians of the nineteenth century, Bohemia becomes the landscape of this betweenness. And, as narrative becomes progressively more focused throughout the century on who is talking and who is listening (Brook 236), so the power of bohemian narratives to energize change or to deflect desires between and among "readers" (not only speakers and listeners but also spectators, or listeners, and performers) becomes the very subject of the narratives themselves. Thematic concerns about the boundaries (or lack of boundaries) distinguishing bohemians and bourgeois, the West and the East, cultural versus subjective agency, or the center and the periphery of society become formally embedded discourses that shuttle between the demands of history and literature, words and music, or cinema and theater.

As in the case of Baudelaire and Rimbaud, this formalizing of thematic concerns finds itself repeated in alternative, or bohemian, art forms such as the hundreds of *Carmen Fantasies* which recompose Bizet's inebriated "Bohemian Song," the recent *Carmen* films that cross social and national cultures in the manner of Mérimée's ethnography, or the various other *Carmen* performances that confuse sexual and racial orientations. Ultimately, as the following *Carmen* case study will illustrate, bohemian narrative becomes a suprageneric phenomenon that, alongside the domesticating energies of a post-Enlightenment prose, continues to theatricalize that agitated political and social plasticity that the modern bourgeoisie stages on the battlefield called culture.

⚘ 2 ⚘ *Carmen*

Novella

TO READ Prosper Mérimée's *Carmen* is to participate in an ideal version of bohemian narrative. The novella, a type of storytelling that parallels the ambiguities of the life of bourgeois bohemians on the eve of 1848, also crosses over or balances between two genres: historical chronicle and novel. In so doing, it troubles our sense of readerly composure by setting up, through opposing modes of address, two narrators, two moral imperatives, two sets of rules for readers to follow. The result is a narrative world of aesthetic anarchy—an oppositional world—which becomes possible not because of the ideological persuasiveness of the tale (all women/bohemians are bad and dangerous, beware!) but because of the tale's moral irresoluteness: Are women and bohemians dangerous, or should we fear the unacknowledged passions of a "closeted" bourgeoisie? It is a formal effect related to the rules of genre and to the audiences that abide by them which accounts for this persistent irresoluteness.

Set in 1830, composed in 1845, amended in 1847, and re-edited in 1852, Mérimée's *Carmen* spans a period of persistent irresoluteness among the French. During this period the liberal ideals of the Revolution were clashing boldly with a new, reactionary conservatism and dividing the suddenly powerful bourgeoisie into bohemian and bourgeois sensibili-

ties (Seigel 29). At the same time, a new sense of historical consciousness, a new way of thinking about ourselves in the world, was causing the
intense scrutiny of the boundaries of literature and history as the pur-
veyors of the existential truths of modern times (White, *Metahistory,*
39–40, 137–39, 152–53).

As Hayden White notes in his study of the period titled *Metahistory,*
in this mercurial atmosphere the discipline of history itself, having been
just recently founded at the Sorbonne in 1812, was, by 1830, attracting a
flow of nationalist energies as well as government subsidies (136). But, as
Linda Orr explains in "The Revenge of Literature," this founding of a
new discipline took place largely in response to the many hybrid Romantic genres whose "main common denominator" was history. That is,
everyone was talking about history. According to Orr, as it found itself
engulfed by fiction both from within and without, the new discipline
sought to redefine history by "rewriting the history of history" in order
to institute its difference from fiction as science (3). One interpretation of
the scientific nature of the new French historical practice appeared the
same year as Mérimée's amended *Carmen* and in the same journal, *La
Revue des Deux Mondes:* "For the past fifty years, in fact, the domain of
history has expanded singularly. This science, lost for a long time in systems, has grown closer to the positive sciences through the strict observation of facts."[1] This pose of objectivity, or the "strict observation of facts,"
is one manifestation of the scientism of the new history. Others include
the rhetoric of reliability, what Orr calls the "eyewitness" account (7–8),
and the rhetorical rules that, according to White, nineteenth-century historical narratives follow (*Metahistory,* 5–42).

Having already written *La Chronique du règne de Charles IX* as well as
La Vénus d'Ille, Mateo Falcone, Tamango, and *La Double Méprise,* Mérimée was clearly aware of how to realize the effects of both objectivity
and reliability by relying upon both his inheritance from the eighteenth
century, often called the "frame narrative,"[2] and the accounting for pre-
cursors typical of historical chronicle. He was also aware of the hotly de-
bated status of the new practice of historical narrative as what White calls
the "neutral middle ground" between the recently divided intents of the
empiricist, inductive methods of the scientist and the liberated fictions,

or "free" art, of Romantic poets (137). As White points out, these debates were not merely academic, since they became charged with the ambivalent political intensities that surrounded them:

> In 1818, both Victor Cousin and Guizot were fired from the Sorbonne for teaching "ideas" rather than "facts" (Liard, II, 157–59).
> . . . In 1850, freedom of instruction was rescinded in the French universities in the interests of protecting "society" from the threat of "atheism and socialism" (234). Michelet and Quinet and the Polish poet Mickiewicz were fired, "dangerous books" were proscribed, and historians were specifically prohibited from departing from the chronological order in the presentation of their materials (246).
> (*Metahistory*, 138)

This censoring of historians may explain the "persistent irresoluteness" of Mérimée's *Carmen*. The issues of "atheism and socialism" add a relevant symbolic dimension to Mérimée's portrayal of the values of the Gypsy community: its anti-Catholic, anticonjugal, but intensely fraternal community spirit and the question of "ideas" rather than "facts" and of strict adherence to chronology bear directly on the form this portrayal takes. In light of this close association between *Carmen* and the covert political concerns of historians, in fact, I shall contend that, in a clandestine manner, Mérimée enters into these debates in *Carmen* by staging the ideological underpinnings of historical narrative itself, that not-so-neutral middle ground between the empiricist objectivity of the historians and the fanciful creations of the writer of literary fictions. Moreover, it is in this regard that Mérimée joins the ranks of other literati, such as Heinrich Heine and, later, Nietzsche, who attack academic historiography for appearing to avoid political realities of the present because the quasi-scientific objectivity of the historian could remain seemingly nonpartisan while, in reality, hiding its support of repressive regimes (White, *Metahistory*, 137–39).[3]

In this politically impassioned, quasi-anarchical prerevolutionary environment the hybridity of the genre of *Carmen* is anything but innocent: What is a *nouvelle*, in the context of impassioned debates and of a new reaction sweeping the country? Is it, like its generic predecessors, a moral parable? And is it a moral parable addressed to women, as a letter of Mérimée's to Eugenie de Montijo suggests: "Après *Arsène Guillot,* je n'ai trouvé rien de plus moral à offrir à nos belles dames" (16 May 1845)? [After *Arsène Guillot,* I found nothing more moral to offer our lovely ladies.] Or is it a "très immorale" [very immoral] novella for the pleasure of men, as he also suggests upon its publication on 1 October (Ollier 114)? Does the address to "toute l'Europe savante" [all of educated Europe] which opens the novella refer to those academic historians who support repressive regimes? And do the epigraph and subsequent references in Greek in that address constitute an exclusionary device (one aimed at excluding women, as Peter Robinson argues [4])? Or does the genre *nouvelle* refer more particularly to the formal constraints of the progressively more self-conscious framed narrative, a story within a story, but, like those of Marguerite de Navarre, for example, one of Platonic undecidedness from which lessons can be both critically and "democratically" gleaned? In other words, does the genre repeat the subversive tendencies of its predecessors while taking on something of the "socially symbolic" quality characteristic of its not-too-distant relative, the prose poem (Combe 105)? As Hayden White might ask, what is the moral value of the narrative? What is the content of the form?[4]

Defined in the *Petit Robert* as both a short novel, from the Latin *novellus,* and as a recent fact or bit of news (as in "Je voudrais de tes nouvelles"), the novella is itself divided, as are the addressees and the messages of *Carmen,* between its role as the appealingly quick-read purveyor of literary fiction so popular in the journals of the day and its role in the "universel reportage" by which Stéphane Mallarmé would later define all prose, a scintillating and capsule instance of public information or historical fact. In this respect the novella is a narrative form that has a synthetic tendency much like that of the newly born historical narrative. In the case of *Carmen,* however, the novella form is used as a self-conscious demonstration of how historical narrative emerges from the novelization of historical chronicle. Like historical chronicle, it follows certain rules designed to insure objectivity and lack of controversy. But the novelization of the traditional chronicle implies, as Mikhail M. Bakhtin explains, a certain radicalization by way of form: "the novelization of other genres does not imply their subjection to an alien generic canon; on the contrary, novelization implies their liberation from all that serves as a brake

on their unique development, from all that would change them along with
the novel into some sort of stylization of forms that have outlived themselves."[5] Without giving into one or the other, Mérimée's novella plays
on the requirements of both the more reactionary effect of historical
chronicle and the more radical effect of novelization, so that its form becomes literally oppositional, that is, forced to oscillate between two sets
of generic requirements.[6]

Carmen dramatizes its reliance upon the requirements of both historical chronicle and the novel through its use of double narrators: the historian who presents his travel memoirs (a doubly problematic figure because of his likeness to Mérimée himself) and the protagonist, Don José.
To use a distinction that White makes in "The Value of Narrativity in
the Representation of Reality," whereas the first narrator, the historian,
employs a discourse that *narrates* (substituting meanings for reality), the
second, Don José, employs a discourse that *narrativizes* (allowing the historian to "stand back" and make the world "speak itself") (White 3).
The result is something akin to what Marie Maclean calls "narrative as
performance" in her discussion of Baudelaire, insofar as the narrator is
both identified with and estranged from the object of his narrative. More
precisely, since both narrators tell essentially the same story, the novella
becomes a setting in which to stage the drama of narrative itself. For, as
White points out, "Narrative becomes a *problem* only when we wish to
give to *real* events the *form* of a story" (4), only when one wants to distinguish real from imaginary events, only when one wants to divide history from literature, both of which had undergone considerable concep-
tual change since the second half of the eighteenth century (Bakhtin 5).

As Bakhtin points out in "Epic and Novel," the novel is the dominant
site of these changing conceptions of history and literature in that it opens
up a "new zone" for structuring literary images—"namely, the zone of
maximal contact with the present (with contemporary reality) in all its
undecidedness" (11). In Bakhtin's analysis these changes are apprehended
in a comparison of the epic, which speaks of a fixed past and terminated
legendary history, and the novel, which tells of an "inconclusive present-
day reality" in its rapport with a possible past and a potential future (39).
According to Bakhtin, in this "genre-in-the-making" (11), "the 'depict-
ing' authorial language now lies on the same plane as the 'depicted' lan-

guage of the hero, and may enter into dialogic relations and hybrid combinations with it" (27–28).[7] This change in the temporal plane of literary representation can be compared to what Fredric Jameson refers to as a shift from a *genetic* to an *existential* view of history—a shift from the idea that the past explains the present and future to the idea that the experience of historicity itself may only be understood as a relativist contact between a historian's mind and the cultural objects that mind chooses to study.[8] Existing only as represented, or as textualized, then, each object or event of the past or present can change before the eyes of each historian and can turn that historian into a writer of so-called realist fiction. Mérimée's novella emphasizes this transformation of the historian as it explores the problematic status of historical consciousness itself.

To set this exploration into the problematic status of historical consciousness in motion, *Carmen* establishes and follows the rules of nineteenth-century historiography in order to be able to transgress and thereby question them.[9] With its division into four chapters *Carmen* becomes, as of 1847, the work of a historian eager to conform to what White identifies as the rhetorical rules, or transformative discursive operations, which govern nineteenth-century historiography. Following a research phase, these rules include: (1) the representation of events as having the order of a chronicle; (2) the *emplotment* of the events into a story with identifiable beginning, middle, and end phases; and, finally, (3) the evaluation or interpretation of these emplotted events (*Metahistory*, 5–42).[10] Although the significance of White's work in this area is to uncover the pervasive and unconscious insistence of these rules in nineteenth-century historiography, Mérimée's *Carmen* consciously cultivates and calculates these same transformative operations so as to burst open the narrative conventions of nineteenth-century historiography and to reveal their limits, primarily the limit of that convention that presumes that historical narrative can be objective and devoid of political force if it adopts a particular rhetorical stance.

During *Carmen's* "research phase," we encounter the voice of a historical chronicler anxious to establish the nature of his character and credibility. As a historical chronicler, the truth value of his chronicle depends entirely, as White explains, upon his character ("Narrativity," 17–18) and upon his capacity to avoid controversy and political maneuvering (*Metahistory*, 137). We might even say that the opening of *Carmen* is irrelevant to the story of Carmen except insofar as it establishes the narrator's upstanding character as a member of the professorate who, like White's example, Richerus of Reims, "situates himself in a tradition of historical writing by citing such classics as Caesar" (White, "Narrativity," 17). The narrator of *Carmen* also refers to Caesar and to the "anonymous author of the *Bellum Hispaniense*" (*Carmen*, 611). Such references to past chronicles suppose that this narrator is a historian who writes chronicles objectively and disinterestedly; they also underscore his conservatism and his sense of national pride. As Peter Robinson points out, they may also be a sign of gender exclusion (4), since this character reference is clearly addressed to those readers—undoubtedly, the "old boys"—who read Greek and who would be amused by a titillating epigraph in scholarly form citing Palladas: "Every woman is bitter as bile, but each has two good moments, one in bed and the other in the grave." It is this introductory epigraph that gives *Carmen* its decidedly misogynistic twist and enlists the "very immoral" quality Mérimée addresses to only some of his readers. It tells those privileged few how to read, but it also tames the more radical aspects of *Carmen*'s appeal to liberty and community.

This establishing of his moral character as a reliable researcher also creates a backbone of logic for the writing of a chronicle: it is the narrator's research that explains why he is in a given place at a given time, and it is this research rather than the logic of the Carmen story he tells which continually restores our sense of chronological development. It is due to the demands of his research, in other words, that the historian is able to represent events as a series of chance encounters, to represent events as *having the order of a chronicle*. After he meets a mysterious stranger in chapter 1, then Carmen in chapter 2, Don José takes over the role of narrator in chapter 3. He retells what appear to be the events of the chronicle in story form and, adding a beginning, middle, and end, emplots the events recounted. It is here that the original *Carmen* ended in 1845, with the abrupt cutting off of Don José's narrative and his attack on the bohemian lifestyle.

The addition of the fourth chapter, in 1847, definitively transformed this historical *chronicle* into a historical *narrative*. Whereas the chronicle is characterized by lack of closure—a chronicle merely terminates or cuts off without concluding (White, "Narrativity," 5)—the newer form of nineteenth-century historical narrative required a sense of temporal closure and an appraisal of moral value. This is precisely the function of the added fourth chapter, although this addition is undoubtedly partly due to "market value" as well. As Jacqueline Ollier suggests, the first version of *Carmen* was too scandalous and so poorly received that certain readers actually canceled their journal subscriptions (114). Yet the addition of the final chapter and its return to the professorial voice of the chronicler who introduces the study also helps complicate the ultimate moral message of the tale. As part of the literary device known as the framed narrative, it draws our attention both to the relative nature of the "present," which opens each chapter, and to the problematic status of the speaking subject. The framing also forces us to reread the tale.

Whereas the *Carmen* chronicle offered a series of more or less plausible events in which one thing literally led to another, the *Carmen* narrative becomes a tale of desire and of human degradation primarily concerned with the nefarious effects of bohemian life on the moral fabric of modern society. Insofar as Bohemia is synonymous, during 1845–47, with a countercultural revolutionary spirit (with one eye, among republicans, toward liberty and another, among monarchists, toward crime), this message emphasizes the persistently destructive influence of the revolutionary ideals of 1830—a reiteration of 1789's liberty, fraternity, equality—on the increasingly unstable contours of a contradictory present. With the 1847 addition offering a return to the voice of authority of the professorial historian, it also promulgates a return to what we may take to be imperial order. In fact, the novella of 1847 closes on the most negative of associations with bohemian values: street slang borrowed from the Gypsies, the underworld of Parisian thieves, the urban crimes of the notorious M. Vidocque and of *Les Mystères de Paris* (665). These are precisely the associations Gautier had hoped to exclude as the propagandistic ravings of an antirevolutionary, conservative bourgeoisie in his 1844 review of *Les Bohémiens de Paris*.[11]

In following the rules of the new historical narrative and leading us to a predictable moral conclusion, however, *Carmen* also dramatizes the ways in which the integrity of a historical consciousness may be unconsciously revolutionized by the destructive forces it seeks to control. That is, the textual disposition of *Carmen*'s narrative may be read as having the theoretical stance that Jameson refers to as "existential history," insofar as both the subject and the object of history appear to glide and shift continually. This gliding and shifting is only apparent and, indeed, only possible because of the formal borders and limits dictated by the rules of historical narrative. In this way following the rules is used as a metacritical device that allows *Carmen* to map out the difficulties inherent both in circumscribing an object of historical research and in restraining the speaking subject of historical discourse. From this perspective *Carmen* echoes Jerrold Seigel's definition of Bohemia as an ambiguous cultural phenomenon associated both with revolutionary spirit and with a reinforcement of bourgeois values (Seigel 7–11). On one hand, *Carmen*'s formal contours work to maintain the status quo by following certain rhetorical rules designed to insure the veracity and objectivity of a historical discourse and to create, thereby, a kind of formal appeal to order and to members of the "Resistance" to change. On the other hand, however, these same contours also disrupt the status quo by unmasking the ideological presuppositions that sustain that discourse and creating, thereby, a kind of formal aesthetic anarchy, an appeal to members of the "Movement," or what I call bohemian narrative.

The Research Phase

At the opening of *Carmen* the historian sets out to correct the geographical details of Caesar's last battle. As a historian depicted in the "research phase of his work," he is, to use White's words, "concerned to discover the truth about the past and to recover information either forgotten, suppressed, or obscured" ("Figuring," 11). Despite the fact that this stance is quickly disrupted by the same narrator's designating himself as a storyteller and despite his marking, thereby, of an uneasy distinction between the official history he purports to correct and the cultural history he has more recently encountered and which will form the basis of most of his chronicle, he begins *Carmen* with the following description of his intent:

> J'avais toujours soupçonné les géographes de ne savoir ce qu'ils disent lorsqu'ils placent le champ de bataille de Munda dans le pays des

Bastuli-Poeni, près de la moderne Monda, à quelques deux lieues au nord de Marbella. . . . Je pensais qu'il fallait chercher aux environs de Montilla le lieu mémorable où, pour la dernière fois, César joua quitte ou double contre les champions de la république. Me trouvant en Andalousie au commencement de l'automne de 1830, je fis une assez longue excursion pour éclairer les doutes qui me restaient encore. Un mémoire que je publierai prochainement ne laissera plus, je l'espère, aucune incertitude dans l'esprit de tous les archéologues de bonne foi. En attendant que ma dissertation résolve enfin le problème géographique qui tient toute l'Europe savante en suspens, je veux vous raconter une petite histoire; elle ne préjuge rien sur l'intéressante question de l'emplacement de Munda. (609)

[I have always suspected geographers of not knowing what they are talking about when they place the battlefield of Munda in the country of the Bastuli-Poeni, close to the modern Monda, approximately two leagues north of Marbella. . . . I thought it necessary to search in the neighborhood of Montilla for that memorable spot where, for the last time, Caesar played for double or nothing against the champions of the republic. Finding myself in Andalusia at the beginning of the autumn of 1830, I made a rather long excursion in order to shed light on the doubts that still remained. A memoir that I shall publish shortly will leave, I hope, no incertitude in the mind of any honest archaeologist. While waiting for my thesis to resolve ultimately the geographical problem that holds all of scholarly Europe in suspense, I would like to tell you a little story; it in no way prejudices the interesting question of the location of Munda.][12]

In this passage doubts about the "official" history of the geographical location of Caesar's last battle center, somewhat ironically, on a simple language problem, the difference between an *o* and a *u* (*Monda* and *Munda*). The supposition is that the events of official history may well have been altered because of a mistranscription or mere typographical error. In this way the unconscious slips of language in any writing or reading of history are already slated to play a determining role in this one.

Though the obscure historical detail may not be as provocative as the historian supposes, it becomes more interesting when considered in light of its association with the "autumn of 1830." Due to this date, marking a second French Revolution, Caesar's double-or-nothing triumph over the champions of one republic necessarily comments upon the unwieldy establishment and subsequent demise of other, more recent republics. With the image of Caesar our historian not only calls to mind the "history of history"; he also recalls the favored self-image of Napoléon I during his rise to power in the waning days of the first troubled French Republic. With the additional notion of a double-or-nothing gamble, he further evokes the duplicity of the conciliatory government of Louis Philippe's July Monarchy which also triumphed, double or nothing, over the modern champions of revolutionary change. Like Caesar's and Napoléon's, Louis Philippe's reign triumphed in a "double," or politically ambiguous, manner by offering the republicans certain new privileges while, at the same time, squashing their revolutionary ideals. Moreover, we know that, during the 1840s, reconciliations between supporters of the July Monarchy and representatives of the ancien régime were being systematically pursued (Seigel 7–8).

Given this subtle suggestion that history repeats itself rather than progressing logically in a linear manner from cause to effect, this writer of 1845 may also be hoping to encourage new republican champions by subtly playing with the sense of an "autumn." To use the expression "the autumn of those years" (the autumn of 1830) is to suggest a waning or dying out of revolutionary politics. In relation to a summer, however, this "autumn" also supposes a new beginning, a movement forward in time and, in relation to a summer monarchy, a new revolutionary call to arms. The double-or-nothing gamble thus confuses and enriches the historical object of research by pitting the present of the historian-writer in 1845 against a historical chronicle that begins in the ambiguously suggestive autumn of 1830 by recalling the waning of the ideals of 1789 while, at the same time, looking forward to the Revolution of 1848. It thereby clues us into the writer's unspoken sense that any attempt to think about a revolution now past may both revise that past and produce repetitive futures.

This double-or-nothing gamble also epitomizes the duplicity of the narrative historian himself, who quickly draws our attention to the fact that he is both a historian and a storyteller. On one hand, his research into the location of Caesar's last battle continues to fuel both his travels and his discourse, causing a productive series of chance encounters designed to insure both the objectivity of his "historical" point of view and the scholarly honesty of his chronicle. On the other hand, the object of the historian's research also takes a literary detour. Since this historian never does get back to the interesting question of Munda, we could say that the object of his research continues to shift away from the historical past toward a more literary present, suggesting that the desire to solve historical dilemmas may itself produce historical fictions. One must also ask if this detour is a detour or a subterfuge. That is, does the little story comment upon recent politics, like many literary fictions of the day, or, is it designed, like good historical narratives of the day, to obfuscate them (White, *Metahistory,* 137)?

The duplicity of the narrator as both a historian and a storyteller causes both the object and the speaking subject of the *Carmen* story to remain unstable or unsettled. We are uncertain, from the start, whether the narrator is an amateur historian, a gentleman geographer, an archaeologist, an ethnologist, or merely a teller of tales, since his goals are varied. First, he sets out to correct the work of geographers but also of "official historians," through on-site fieldwork, so as to retrieve the location of Caesar's last battle. But the geography project soon becomes an effort at cultural geography, a study of the Bastuli-Poeni and later a study of the customs of Andalusia and ultimately of bohemians. Far from establishing his character, then, the opening paragraph offers the image of an ambiguous figure who is both an amateur historian cum official spokesman—a writer of memoirs much like Mérimée himself— and a questioner of official boundaries and disciplines whose focus and expertise wander.

Complementing the duplicity of the narrator as both an official spokesman and as a spokesman who transgresses boundaries, the text also pulls its reader in two by self-consciously diminishing the credibility of the presumed professorial savant through a textual overabundance of "doubts," "suspicions," "conjectures," "uncertainty," "suspense," and "prejudice." Through this textual luring by way of unanswered questions, this amateur historian, gentleman geographer, archaeologist storyteller, has, like many good nineteenth-century narrators of "readable," or "readerly," and "realist" texts, already created the persona of a detective-tourist. This last suggested designation only complicates the ambiguity of the narrator's persona, since the detective is motivated to observe details—there is clearly the premonition of a crime to solve—while the tourist observes passively and is prey, as our narrator will soon be, to the effects of foreign *charme*. As the object of an "official" historical narrative moves, in the opening paragraph, from a faraway imperial history of a past Europe,[13] through the autumn of 1830 and by way of a detour or subterfuge, into a kind of suggestive musing about a renewed, present-day debate over imperial and republican politics in 1845, the historian who unearths the treasured facts of the past becomes an entirely unstable subjectivity. Thrust from a "positivist" and comfortable study of texts, maps, and documents into a constantly shifting cultural geography, from a desire to seek a past singular truth to a set of multiple, purely potential, and present-day truths, our narrator also moves from the secure authoritative figure of one who writes to the indecisive conjectures of one who reads.

This shifting from the position of authority of one who writes to that of a reader of signs introduces the first transformative operation characteristic of the rhetorical rules of the new historiography. Moreover, this rhetorical transformation occurs precisely, as the *English Historical Review* proposes, "to avoid contemporary controversies, to treat the subjects science demands, and not to seek arguments for or against doctrines which are only indirectly involved" (173; as quoted by White, *Metahistory*, 137). In relation to the prevailing view, at midcentury, that history was either another form of political analysis or an exercise in human studies (ibid.), Mérimée's novella walks a center line; it plays double or nothing.

Writing a Chronicle

The narrator becomes an ideal historical chronicler as he details a series of chance encounters that shape the logic of his storytelling into what, in 1845, were originally three chapters. Though the actual reader learns ultimately that the three chapters are not chronologically accurate, the tale is, nonetheless, structured as a historical chronicle, which only later appears to us to have gone awry. The first encounter is with a noble stranger whom the historian refers to as a "voyageur comme moi, moins archéologue seulement" (611) [traveler like myself, though a bit less of an archaeologist]. The fact that this historian sees the stranger as being a traveler like himself is an initial clue that the objectivity of his point of view is already in peril. Nonetheless, the historian proceeds to outline a new object of study. Due to his knowledge of Spanish culture, he quickly establishes a cultural fraternity with the stranger which allows a detailed study of the physiognomy and linguistic habits of his specimen. His cultivated distance from this new object of study is underscored through his use of explanatory footnotes such as "Les Andalous respirent l's" (611), [The Andalusians breathe in their esses].

This scholarly objectivity is soon thwarted, however, as the historian decides that he recognizes, in this traveler, the face of the infamous bandit José-Maria.[14] As a tourist, the narrator is intrigued and naïvely charmed by what may well be an armed and dangerous criminal; as a detective, he shows himself to be a very bad reader of signs, for it is on the basis of a detailed observation of physical attributes that he determines the stranger to be the celebrated criminal (611–13). It is not until the opening of the third chapter that the bandit is identified as Don José. Nonetheless, the interesting result of his misreading of the signs is a slip in assumptions and, therefore, in the factuality of his chronicle which recalls the suspected slip in vowels which got him started in the first place.

The historian's effort to rectify one error leads to the production of new ones, as scholarly observation gives way to excited fascination: "à force de considérer mon compagnon, j'étais parvenu à lui appliquer le signalement de José-Maria, que j'avais lu affiché aux portes de maintes villes d'Andalousie. —Oui, c'est bien lui. . . . Cheveux blonds, yeux bleus. . . . Plus de doute! Mais respectons son incognito" (613) [having considered my companion at length, I managed to see in him José-Maria's mug shot that I had seen posted on the doors of many cities in Andalusia. —Yes, it is truly he. . . . Blond hair, blue eyes. . . . No doubt about it! But let us respect his incognito]. In what appears, momentarily, to be a respite from the unsettling conjectures and suppositions of the opening of the tale, the narrator is excited to have encountered some real local color and has forgotten his earlier, more realistic appraisal of the stranger as "a traveler like me." As we shall see repeatedly throughout the tale, it is excitement and fascination—the work of desire—which transforms sameness into a falsely desirable difference. More significantly, however, the narrator divides his discourse, for the first time in this recitation, into two separate scenes. The interior dialogue of his own intimate thoughts, "Oui, c'est bien lui . . ." [Yes, it is truly he . . .], is a silent response to himself, whereas the narrative discourse by which he represents himself to others, "Mais respectons son incognito" [But let us respect his incognito], is an injunction to the implied reader to join him in his friendly, fraternal infraction. The latter is a public stage upon which he has already played a series of roles—roles that will shift according to his audience, whether the "old boys," José, Carmen, or the authorities, religious and legal.

The importance of this double scene representing the mind of the narrator as divided between narrative and dramatic discourses (besides the fact that the narrator continues, quite seriously, to play double or nothing) is the way that these two modes of discourse relate to Jerrold Seigel's sense of the relationship between the bourgeois and the bohemians. Seigel insists not only that the borders separating the two social identities are malleable but that, as the bourgeoisie opposes bohemians, or constitutes them as other, that same bourgeoisie seeks to define itself publicly by hiding its bohemian behaviors in the private hollows of its own dangerously individualized subjectivity (10). In other words, the "counterimage of Bohemia" was one way to dramatize ambivalence within the bourgeoisie toward its own social identity, one way to respond to the dilemmas posed by the question of individuality as the expression of a conflict at the very heart of the bourgeois life, a place to probe social margins and frontiers (9–10). Seigel's sense that "Bohemia has always exercised a powerful attraction on many solid bourgeois, matched by the deeply bourgeois instincts and aspirations of numerous Bohemians" is enacted dramatically, in *Carmen*, as a relationship that defines the narrator's own subjectivity as a divided discursive scene.

Relations between his split bourgeois and bohemian identities poses a moral dilemma for the narrator at the close of *Carmen*'s first chapter. Having decided not to denounce his exciting pseudoforeigner to the authorities, the narrator has second thoughts in what has become a relatively frequently cited passage:

> Je me demandais si j'avais eu raison de sauver de la potence un
> voleur, et peut-être un meurtrier, et cela seulement parce que j'avais
> mangé du jambon avec lui et du riz à la valencienne. N'avais-je pas
> trahi mon guide qui soutenait la cause des lois; ne l'avais-je pas
> exposé à la vengeance d'un scélérat? Mais les devoirs de l'hospitalité!
> . . . Préjugé de sauvage, me disais-je; j'aurai à répondre de tous les
> crimes que le bandit va commettre. . . . Pourtant est-ce un préjugé
> que cet instinct de conscience qui résiste à tous les raisonnements?
> (618; elisions in original)

> [I asked myself if I had been reasonable to save a thief, and perhaps
> a murderer, from capture and that only because I had eaten ham with
> him and some rice *à la valencienne.* Had I not betrayed my guide,
> who was upholding a lawful cause; had I not exposed him to the vengeance of a scoundrel? But the responsibilities of hospitality! . . .
> Prejudice of a savage, I said to myself; I will have to answer for all
> the crimes the bandit is going to commit. . . . On the other hand, is it
> a prejudice, this instinct of conscience which resists all reasoning?

In this passage the narrator's moral dilemma pits his bourgeois values against those of the bohemian. He fears he is guilty of "treason" (a crime against the laws of the state), of "vengeance" (a crime against those of the church), and of irrational behavior (a crime against the enlightened subject of Cartesian rationalism). These fears are dismissed, however, in favor of the "duties of hospitality" dictated by the unwritten cultural codes of Spanish fraternity (shared food), the "prejudice of an [uncivilized] savage" (but here in the sense of the *bon sauvage*), and instinctive mental behavior. Not only are these the values typically associated with an antiestablishment Bohemia which recur, in a rather different light, in the narrator's closing chapter 4 discussion of Gypsies and their practices, but these values are neatly inserted into the innermost space of private dialogue. On the outside the self-conscious agitation of the private mental space will be quelled in the manner of a good bourgeois. The narrator will save face by "exhibiting my passport, and signing a [false] declaration before a judge" (619). And, as he coldly terminates an otherwise agitated mental dilemma, the same agitation is quieted or resolved formally by the marking of a chapter ending in the manner of a true historical chronicle. The closures, both mental and formal, are in each case entirely artificial. Yet as White notes, citing Hegel, history is always the tale of a conflict between desire (culture, religion, sexuality) and authority (the law, the state, that which founds the subject's legitimacy) (White, "Narrativity," 12). In other words, this conflict between desire, or bohemian tendencies, and authority, or bourgeois sensibilities, stages the very nature of historical consciousness itself.

It is because the narrator believes himself to be opposed to bohemian values that he is able to construct his exotic foreigner as an other and to identify with that otherness, unconsciously, with a view to justifying his own criminal comportment. Ironically, however, he is able to identify with José not because his rigid exterior contains the heart of a bohemian but, instead, because the bourgeoisie is a cross-cultural, international community that, in curious ways, actually mimics the supranationalism of Bohemia. The two men are culturally and socially similar, even if they are of different nationalities. In both cases unconscious alliance to the values of Bohemia permits and contributes to a dissolution of moral character. From the ranks of the professorate the historian has been rather quickly reduced to the status of a bad detective, a naive tourist, and from there to that of a moral criminal (only to be reduced further, after having met Carmen, to premeditating a truly murderous crime [623]). The same will be true of Don José. In other words, the narrator mimics the dissolution of José's moral character quite literally "avant la lettre," before the telling of that life in chapter 3.

The historian's unconscious identification with this supposed bohemian he himself has constructed calls to mind a phenomenon that psychoanalysis refers to as *Verleugnung* (denial, disavowal, denegation). In *Clefs pour l'Imaginaire ou l'Autre Scène* Octave Mannoni relies on this phenomenon to explain that belief in dream scenes or in phantasms—that is, in unconscious fantasy scenarios—is only possible because the subject in question is able to deny any real participation in the events of the scenario (166). Mannoni uses the formula "Je *sais bien* mais *quand même* . . ." [I *know very well* but *even so* . . .] to illustrate the way that patients begin to tell of their dream scenes or fantasy scenarios as if already denying them. This unconscious mechanism is applicable to the historian and perhaps to the nature of nineteenth-century historical consciousness in general. In this case, however, it is because the historian believes that the cultures of the bohemian and the bourgeois are distinguished that he is able to participate in his game of fantasy role-playing. It is because he can deny any association with Bohemia that he is able to identify, on an unconscious level, with the fascinating bandit and to justify moral infractions of the law. This identification necessarily transports this or any object of research into the world of the subject's desiring fantasies. It is not surprising, therefore, that this same phenomenon applies to Edward Said's Orientalism.

In *Carmen* this identification on the part of the historian with the object of his research supposes that the dissolution of the narrator's moral character is accompanied by an even more compelling dissolution of the speaking subject's authority creating, in the end, two morals of the story. There is the moral value of the tale itself, the lesson the historian and José both want to teach us: interaction with Bohemia weakens moral fiber. Then there is the moral value of its form, the lesson we learn by tracing the identification of narrator and protagonist: unanalyzed desires and identifications can lead us astray. Consequently, just as the narrator of this history is pulled in a conflict between his inner bohemian tendencies and the responsibilities of his public persona, so too is the story's form.

An interrogation into the power of unanalyzed desires follows the arrested agitation of the end of chapter 1. Returning to his research at the Dominican library in Córdoba on manuscripts relating to the "interesting problem" of Munda, the historian opens his second chapter by relating a new exciting encounter: thinly clad working women bathing by the banks of the Guadalquivir. As the historian puts it: "On y jouit d'un spectacle qui a bien son mérite" (619) [There one takes pleasure in a spectacle that is particularly noteworthy]. As he describes this "spectacle," the historian recultivates his distant gaze, transforming the sounds of an "infernal" din into a silent, almost balletic vision of "white forms" against an azure backdrop.[15] He also comments upon the ways in which a literary (and fantasy-oriented) imagination may contaminate what attempts to be an objective relation of facts. His choice of the pronoun *on*, or "one," is already suggestive of his simultaneous distance from and involvement in the spectacle, and his use of the verb *jouir* (to partake in an erotic pleasure) predicts something more than an indifferent attitude toward the scene. Indeed, his description of the bathers reeks of unconscious desire:

> Au dernier coup de cloche, toutes ces femmes se déshabillent et entrent dans l'eau. Alors ce sont des cris, des rires, un tapage infernal. Du haut du quai, les hommes contemplent les baigneuses, écarquillent les yeux, et ne voient pas grand'chose. Cependant ces formes blanches et incertaines qui se dessinent sur le sombre azur du fleuve, font travailler les esprits poétiques, et, avec un peu d'imagination, il n'est pas difficile de se représenter Diane et ses nymphes au bain, sans avoir à craindre le sort d'Actéon. (619–20)

> [At the last stroke of the clock, all of these women undress and go into the water. Then there are cries and laughter, an infernal noise-making. From the top of the quay, the men contemplate the bathers, squint their eyes, and don't see much. Yet the white, uncertain forms drawn upon the somber azure of the river put poetic minds to work, and, with a little imagination, it is not difficult to see before oneself [literally, to represent before oneself] Diana and her nymphs bathing, without having to fear the destiny of Actaeon.]

In this description the infernal noise-making of what can only be prostitutes bathing becomes a poetic vision of the goddess Diana and her nymphs. Both the erotic and the political force of these female workers is tamed by a poetic reading of mythic proportions.

Though this poetic reading tends to reinsure the objective distance of the historian's discourse, it also works to hide the energetic, if disavowed, work of desire. The historian once again denies reality, here the eroticism of the scene, in order to replace it with a personal poetic fantasy. And, once again, the formula for fantasy based on denial is set in operation: he *knows* he need not face the destiny of Actaeon—to be devoured by the dogs of the huntress—and this safety allows him to justify and to deny his own personal voyeuristic pleasure. He is not like those other men who strain their eyes to see and see little. By concentrating on the painterly aspect of these clair-obscure drawings in space, he sees much more than what is actually there. Evidently, the contrast between the Dominican fathers and this spectacle of "infernal" prostitution which their teachings would both forbid and promote is obviously too much for this ethnographer to reconcile. He poeticizes the scene and, quite literally, re-presents it for himself in such a way as to sublimate an erotic experience into an artistic vision.[16]

It is ironic that Jacques Lacan uses the image of Actaeon to describe Freud (and indeed all analysts) as well as the transformative and destructive power of desire as it links subjects back to themselves rather than to any object of their desires, destroying the very integrity of subjectivity itself.[17] Furthermore, an analogy can be drawn between this instance of subtle denial and the historian's earlier examination of motives which also justified and denied a loss of personal integrity. It is once again an effort to constitute Bohemia as other, and thus to distinguish himself from it, which summons the energy of desire. This denied desire unleashes the historian's own bohemian tendencies and causes the un(self)conscious historian to misread or slip up. As a result, the objectivity of a scholarly account of Guadalquivir is undermined by a literary and phantasmatic productivity.

The historian's misapprehension of the bathing scene and denial of his own capacity to play the role of Actaeon serve as a prelude to a magical and charming encounter with Carmen, one of the engaging bathers our researcher wants to misrepresent. Curiously, though this third encounter with Bohemia appears to move the chronicle forward, it also twists itself into a repeat of the encounter with José. It is the strange and, once again, "savage" beauty of this Gypsy which charms and finally seduces him: "C'était une beauté étrange et sauvage, une figure qui étonnait d'abord, mais qu'on ne pouvait oublier" [622] [It was a strange and savage beauty, a face that was astonishing at first, but a face one could never forget]. And, just as José reminds him of Milton's Satan, Carmen appears as a "sorceress," a "servant of the devil" (621). He smokes with Carmen, as he did with José, and eats with her.

Though the jasmine in her hair is "intoxicating" and her beauty alluring—"*à l'obscure clarté qui tombe des étoiles*" (620; Mérimée's emph.) [in the obscure light that descends from the stars]—the historian makes excuses and again calculates his distance by punctuating his thoughts with footnotes. Unfortunately, the footnotes give way to "savage prejudices," to an overemphasis of his own poetic sensibilities, and thus, once again, to a denial of Bohemia's seductive powers and a renewal of criminal thoughts: "Déjà j'avais la main sur le pied d'un des tabourets, et je syllogisais à part moi pour deviner le moment précis où il conviendrait de le jeter à la tête de l'intrus" (623) [Already I had my hand on the foot of one of the bar stools, and I was syllogizing to myself to determine the precise moment at which it would be appropriate to throw it at the head of the intruder]. The potential murder is only staved off by the fact that this jealous intruder is none other than the bandit Don José, whom "je regrettais un peu de ne pas avoir laissé pendre" (623) [I regretted a bit not having let hang]. What was once only a fantasy fascination with crime now becomes a reality, and the identification with an imaginary version of the "bandit" José is thoroughly complete. This identification throws a different light on the association of criminals and bohemians which closes the tale.

Emplotment

In the third chapter the historian learns that the bandit is named Don José Lizzarrabengoa (a name that identifies him, ironically, as a bourgeois gentleman "much like myself") and that he has been imprisoned and sentenced to death for the murder of Carmen. In this third chapter Don José takes over the discursive function of storyteller as the historian listens to a tale of moral dissolution disquietingly similar to the one he himself has just experienced. Although José tells his own story, he also rectifies the details of identity and chronology contained in the historian's chronicle of events. Therefore, José's narrative can be called, in White's words, a transformation by way of *emplotment*, a chronicle recast as a "story with identifiable beginning, middle, and end phases" ("Figuring," 12). By the end of this third chapter it is clear that José has recounted the story that our historian has just lived and that the exchanging of narrators signals a more interesting exchange of identities.

The parallels between the two stories are subtle but regular and are often as much a question of textual echoes or stylistic similarities as they are of shared character or psychological traits.[18] Psychologically, José, like the historian, is a bad reader of signs, the result being that he, too, idealizes and is seduced by his own personal version of Bohemia: "J'avais entendu souvent parler de quelques contrebandiers qui parcouraient l'Andalousie, montés sur un bon cheval, l'espingole au poing, leur maî-tresse en croupe. Je me voyais déjà trottant par monts et par vaux avec la gentille bohémienne derrière moi. Quand je lui parlais de cela, elle [Car-men] riait à se tenir les côtes" (643) [I had often heard talk of contraban-dists who traveled Andalusia, mounted on a good horse, blunderbuss in hand, their mistress riding behind. I saw myself already trotting along hills and valleys with the gentle bohemian woman behind me. When I spoke of that, she (Carmen) laughed enough to split her sides]. This image of the tourist's bourgeois naïveté is reminiscent of the progres-sively more excited nostalgia with which the historian describes his first encounter with José; it too has to do with identifying with a romanticized version of an other who, like all others populating the Imaginary, is really only designed to complement a fantasy image of oneself. Indeed, José's bohemian fantasy includes the bourgeois desire for easy money and a mistress all to himself.

Accompanying this mistaken sense of other and of self is the idea that one can master or sublimate sexual impulses in such romantic fantasies. Just like the narrator who describes bathing prostitutes with a certain po-etic distance, for instance, José remains sexually indifferent as the other guards watch thinly clad young working women return to work at the tobacco manufactory. Textually, José's remark "Pendant que les autres regardaient, moi, je restais sur mon banc" (628) [While the others watched, me, I remained on my bench] echoes an earlier one by the nar-rator: "Bien qu'il fît encore grand jour, les nymphes du Guadalqui-vir . . . firent en sûreté de conscience leur toilette de bain. . . . Je n'y étais pas" (620) [Though it was still bright daylight, the Guadalquivir nymphs . . . bathed with total confidence. . . . I wasn't there]. In José's scene, moreover, the "ringing of the bells" recalls the earlier bathing scene at the sound of the *angélus* quite deliberately: "Voilà la cloche qui sonne; les filles vont rentrer à l'ouvrage" (627) [There's the bell ringing; the girls are going to go back to work].

José's attitude of bourgeois indifference persists in his description of his first meeting with Carmen. He focuses on her animal qualities and her intoxicating flowers (628, 633), and his description, like that of the narrator, is peppered with the distanced objectification of scholarly remarks and explanations. For example, "La *Bar lachi,* monsieur, c'est la pierre d'aiment, avec laquelle les bohémiens prétendent qu'on fait quantités de sortilèges" (630) [The *bar lachi,* sir, is the magnetic stone, with which the bohemians maintain one can do a lot of sorcery"]. Or "Vous savez que les bohémiens, monsieur, comme n'étant d'aucun pays, voyagent toujours, parlent toutes les langues, et la plupart sont chez eux en Portugal, en France, dans les provinces, en Catalogne, partout; même avec les Maures et les Anglais, ils se font entendre" (631) [You know that the bohemians, sir, being from no country, travel all the time, speak all languages, and that most are at home in Portugal, in France, in the provinces, in Catalonia, everywhere; even with the Moors and the English, they make themselves understood"]. It is significant that this sort of information, gleaned from Don José, later informs the more ethnographic discussion of bohemians and their lifestyle, in chapter 4. Even though Don José should be read as a mirror image of the narrator in terms of his social class, race, gender, and cultural identity, the narrator continues to think of him as an unruly foreigner and uses as fact, in his cultural history of bohemians, knowledge appropriated from José's limited experience among them.

Among their parallel relations, however, most important is the way that José, like the narrator before him, is pulled by two opposing moral senses when he liberates a different bohemian prisoner, the infamous Carmen, with whom he also identifies. José explains:

> Elle estropiait le basque, et je la crus Navaraise; ses yeux seuls et sa bouche et son teint la disaient bohémienne. J'étais fou, je ne faisais plus attention à rien. Je pensais que, si des Espagnols s'étaient avisés de mal parler du pays, je leur aurais coupé la figure, tout comme elle venait de faire à sa camarade. Bref, j'étais comme un homme ivre.
> . . . Et pourquoi me suis-je fait punir? Pour une coquine de bohémi-

enne qui s'est moquée de moi, et qui, dans ce moment, est à voler dans quelque coin de la ville. (632–33)

[She spoke a broken Basque, and I believed she was Navarrese; her eyes alone and her mouth and her skin tone said she was bohemian. I was crazy, I was no longer paying attention to anything. I thought that, if some Spaniards had decided to speak poorly of my country, I would have cut their faces, exactly as she had just done to her comrade. In short, I was like a drunken man. . . . And why did I let myself be punished? For a Gypsy floozy who had made fun of me and who, at this very moment, is out stealing in some corner of the city.]

Reactions that parallel those of the narrator facing a similar moral dilemma include: identification despite or because of the denial of a reality he knows to be otherwise, dismissal of his sense of responsibility, misapprehension of character, charmed naïveté like that of a tourist, and a kind of intoxicated following of animal instinct, or "savage prejudice," rather than reason, religion, duty, or the law. In both cases bohemian instincts rather than bourgeois conventions win out. With regard to textual or stylistic echoes one notices as well that José's attempt to justify his behavior also leads to the self-questioning of inner dialogue.

Finally, in this outlining of parallels, it is useful to return one more time to the similar degradation of both moral and social standing I suggested earlier. Like the historian, José's life is summed up by a series of degradations from officer to brigadier to soldier to naive tourist to contrabandist to jealous lover to murderer to condemned man, so that he, too, takes on a multiplicity of different roles to play which are, once again, the result of an unresolved choice between bourgeois and bohemian values. At the conclusion of his story José condemns Bohemia, making it clear that neither he nor Carmen is at fault but, rather, the nefarious Bohemia, which always corrupts (660). In his final evaluation this reading is reiterated by our supposedly objective historian, in the shape of what we might call on-site documentation or data gleaned from fieldwork. The supplementary chapter 4 thus rounds out the series of associations that make the historian the mirror image of his protagonist and prove that José's story is nothing but an emplotted version of historical chronicle.

Moral Evaluation

In the final chapter of *Carmen* a formal argument is adduced in order to establish, as White suggests, the ethical, cognitive, and aesthetic meaning of the now emplotted chronicle (*Metahistory*, "Figuring"). Both José's story and the historian's original object of research are temporally and emotionally distanced as the cool voice of the historian returns, but in an even more anthropological tone, to give an impersonal but erudite evaluation of bohemian life. This new conclusion offers a sense of formal coherence and closure as it determines the moral value of the historical narrative. More important, however, this evaluation essentially repeats José's indictment of Bohemia by recasting elements of the story we have just read into the shape of a scholarly interpretation.

Though not all of the historian's information has come from Don José, it is clear that much of it generalizes the facts based on José's emplotted version of the *Carmen* story in much the same way that José's version generalized the one already suggested in the narrator's chronicle. Echoes from his previous discussions and experiences inform, for example, the following remarks about Gypsies: "La plupart . . . mènent une vie errante dans les provinces . . . en Andalousie . . . en Catalogne. Ces derniers passent souvent en France"; "Sans parler de la contrebande. . . . Les femmes disent la bonne aventure"; "On ne peut comparer leur regard qu'à celui d'une bête fauve"; "Le caractère de la nation, rusée, hardie"; as for the women, "Il faut leur plaire, il faut les mériter"; "Il est certain que les Gitanas montrent à leurs maris un dévoûment extraordinaire"; and, finally, "La vie de ces gens est si misérable, que l'annonce de la mort n'a rien d'effrayant pour eux" (660–61) [Most lead a wandering life in the provinces . . . in Andalusia . . . in Catalonia. The latter often cross into France; Without speaking of contraband. . . . The women tell adventure stories; One can only compare their gaze to that of a wild beast; The character of the nation [is] wily, strong; as for the women, You have to please them and merit them; It is certain that Gypsies show their husbands an extraordinary devotion; and, finally, The life of these people is so miserable that the announcement of death is not at all frightening to them]. The interest of these textual echoes of remarks made previously by José or the historian is that, whereas the final moral evaluation is designed to render the objective facts of the case by following the rhetorical rules of historical narrative, the literary, almost musical nature of these echoes coupled with the uncertain moral character of their source leads us to question the linear logic of the unfolding narrative and causes readers to see that logic as one of repetition and obsessive re-reading.

In reiterating "facts" in this manner, this historian does not correct the geography of Caesar's last battle but, rather, that of the official history of Bohemia. Whereas previous research in the field, primarily that of the Englishman George Borrow, extolled the positive virtues of bohemian life—liberty, fraternity, equality, and virtue (661)—the historian has made it his business to guard us against its evils. The final reference, at the end of the chapter, to the contagious nature of Romany, the Gypsy language, forges a link between common Parisian thieves and these "savage" bohemian nomads (665). It sends a clear message of condemnation to the average Parisian reader of 1847 insofar as this same association will have been regularly referred to in the popular media. It is precisely this association, for example, which was popularized by Eugène Grangé and Adolphe d'Ennery's *The Bohemians of Paris* in 1843 and decried by Gautier's review in 1844. We could say of *Carmen,* as Seigel does of the play, "The play called attention to a phenomenon that merged traditional images of gypsies with new specters rising from the shadows of modern urban life; it also emphasized how thin was the line between imagining and inventing on the one hand, and piercing the limits of socially or legally sanctioned behavior on the other" (23). In this light the citing of a Gypsy proverb at the end of *Carmen*—"*En retudi panda nasti abela macha.* En close bouche, n'entre point mouche" [Into a closed mouth enter no flies]—seems less oriented than the historian maintains toward giving us "une idée avantageuse de mes études sur le rommani" (666) [an advantageous idea of my studies in Romany] and more toward presuming, with his readers, that the obvious dangers suggested by the association of Gypsies and the underworld need not be stated.

On a formal or textual level, however, the "moral of the story," or what White has referred to elsewhere as the "content of the form," is quite different. First, the mirror effect that plays across a narrative frame both to distinguish and to ally the historian and José works, as a "read-

erly," or literary, effect, against both the historian's reactionary evaluation and the only formally cohesive closure of the tale. Although the historian uses the form of the historical narrative to conquer, dominate, or
tranquilize the revolutionary forces that the nefarious Bohemia has come
to represent (Robinson makes this point [13–14]), he also shows us that a
program of cultural classification such as the one in which he is engaged
may force an identification of a historian and the object of his research.
Indeed, in his setting up of Bohemia as a dangerously seductive other,
the historian proves, by way of his own actions, that it is impossible to
escape its alluring appeal. Looking outward, the historian merely finds
himself projected into a world inevitably reorganized by his very attempt to organize and study it. He does, in other words, precisely what
Lacan suggests is useful about the Actaeon syndrome. Despite his ethical
evaluation of Bohemia, therefore, the historian's cognitive contact with
it nurtures the very destructive forces his discourse would guard against.
He, like Caesar, has also gambled double or nothing.

This constant insistence on the unconscious reorganization by readers
(historians, lovers, ethnologists) of the objects of their (re)search sends
an opposing political message to the reader of *Carmen*. It suggests that it
may not be Bohemia that is dangerous but, more precisely, the constraints
of an ordered vision of society (and of historiography) which actually
cause revolutions or, at least, productive disruptions. The idealizations,
misreadings, and unanalyzed desires provoked by Bohemia actually push
Carmen forward and program new identities releasing the intense utopian
energy of an aesthetic violence. These idealizations and unanalyzed desires of both the narrator and his protagonist are only rendered possible,
however, because the rules of form and the affective distance between
readers or researchers and the objects of their gaze are secured and maintained. That is, the men identify with Bohemia only because they are
"closeted" and can deny their innermost affinities for it; readers of *Carmen* seem to rewrite the tale because it sets up the culture of Bohemia as
a distant other place in which we somehow find ourselves. To secure the
borders of the story by following the rules of nineteenth-century historiography is to believe that one secures those of society as well, but, as
the story is reordered by the transformative operations of discourse, so
are the lifestyles and identities of its readers.

Second, the play of textual echoes throughout *Carmen* along with the confused chronology of the tale at the level of its narrative structure permit an unresolved sense of the present and tacit speculations about the future of France. Insofar as José, the only slightly wayward bourgeois gentleman, can be read as both supportive of the hierarchical values of the ancien régime—church, military, and state—and, at the same time, corrupted and seduced by the bohemian champions of a republican lifestyle, it is clear that, situated in 1830, his lifestyle can be equated with the compromise and duplicity of the bourgeoisie itself. The traveling historian then condemns those revolutionary forces that destroyed Don José in 1845. But in his critique of those forces our historian also borrows them, promulgating liberty, fraternity, and an unconscious equality, an invitation to identify with the bohemian values of a countercultural lifestyle. This leaves us with the writer of 1847, whose nostalgia for those revolutionary ideals waning since 1830 releases a utopian energy that looks forward to '48 by showing us his poetic capacity to rewrite the world that he sees. Indeed, he may be said to represent a world violently reordered by a disavowed, and thus inevitable, identification with bohemian style. Like the bohemians, his style wanders across the frontiers, or borders, of historical narrative, cultivating visions of Bohemia which confuse art and life, imagination and invention, criminality and legality.

In this ambivalent mixture of settled and lack of settled values and meanings, of closure and of repetitive rereadings, Mérimée stages and interrogates the moral value of narrative form itself by disrupting what White calls the "appeal of historical narrative," the offer of an ordered, "concluded" world to readers for whom that is necessarily not the case ("Narrativity," 20). Readers, like their models, the narrator, José, and the historian at the end, finish by finding themselves pulled between the social duties and cultural values of an international Bohemia and the rules, comfort, order, or formal coherence of narrated realities and of dominant popular values associated with bourgeois conformity. It is this pull, I shall contend, that causes us to continually reappropriate and rewrite Carmen and her story, for their bohemian irresoluteness is also our own.

Finally, on the subject of the doubled exigencies of *Carmen* creating a form of literary oppositionality which actually causes future readers to respond, it is clear that Bohemia does indeed become an artistic call to freedom and a social force for change, as the participation of poets and artists in the insurrection of '48 demonstrates (Seigel 404).[19] More important, however, beyond '48, *Carmen* continues to program innovative revolutionary art forms and creative critical responses that, beyond those I will consider in the work of Georges Bizet and Carlos Saura, proliferate and find new followers as I write.

⅍ 3 ⅍   Carmen

Opéra-comique

ONE OF the most elusive and illusory aspects of opera is the place of narrative in the peculiar dramatic and musical exigencies of operatic form. Though we all presume narrative to be the overriding operating principle of operatic textuality, as Carolyn Abbate points out in *Unsung Voices*, the questions of what constitutes the narrative, where it is located, and, indeed, who narrates need to be systematically considered in the case of each individual opera.[1] As in film narrative in which an accumulation of individual and often highly disparate shots contribute to a continuity that is largely imaginary—a mere "effect" of narrative created by the cinematic apparatus rather than an actual telling of a story by one person to another, that is, rather than an actual speech act[2]—operatic narrative may only "unfold" or take place as a similar kind of imaginary effect within the minds of its listener-spectators. In the context of late-nineteenth-century operatic politics this chapter will "listen" to Georges Bizet's *Carmen* and to some of its imaginary effects among readers such as Friedrich Nietzsche and Catherine Clément and others who speak from inside the opera itself.

Although the peculiarly heterogeneous concatenation of practices, disciplines, and materials that make up operatic textuality—song, dance, dialogue, music, costume, landscape, architecture, and so on—continue to adapt stories, and seem, indeed, to tell them, it is also true that we do not necessarily hear these stories. In other words, that which we imagine to be operatic narrative may be less like literary narrative, in which someone tells something to (an at least implied) someone else, and more like film narrative, in which a general force, logic, energy, or rhythmic design only seems to narrate because of the anticipations and recollections (or desires and temporary satisfactions) solicited among its "readers" by its textual effects.[3] If it is true that narrative in opera is indeed dependent upon this kind of purely imaginary effect, then it is the perfect potential setting for the "deflecting of desires" characteristic of bohemian narrative. The question remains about how the rhythmic designs of operatic textuality figure the imaginary effect of narrative continuity and logic from within the heterogeneous fragments—what Abbate and Roger Parker call the ambiguities, irresoluteness, eclecticism, and systematic mishaps that characterize operatic composition.[4]

In this context of opera the concept of bohemian narrative proposes to uncover some of the textual strategies by which opera induces the sense of continuity and logic we call operatic narrative and to suggest some of the ideological purposes behind these strategies in the particularly self-conscious example of Bizet's *Carmen*. As in the case of Mérimée's *Carmen*, then, bohemian narrative supposes both the telling of a story about Bohemia in its indistinctiveness from the bourgeoisie and a certain kind of metacritical, or self-reflexive, narrative behavior that has the peculiar status of playing a textual function against a narrative function in order to tempt a reader's duplicity. There are, in other words, always at least two reading strategies inscribed in a bohemian narrative: one that encourages attention to narrative discourse, to intrigue, plot, and character, and appears to play into a set of dominant cultural values; and another whose goal is to make this play available to its readers, or open to their scrutiny, in a kind of counterdiscursive unmasking of the ideological imperatives of narrative and, in this case, of operatic form itself. The strategies that make this second kind of reading possible also reveal the necessary complicity of the form with the values it purveys. In the case of nineteenth-century opera it may be that the ideological effects of narrative form are the same as or are equal to what it is we sense to be operatic narrative. It is this "equality" that the concept and study of bohemian narrative proposes to disclose.

In Bizet's *Carmen* this double set of strategies for how to read becomes, as in Mérimée's *Carmen*, the very subject of the narrative, representing itself in a variety of double contradictory binds. These contradictions take various familiar configurations including: bourgeois/bohemian and Resistance/Movement (these being the names of two major political parties opposed during the 1830s and '40s in Paris, while Prosper Mérimée was writing the original *Carmen*) and, in addition, Oriental/Occidental, feminine/masculine, dominant/marginal, central/peripheral (these being more in keeping with the racial terms at stake in French nationalism, whose inception, during the 1870s, parallels Bizet's revision).[5] Yet, insofar as the textual function of bohemian narrative displays the ideological allegiances of narrative itself, the bohemian narrative of Bizet's *Carmen* repeats the capacity of Mérimée's to reach outside of these self-contained, mutually exclusive systems to what Ross Chambers, in *Room for Maneuver*, calls a potential community of future readers. In some sense the very fact of the operatic adaptation, as well as of the critical reactions to its opening and subsequent performances and its renewed popularity today, prove this capacity of Mérimée's original to solicit repetitive reinterpretations among future readers. Likewise, the similar capacity of Bizet's *Carmen* is best demonstrated by later readaptations of it among its future readers.

Carmen's tendency to inscribe within itself the futurity of interpretive openings proposes, however idealistically, to work within a narrative system, not to overthrow its values but to realign or reappraise them, by catching the reader within a narrative anarchy in which actual political alliances may have an opportunity to shift. In the case of *Carmen* the adaptation of the novella to the opera seems to occasion another shift away from something like Mazzini's imagined community of Romantic nationalists toward an equally idealized image of an ethnically or "racially" diverse modern bourgeoisie, in response to the political xenophobia characteristic of domestic nationalism in the 1870s (Hobsbawm, *Nations and Nationalism*, 104–5).

In this context of opera analysis, however, the association of opera and bohemian narrative poses two distinct dilemmas. First, which blue-print constitutes an operatic text? A recording, a score? A mise-en-scène? A libretto? And do we hear this text, or does it only exist in each reader's subjective encounter with the effects of textuality? For my purposes the text of opera—like any text, in Roland Barthes's sense of the term—grows out of an individual and perhaps shifting combination of each of these physical experiences but remains a purely virtual coherence produced by each reader's or spectator's imaginary interaction with them. It is only analyzable through attention to a variety of formal strategies.[6] Second, where is the narrative in opera? Is it in each aria? Is it carried by recitativos or dramatic dialogues? Is it, rather, the domain of some kind of orchestral voice? And, as Carolyn Abbate asks in the introduction to *Unsung Voices,* whose voice speaks? That of an always already acculturated composer, those of characters, those of singers and musicians, or those of operatic readers? Though answers to these questions remain, as I have already suggested, both elusive and illusory, insofar as the textual strategies of bohemian narrative seek to reveal the ideological underpinnings of narrative form, I shall demonstrate how the textuality of Bizet's *Carmen* exposes and offers for our consideration the modes of behavior characteristic of operatic narrative itself.[7]

To understand *Carmen*'s exposition of the ideological allegiances or dominant discourses of nineteenth-century operatic narrative, we must understand the opera's place in the cultural politics of French opera during the late nineteenth century as well as in the larger phenomenon of a French response to Richard Wagner after 1860. Indeed, the French have been as obsessed with Wagner's "symphonic web" or what they call his "poetry," for almost as long as German musicologists.[8] This obsession has been largely concerned with the question of a "subject effect"—the effect of Wagner's poetry on its listeners—and with a desire to rival that effect with written words. Since the earliest large-scale reaction to Wagnerian sound among his first French audiences, of *Tannhaüser* in 1861, Wagner's music is as celebrated or scorned for the newness of its effect on listeners as it is for its revolutionizing of modern opera, the internationalization of its repertoire, or its specific participation in a larger cultural project to forge or form, aesthetically, a German national identity. So overwhelming is this response to Wagner, in fact, that generations of

French thinkers have been trying to come to terms with "l'effet Wagner," or the Wagner effect.[9]

In the context of bohemian narrative the Wagner effect needs at least two working definitions, which I shall label "acoustic" and "poetic." By acoustic effect I mean what you hear both outside and inside, both what a sonic surface executes, realizes, or effects and the consequences, results, or follow-up impressions produced as a subjective, imaginary sound. This effect is both material and virtual, then, both sonic and subjective. By poetic effect, however, I seek to evoke efforts to repeat these acoustic effects in writing, imitations of Wagnerian style which use literary rather than musical form to react to or oppose Wagner's project. Charles Baudelaire, admiringly; Stéphane Mallarmé, scornfully; and Arthur Rimbaud, perhaps unwittingly, as we have already seen, have all sought to execute, replay, and rethink this Wagner effect.

What interests me in the context of this discussion, however, is not the repetition on paper of "continuous music," thwarted cadences, or recurring motives but, instead, the poetic re-execution of Wagner's acoustic effects in the domain of another acoustic environment, namely, that of Bizet's *Carmen*. Considered from within the same time frame as the aforementioned poetic revisions of Wagner, Bizet's *Carmen* appears to stage this effort at poetic rethinking from within the context of operatic form. This may explain why Friedrich Nietzsche evokes Bizet's *Carmen* as an antidote to his later perception of the surreptitious politics of Wagner's Dionysian music. In the same vein I evoke the French response to Wagner, that is, French sensibility and theory, as an antidote or rival to the hegemonic effect of Wagnerian sound among modern musicologists.[10]

L'*Effet* Wagner

To understand the capacity of Bizet's "light" comic-opera to rival the heavy redemptive hegemony of Wagner's symphonic web, we must consider this effort in light of French operatic politics and of the more general relations of operatic pleasure to the formation of national cultural identities. In *The Nation's Image* Jane Fulcher concludes her study of French opera during the nineteenth century by focusing on the opera house as a setting for opposition to the French Empire's cultural politics during the reign of the so-called democratic emperor, Napoléon Bonaparte III (164–200). In the 1860s, according to Fulcher, the French Opera House maintained an image (or ideology) of public accessibility while stratifying society quite distinctly by pandering to a bourgeois cultural elite. While all members of society were theoretically invited to attend, in other words, the actual audiences of the empire's operas were made up of essentially homogeneous members of a social class likely to help tranquilize national political debate: the *grande* and the *petite* noblesse, diplomats, foreign dignitaries, and political figures rather than artists and journalists (167, 170). Moreover, whereas opera houses and theaters in Paris have long been settings for intense political rivalries, the empire's operatic politics insured that any real political issues were obfuscated by a repertoire that was foreign and old. Revivals of Rossini, Meyerbeer, and Verdi were divorced from their original political actualities and staged in the diaphanous fogs of a remote and dusty past (179–80). Issues of actual political debate were thereby removed to the streets (as much as possible), only to be replaced by a more insidious form of institutional control which Fulcher refers to as "cultural politics."

The effects of this kind of institutionalized cultural politics are explored in chapter 15 of the second part of Gustave Flaubert's *Madame Bovary,* when Emma Bovary goes to the Opéra de Rouen to attend a performance of *Lucia di Lammermoor.*[11] As she enters the theater, Emma is delighted by what she sees; high society in a self-serving parade of beautiful dresses and gallant gentlemen makes Emma feel both like a child and a duchess. Though Emma is immediately caught up in the imaginary roles to be played in this social drama, Flaubert remains ironical about the cultural elite on parade, pointing out that the season ticket holders, so white haired and inexpressive that they appear to be pressed on coins, are not really there to listen to the music: "Ils venaient se délasser dans les beaux-arts des inquiétudes de la vente; mais n'oubliant point *les affaires,* ils causaient encore cotons, trois-six ou indigo" (247) [They came for respite, in the arts, from the concerns of their sales; but never forgetting *business,* they still spoke of cottons, of thirty-sixes, or of indigo].[12] The opera house is, then, as Fulcher supposes, a setting in which the cultural elite may carry on their business affairs, unaffected by any unruly working-class mob. Once the opera begins, however, Flaubert focuses on Emma's relation to the performance of *Lucia di Lammermoor* and on the insidious molding of identities nurtured by the institutionalized values of the empire's cultural politics. Well versed in the novels of Walter Scott, Emma's knowledge of Lucia's story results in a phenomenon of double reading:

Elle se retrouvait dans les lectures de la jeunesse, en plein Walter Scott. Il lui semblait entendre, à travers le brouillard, le son des cornemuses écossais se répéter sur les bruyères. D'ailleurs, le souvenir du roman facilitant l'intelligence du libretto, elle suivait l'intrigue phrase à phrase, tandis que d'insaisissables pensées qui lui revenaient se dispersaient aussitôt sous les rafales de la musique. Elle se laissait aller au bercement des mélodies et se sentait elle-même vibrer de tout son être comme si les archets des violons se fussent promenés sur ses nerfs. (248)

[She found herself transported to the reading of her youth, into the midst of Walter Scott. She seemed to hear through the mist the sound of the Scotch bagpipes repeating across the heather. Besides, her memory of the novel helping her to understand the libretto, she followed the story phrase by phrase, while inaccessible thoughts that came back to her were dispersed at once beneath the bursts of music. She gave herself up to the lulling of the melodies and felt herself vibrate with all her being as if the violin bows were being drawn over her nerves.]

According to this passage, Emma's "reading" of the performance supposes two distinct ways of participating. First, she actively follows the libretto, "phrase by phrase," remembering a story line she already knows. Then, she is intermittently lulled, across the diaphanous fog of the Scottish landscape, into a passive demisleep state—or what the French call *rêverie*—becoming like an instrument vibrating at the touch of violin bows across her nerves. Calling forth inaccessible, we might assume, unconscious thoughts, which recur and scatter like the waves of music she hears, the bagpipes echo in the fog of the stage setting and within the "fog" of her own thoughts.

This exercise in double reading structures the remainder of the chapter. Emma oscillates between being swept away by the sounds emanating from the stage, as she identifies with Lucia, and denying the appropriateness of that identification: "La voix de la chanteuse ne lui semblait être que le retentissement de sa conscience, et cette illusion qui la charmait quelque chose même de sa vie. Mais personne sur la terre ne l'avait aimée d'un pareil amour" [The voice of the prima donna seemed to her to be only the reverberation of her conscience, and this illusion that charmed her, as some very thing of her own life. But no one on earth had ever loved her with such love]. Later, though Emma remains critically attuned to the illusory nature of the identification, despite or because of her sense of distance from Lucia's life, Emma screams, during the love duet, blending herself into the vocal sound in a kind of cathartic release: "Emma jeta un cri aigu, qui se confondit avec la vibration des derniers accords" (249) [Emma hurled a strident cry that mingled with the vibrations of the final chords].[13]

As the opera continues, Walter Scott's story becomes more and more remote and Emma more and more indifferent to it, finally leaving before the end at the thought of a new romantic tryst with Léon. She concentrates, instead, either on how the sound is produced or on the life of the celebrated opera singer, Edgar Lagardy: "S'efforçant donc d'en détourner sa pensée, Emma voulait ne plus voir dans cette reproduction de ses douleurs qu'une fantaisie plastique bonne à amuser les yeux, et même elle souriait intérieurement d'une pitié dédaigneuse quand, au fond du théâtre, sous la portière en velours, un homme apparut en manteau noir" (250) [Striving thus to divert her thoughts, Emma no longer wanted to see in this reproduction of her misfortunes more than a plastic fantasy, adept at delighting the eye, and she smiled to herself internally with disdainful pity when, at the back of the theater, beneath a velvet curtain, a man emerged in a black coat]. It is as if her attention to the "plasticity," or materials of expression, of the performance aids her ability to distance herself from an identification with the lives of the characters only to force her attention to the real people who realize operatic effects.

Although Emma's attention to how sound is produced and to who produces it leads her away from any identification with the characters or the story line, it does promote an imaginary fantasy scenario in which she becomes the lover of Lagardy, the man in the black coat, living the

Parisian high life, among a cosmopolitan and bourgeois cultural elite. As is often the case in *La Tentation de Saint Antoine,* Flaubert uses the conditional past to transport the fantasy into Emma's present circumstances:

> Entraînée vers l'homme par l'illusion du personnage, elle tâcha de se figurer sa vie, cette vie retentissante, extraordinaire, splendide, et qu'elle aurait pu mener, cependant, si le hasard l'avait voulu. Ils se seraient connus, ils se seraient aimés! Avec lui, par tous les royaumes de l'Europe, elle aurait voyagé de capitale en capitale . . . ramassant les fleurs qu'on lui jetait . . . elle eût recueilli, béante, les expansions de cette âme qui n'aurait chanté que pour elle seule. . . . Mais une folie la saisit: il la regardait, c'est sûr! (251)

> [Beckoned toward the man by the illusion of the character, she tried to imagine [*se figurer:* to etch or figure mentally] his life, the reverberating, extraordinary, splendid life, and which she could have led, nonetheless, had chance so deemed it. They would have known each other, they would have loved! With him, in all of the kingdoms of Europe, she would have traveled from capital to capital . . . gathering the flowers thrown to him . . . she would have gathered to herself, wide open, the expansions of this soul, which would only have sung for her alone. . . . But a wild thought seized her: he was looking at her, it's certain!]

Having figured herself into his life in a magnificent fantasy scenario all her own, it is clear that Emma has virtually missed the remainder of the performance of the act. Having mixed her own inaccessible thoughts into the rhythms of the music, the curtain falls almost unexpectedly on what seems to Emma to be a moment of intentional eye contact. As is typical in Flaubert's writing, the conditional past of Emma's personal fantasy gives way slowly to the imperfect past and, then, to a present whose certainty is purely subjective. But in this example Emma's conviction about the reality of the fantasy offers a particularly good image of what can happen, intermittently, to any opera listener.

This shift from an identification with the lives of characters to an identification with the lives of performers foregrounds an imaginary effect occasioned both because of and despite the opera performance. We might say, following Octave Mannoni's discussion of theatrical illusion, that because Emma is aware that the story is an illusion—she knows she is not Lucia—she is able to identify with those people who regularly perform and attend opera performances. In other words, the imaginary effect described by Emma's fantasy is an identification nurtured by the institution itself, one designed to promote a kind of capitalist or industrial programming of consumer instincts. As Flaubert put it earlier, we forget about sales, but we do not forget about business. So, although Emma may be unaware of this "cultural programming" of tastes and identities, Flaubert exposes it by showing how Emma's subsequent life "buys into" this fantasy of the bourgeois duchess.

The notion that Flaubert is exposing the empire's operatic politics brings us back to Jane Fulcher, who closes her book with a look at two modes of opposition to this kind of cultural politics. The first, allied with Flaubert, or at least with the politics of literary realism as well as with *charivari,* a journalistic style that turns political values topsy-turvy, is associated, on the operatic stage, with the trenchant political satires of Jacques Offenbach. The second, more significant for my purposes, is associated with Richard Wagner and with the taking up of Wagner's name in the service of a politically progressive egalitarianism. As Fulcher points out, the first performances of Wagner's music produced dramatically opposed reactions to what was seen as its appeal to a broad spectrum of society (185–97). In effect, Wagner's music appeared to do what the empire's operas only said they did—offer "authentic democratic representation" (Fulcher 196).

In relation to the exigencies of Italian opera listening such as we understand them in the example of Emma Bovary, both admirers and critics of Wagner focused on a new effect on listeners. They repeatedly underscored that this new music, with its innovative orchestral voice, its long, continuous melodies, and its striking new sounds, facilitated a kind of release or catharsis among its spectators. Political liberals spoke about this release as a "counter-image," a new liberty that would unleash the "true community" and its capacity for autonomous social action (ibid.). Conservatives, on the other hand, rekindled memories of opera houses in flames, arguing that such a release of popular energies would lead to wild mobs and moral anarchy (194).

Without reiterating what countless numbers of Wagner scholars have repeatedly detailed, Wagner clearly set out to achieve this effect of release.[14] Reacting in particular to the frivolous and commercial social setting we see in Flaubert and to the stodgy formal constraints of an Italian opera which juxtaposed dramatic songs, or arias, and recitativos, or words set to music, Wagner also sought to put an end to the kind of double reading Emma performs at *Lucia*. At Bayreuth he shut off the lights and hid the orchestra, not only to keep his audience from reading librettos but also to hide the means of expression which produce operatic sound. Moreover, to realize a mass of theoretical notions idealizing relationships between art and community, and with the distinct aim of rewriting the history of opera, he blended characters into a network of orchestral fibers and wrote librettos creating a kind of remote medieval German national past and myths or legends singing the nobility and glory of the German character. These characters and myths undoubtedly reached into the depths of German fears about national fragmentation and dismemberment and offered new identities into which one might be released.[15] Above all, however, Wagner sought to replace individual appetites with a religious experience of communal pleasures, through the creation of a hypnotic, even regressive, atmosphere.

In "Richard Wagner et *Tannhaüser* à Paris" Charles Baudelaire wholeheartedly espouses the effects of this new Wagnerian sound in terms that recall the second way in which Emma Bovary participates in the performance of opera: lulled into a demisleep state, violin bows play upon her nerves. Unlike the individual response that Flaubert attributes to his heroine, however, Baudelaire finds in Wagner's music an ideal image of both psychical and communal *correspondence*.[16] He writes: "Je n'oserais certes pas parler avec complaisance de mes *rêveries* précedentes. Le lecteur sait quel but nous poursuivons: démontrer que la véritable musique suggère des idées analogues dans des cerveaux différents" (206) [I would certainly not dare to speak smugly of my preceding *daydreams*. The reader knows what goal we seek to attain: to demonstrate that true music suggests analogous ideas in different brains]. Instead of a uniquely individual response, then, what interests Baudelaire is a more generalized "subject effect." To demonstrate it, he points out analogous associations with the music of a previous performance (of *Lohengrin*) which include spiritual and physical beatitude, isolation, infinite space, and intense white light among listeners as varied as himself, Liszt, and Wagner in his own program notes (208).

Although this analogous thinking supposes a distinctly Baudelairean duplicity of basic mental aspirations toward heaven and hell, the essential conflict of subjective or individual mental dualism leads, by way of innately intelligible spiritual myths and legends (216–18, 225–26), to common moral analogies (230):

> Dès les premières mesures, les nerfs vibrent à l'unisson de la mélodie; toute chair qui se souvient se met à trembler. Tout cerveau bien conformé porte en lui deux infinis, le ciel et l'enfer, et dans toute image de l'un de ces infinis il reconnaît subitement la moitié de lui-même. . . . Quand le thème religieux, faisant invasion à travers le mal déchaîné, vient peu à peu rétablir l'ordre et reprendre l'ascendant, quand il se dresse de nouveau avec toute sa solide beauté, au-dessus de ce chaos de voluptés agonisantes, toute l'âme éprouve comme un rafraîchissement, une béatitude de rédemption. (222)

[From the very first measures the nerves vibrate in unison with the melody; any flesh that remembers begins to tremble. Any well-conformed brain carries in it two infinities, heaven and hell, and in every image of one of these infinities, it suddenly recognizes half of itself. . . . When the religious theme, invading the unleashed evil, begins little by little to restore order and to recover its ascendancy, when it rises again with all of its solid beauty, above this chaos of agonizing voluptuousness, every soul feels a refreshment, a beatitude of redemption.]

The tensions of human aspiration toward heaven and hell, the pleasures of the flesh and those of the spirit, are not only echoed by Wagner's music; they also lead to a redemptive resolution.

After 1871, after the formation of the German nation and the defeat of France by the Prussians, Baudelaire's sense of Wagner's redemptive releasing of moral analogies among listeners presents a more frightening specter of the ways in which music drama can be used to further tranquilize or silence individual appetites in the name of community. A long while before Martin Heidegger's *Volksgemeinschaft*, the religious communion of spirits, and its subsequent uses in Nazi Germany, Wagner's musical effects roused ethical concerns about the nature of this community. In fact, the cultural politics of this release became the focal point of Stéphane Mallarmé's biting critique of both the biblical legends cast in Germanic tones which Baudelaire admires (218, 229–30) and the so-called union of the arts, or *Gesamtkunstwerk*. In "Richard Wagner: Rêverie d'un Poëte français" and perhaps, as Philippe Lacoue-Labarthe argues convincingly, throughout his entire poetic career, Mallarmé would attempt to counter this threat of Germanic cultural hegemony—or, more generally, that of nationalism and its specifically racial terms. To do so, he would reassert the primacy of poetry, and of reading, and insist upon the ways in which the acts of individual readers contribute to a different kind of democratic community. Rather than producing a "stupor mixed with intimacy that erases the past in a religious communion of self-abnegation," Mallarmé would foreground each individual's capacity to forge a "personal instrument."[17] Now, writes Mallarmé, the French sensibility and the writer of verse will attempt to rival Wagner: "Oui, en tant qu'un opéra sans accompagnement ni chant, mais parlé; maintenant le livre essaiera de suffire, pour entr'ouvrir la scène intérieure et en chuchoter les échos" ("Planches et feuillets," OC 328) [Yes, as an opera with neither accompaniment nor song, but spoken; now the book will try to suffice in order to half-open the interior stage and whisper its echoes].

Whether Mallarmé's poetic "operas," such as *Hérodiade* and *Un Coup de dès* [*A Throw of the Dice*], actually rival the Wagnerian experience may well be a matter of national opinion. It is certain, however, that Mallarmé's poetic dramas, like Rimbaud's "*opéra fabuleux*" and Nietzsche's *Also sprach Zarathustra* (*Thus Spoke Zarathustra*), did seek to contest or subvert Wagner's project to program cultural identities by repeating or imitating certain qualities of Wagnerian sound. As we have already seen in the case of Rimbaud's "Bad Blood," musical strategies such as thwarted cadences, continuous and circular "melodies," reminiscence motives or leitmotivs, proliferate in the poetic prose of the late century. More generally, these authors were responding to what they perceived to be the growing threat of an institutionalization of national cultural values through popular media and entertainment. It is in this light that it is useful to reconsider Nietzsche's late reappraisal of Wagner and his setting up of Bizet's *Carmen* as an antidote to the Wagner effect.

Nietzsche's *Carmen*

In *Musica ficta* Philippe Lacoue-Labarthe studies the political dimensions of the Wagner effect in poetry and philosophy by revisiting Nietzsche's reappraisal of Wagner in a light cast by Baudelaire, Mallarmé, Heidegger, and Adorno. Situating this study between two paradoxically repetitive theatrical events, Plato's expulsion of the actor from the Republic and Nietzsche's repulsion by the ethics of Wagner's aesthetic project, Lacoue-Labarthe argues that in both Plato's dialogues and Nietzsche's *Zarathustra* (as well as in Baudelaire's prose poems and Mallarmé's theaters) music haunts thought in a fundamentally political preoccupation (165–68). Politics should be understood, in this context, both in a larger sense as that which determines the destinies of nations and in the more specific sense of the effects produced upon a community of spectators drawn together in a theater; this is the politics, in other words, of mass, or popular, art (20). But in Lacoue-Labarthe's discussion of four reactions to Wagner it is the "aestheticization," or *figuration*, of politics which is in question—the capacity of art to forge, form, mold, or sculpt those political destinies in the only potentially political setting of popular culture (11–15, 17–18).

In the case of Wagner this political figuring is a phenomenon to be distinguished both from the art of politics and from political art, in that it supposes the presence of hidden voices, discursive plots, which seek by way of ideologically influential aesthetic principles to disarm our capacity for logical reasoning (51). Through the irresistible persuasion of one's musical sensibilities, in other words, the goal of the Wagner effect is to blur intelligibility and to supplement it with feelings that encourage a form of spiritual submission, enchantment, or "transfiguration." Though this effect is at least partially characteristic of much nineteenth-century opera—indeed, Catherine Clément insists that the opera form itself links words and music in such a way as to obfuscate the intelligibility of the dominant cultural values that give its intrigues shape (22–23)—Nietzsche's anxious rejection of Wagner's project brings this surreptitious manipulation to light by underscoring the ethical concerns of a cultural project that reaches into the inaccessible recesses of unconscious thought to reshape conscious identities.

In *Nietzsche contra Wagner* the German philosopher, like his French contemporaries, focuses on the "physiological" effects that contribute to a listener's response to Wagnerian sound, "the convulsions of his 'moral' ecstasies which give the people—and who is not 'people'?—satisfaction."[18] Whereas "older music" required a "continual *wariness* of the listener's soul," writes Nietzsche, listening to Wagner's "infinite melody" is like swimming: "One walks into the sea, gradually loses one's secure footing, and finally surrenders oneself to the elements without reservation: one must *swim*. In older music, what one had to do in the dainty, or solemn, or fiery back and forth, quicker and slower, was something quite different, namely, to *dance*" (666). In this passage a rhythmic "back and forth," similar to Emma's double reading strategies, pits itself against a surrendering of self-consciousness to swimming. Later reiterated in Theodor Adorno's post-Freudian idea that Wagner's music dramas place their listeners in a state of "oceanic regression," Nietzsche's "swimming" is particularly striking in that it is opposed to "dancing," in which one remains conscious of the physical reenactment of musical rhythm in an art form that is essentially antirepresentational. In other words, Nietzsche is focused on the way in which "one leaves oneself at home when one goes to Bayreuth" (665), because one surrenders to the musicodramatic effects of a purely representational art form. In lieu of any attention to the plasticity, or materiality, of theatrical "forms, tones, words" (683), Wagner's music dramas offer satisfaction to the people by representing, as if transparently, or "naturalistically," "a certain catholicism of feeling and a delight in some old indigenous, so-called 'national' sense and nonsense" (668). Though the terms in question recall Baudelaire's, Nietzsche's association of religious feelings with national feelings is more explicit.[19]

When we consider the characteristics that would ideally define an antidote to this swimming of "moral ecstasies," it is not surprising that Nietzsche would ultimately see the "southern, brown, burnt sensibility" of *Carmen*'s "African" rhythms in this role.[20] Not only does his emphasis on supposedly non-European rhythms remind us of *Carmen*'s constant recourse to dance and body language, but the cultural otherness of *Car-*

men so compelling to Nietzsche is a way of describing the "fiery back and forth," a capacity among spectators to resist an immediate identification with the characters onstage.[21]

In *Nietzsche contra Wagner* he continues: "No, if we who have recovered [from Romantic art] still need art, it is another kind of art—a mocking, light, fleeting, divinely untroubled, divinely artificial art . . . *for artists only!* . . . One should have more respect for the bashfulness with which nature has hidden behind riddles and iridescent uncertainties. Perhaps truth is a woman who has reasons for not letting us see her reasons?" (682–83). The notion of a mocking, light, essentially artificial art—one aware of its own materials of expression, "forms, tones, words"—evokes what semioticians distinguish as a "presentational" rather than a "representational" text.[22] Associated with the ambiguities of nature and of woman, against culture and spiritual satisfaction, this image of truth as a woman may present a problematic figure from a feminist perspective, but it also emphasizes the idea of a logical, or rational, justification for remaining all riddles and uncertainty and, therefore, open to interpretation. This woman offers a striking likeness to the Carmen of *The Case of Wagner*, whose destructive sexuality underscores the fundamental duplicity of desire and satisfaction as it pits one mode of political figuring against another.

In relation to Wagner's use of continuous melody in the service of spiritual satisfaction, of mass hypnosis, and of the aesthetic forging of a German national identity, Nietzsche's Carmen exposes Wagner's "catharsis for the weak" by helping us to recollect opera's lack of intelligibility and to intellectualize or remain wary, precisely, of that potentially mesmerizing dimension of operatic sound. From Nietzsche's perspective, whereas Wagner forces us to "swim in the sea," Bizet asks us to view it from a distance (*Case*, 159). Or, put otherwise, whereas Isolde demands the Buddhist-like self-abnegation of a musical communion in death, a "fathomless oblivion," or *Ur-Vergessen* (Kerman 195–99), Carmen warns against the effects of hypnotic inebriation or spiritual intoxication. Indeed, she continually repeats it for us: "Prends garde à toi!" [Beware!].

The hypnotic subject effect described by Nietzsche's swimming is reminiscent of the one Baudelaire describes in terms of release and redemption. In its evocation, for both thinkers, of losing oneself in ecstasy, rather than contemplating it from afar, this effect anticipates the trance-like pleasure of *jouissance* which Jacques Lacan identifies with the unlo-calized, mystical pleasure of Saint Theresa. In *Encore* Lacan writes:

Comme pour Sainte Thérèse—vous n'avez qu'à aller regarder à Rome la statue du Bernin pour comprendre tout de suite qu'elle jouit, ça ne fait pas de doute. Et de quoi jouit-elle? Il est clair que le temoignage essentiel des mystiques, c'est justement de dire qu'ils l'éprouvent, mais qu'ils n'en savent rien. (70–71)

[As for Saint Theresa—you have only to go see the statue of Bernini in Rome to understand right away that she's coming, no doubt about it. And what is she coming about? It is clear that the essential eyewit-ness account of mystics is precisely to say that they feel it, but they do not know anything about it. (My trans.)]

Lacan's pleasure of mystical *jouissance* is characterized by the mystic's capacity to feel it, physiologically, without knowing anything about it, intellectually; it is a kind of knowledge without acknowledgment.

This self-abnegating intensity constitutes a kind of empty or undesig-nated affectivity which thereby leaves itself open to individualized inter-pretations already shot through with the distortions of desire. Lacan iron-ically situates this desire behind the spectator's gaze, both that of the "you" who has "only to go *see* the statue" and that of the mystic's "eye-witness account," implying that Theresa's ecstasy is also Bernini's, also Lacan's, also my own, and that "catholic feelings" could be "national de-light" or aesthetic wonder. In other words, the suggestion is that the un-designated affectivity of the mystic's ecstasy can be made immediately available to the creation of more generalized ideological effects because of individual tendencies to appropriate or assimilate objects of the gaze. To the extent that a properly ideological effect, as Slavoj Zizek describes it in *The Sublime Object of Ideology*, requires precisely this affectivity in subjects unaware of the political maneuvering surreptitiously at work in their desires (87),[23] the mystic's unconscious pleasure lends itself to the kind of mass enchantment we can infer from both Nietzsche's and Baude-laire's appraisals of Wagner's project.

Lacan himself seems to point out this association between the mystic's affect and the politics of the Wagner effect, if ambiguously: "La mystique, ce n'est pas tout ce qui n'est pas la politique. C'est quelque chose de sérieux, sur quoi nous renseignent quelques personnes, et le plus souvent des femmes" (*Encore,* 70) [Mysticism: it is not everything that is *not* politics. It's something quite serious about which some people can teach us *some* things, and most often women" (my emph. and trans.)]. The double negation of Lacan's sentence insists that mysticism is *not* everything that is *not* politics. It is not, in other words, "opposed" to politics as a separately defined realm. On the contrary, the pleasurable subject effect described as a mystical trance is akin to the powerful aesthetic response summoned by Wagner's project insofar as the latter's political dimension must be denied in the very moment of its production. And, just as Lacan's reading of the mystics supposes that it is women who teach something about this affective subject of politics, Nietzsche focuses on Carmen's love-hate relations, not in the service of some kind of protofeminist appeal to cultural critique but, rather, because they emphasize the surplus affect at stake in ideology and the extent to which that surplus can be exposed and diffused by musical ambiguities or made available to reappropriation for "decadent" political ends.

Ultimately, whereas Wagner exploits the ideological potential of *jouissance* in order to substitute "national delight" for "catholic feelings," Bizet exposes it, substituting self-conscious resistance for Wagner's totalizing gesture toward restoration.[24]

The *Carmen* Case

Georges Bizet is fully aware of Wagner's appeal, and in terms that recall Lacan's he refers obliquely, in 1871, to the phenomenon of enchantment associated with the total art form:

> Wagner n'est pas mon ami, et je le tiens en médiocre estime; mais je ne puis oublier les immenses jouissances que je dois à ce génie novateur. Le charme de cette musique est indicible, inexprimable. C'est la volupté, la tendresse, l'amour.
>
> Si je vous en jouais huit jours, vous en raffoleriez! . . . L'esprit allemand du XIXᵉ siècle est incarné en cet homme.[25]

[Wagner is not my friend and I think little of him; but I will never forget the immense pleasures *[jouissances]* I owe to this innovative genius. The charm of this music is unspeakable, inexpressible. It is voluptuousness, tenderness, love.
If I played it for you during eight days, you'd go crazy. The German spirit of the nineteenth century is incarnate in this man. (My trans.)]

In terms parallel to Lacan's, Bizet associates a musical pleasure that, after long days of listening, would "drive you crazy" because of its inexpressible, at once illogical and unspeakable *charme*. This undesignated *charme* evokes, in French, a magical kind of force reminiscent of the mystic's affect. Moreover, in his discussion of this *charme*, Bizet's letter muses openly about the nationalist politics of Wagnerian sound by noting that it incarnates the nineteenth-century German national "esprit," that is, spirit and mind, or identity.

Despite his own reservations, Bizet was himself plagued by the appellation *wagnériste* beginning in 1863 with his *Pêcheurs de Perles* and during most of his short operatic career.[26] Although for many years French music reviewers continued to try to understand what was Wagnerian about Bizet's orchestral tendencies, it is important to remember that the term *wagnériste* had less to do with his musical style than with his participation in what Jane Fulcher calls the "operatic opposition culture" of Paris in the 1860s and 1870s (183–84, 189). In essence, the label *wagnériste* was applied to any apparent reaction against the exploitation of opera to project a false politics of democratic accessibility while celebrating social privilege for the few (166–67).

Against this political backdrop Nietzsche's reference to *Carmen* helps to restore a more appropriate relation between the two composers by opposing them on the question of the aestheticization of politics. In relation to Wagner's totalizing, even totalitarian, aesthetic politics, Bizet's propose a Romantic version of social enlightenment which would make opera's capacity for ideological persuasion apparent to those cultured bourgeois opera-spectators most likely to be hypnotized because most likely subject to a kind of generalized psychology of popular escapism. These were also the people most likely to attend the Opéra Comique theater after the opening of the Palais Garnier in 1875, people eager to see the new and unique alternatives to national opera which that theater regularly subsidized.

In relation to Nietzsche's philosophical rivalry with Wagner, Bizet offers what we could call a performative version of this rivalry in *Carmen*, one that takes the form of a "meditation in action" on the relation of words and music.[27] This meditation in action is accomplished through an open attention to the generic conventions of the *opéra-comique* form, with its distinct capacity to move between two genres, opera and drama (i.e., *comédie*); between two ways of telling, speaking and singing; and between two ways of listening, anticipating and recalling. Moving between the two genres, Bizet's displays its own internal workings, as if ironically looking at its own materiality, by disrupting the continuity of its own narrative. This internal disruption can be seen, in the score, both in its oscillation between Mérimée's dialogues and Bizet's comic-opera numbers and in its division of those numbers into tableaux, songs, choruses, dances, and dialogues, or melodramas. Few people are aware, in fact, of how much of Mérimée's original dialogue interrupts the music of the first comic-opera *Carmen*, recalling passages from a text that had become decidedly familiar. The internal disruption is also apparent, however, in the opera's mapping of formal tensions onto José's tendency to speak and Carmen's diversity of musical discourses; in its emblematic use of narrative songs; and in its play of textual reminiscences and motivic correspondences. The latter work constantly to remind us that a multiplicity of materials of expression—vocal, verbal, symphonic, iconographic, and choreographic—are at work in the staging of the conflict borrowed from Mérimée between Carmen's bohemian pleasures and José's (and the narrator's) border patrol.

The formal conflict of speech and singing is not limited, however, to a formal dimension; it repeats itself as well in the operatic narrative of *Carmen*. By weaving the concerns of the form into a narrative about pleasurable abandon and self-control, the two ways of telling, song and speech, become associated with two hostile modes of desire characteristic of its two principal protagonists. Carmen's is a Lacanian form of desire based on lack and therefore productive of an endless substitution of new objects of desire. In the "Habañera" Carmen sings:

L'amour est enfant de Bohême,
Il n'a jamais connu de loi;
Si tu ne m'aimes pas, je t'aime;
Si je t'aime, prends garde à toi![28]

[Love is a child of Bohemia,
It has never known any law;
If you do not love me, I love you;
If I love you, beware!]

And in the "Seguidilla" she adds:

Mon coeur est libre comme l'air . . .
J'ai des galants à la douzaine,
Mais ils ne sont pas à mon gré;
Voici la fin de la semaine,
Qui veut m'aimer je l'aimerai.
Qui veut mon âme . . . elle est à prendre (29).

[My heart is free like the air . . .
I have dozens of admirers,
But they are not to my liking;
Here is the end of the week,
Who wants to love me I will love him.
Who wants my soul . . . it is for the taking.]

In this mode, Carmen's proverbial freedom from laws or limits of any kind is all-important. The goal of her love affairs is neither satisfaction nor the security of any one particular love object but, rather, the constant changing of partners and the sheer intensity of an unrequited desiring passion, or *jouissance*.

In José's mode, on the contrary, the goal is satisfaction and closure through self-control and the securing of emotional and linguistic borders. His "Flower Song" is introduced by an intense "Tu m'entendras, Carmen, tu m'entendras!" (54) [You will hear me, Carmen, you will hear me!], indicative not only of his reliance upon speech but also of his desire to communicate clearly and to stop the flow of uncertain musical messages.[29] Likewise, near the very end he implores Carmen to mediate the uncertainty of their relations, promising her anything: "Tout, tu m'entends . . ." (85) [Anything, do you hear me . . .]. But, because they speak different languages of desire, the question is moot.

Similar versions of these two distinct modes of desire are identified by Lawrence Kramer, who understands the passage from one to the other as a crucial shift in late-nineteenth-century cultural practices.[30] For Kramer these modes are defined a bit differently and include the "instinctual," in which desire is "aroused in the subject by a specific sexual object, and still seeks extinction like a flame in its physical consummation" and, on the other hand, the "free, unattached force" of the Freudian libido which "always exists in excess of its objects, and . . . cannot be fully satisfied by any object whatever" (139–41). In Kramer's discussion the "classical, instinctual" model is associated with flame and "permanent extinction" and therefore describes the "*Lust* trope" in the Transfiguration from Wagner's *Tristan und Isolde* (153), whereas the more modern model is associated with fluidity and with the "self-delighting flow of desire" characteristic of the *Lust* tropes in Hugo Wolf's "Ganymed" (169). Whether or not Kramer's *Lust* trope examples are accurate, these two modes clearly approximate the conflictive distinction I am trying to underscore in Bizet's *Carmen*—José's mode resembling the "instinctual" and Carmen's the free-flowing libidinal. By referring to the latter as Lacanian rather than Freudian, however, we take one step further toward the notion of a purely self-interested desire without objects. What is most significant, of course, is that the two modes appear together and in conflict in the one piece.

The importance of these two modes of desire as ways of representing the formal conflict of dialogue and song in the opera is most clearly revealed in the context of Michel Poizat's affective history of opera, titled *L'Opéra ou le cri de l'ange*.[31] Although the entire history of opera and of opera criticism is marked by heated debates about the preeminence of song or words, music or drama, Poizat focuses on the use of the two aesthetic forces to regulate the use of pleasure in the service of authority: religious, imperial, national. From this perspective the history of opera may be refined into a series of cultural apparatuses or systems (*dispositifs*) which regulate tensions created by the production of lyric pleasure (*jouissance*) and its control (*maîtrise*). This regulation occurs through the constantly monitored interplay of the power of music (of pure voice and/or material sonority) and the power of words (their intelligibility or signification). As a model for this regulation of affective tensions, Poizat begins his history with a discussion of the church's dictates, during the Renaissance, regarding the social control of music and of singing. In relation to the church's need to maintain intelligibility so as to maintain authority and the clarity of the Word of God, the pleasure of music or of pure voice offered a source of potential danger where the maintenance of authority was concerned because it encouraged an overload of musical pleasure (Poizat 70–73).

The perceived danger of musical pleasure becomes evident, historically speaking, upon perusal of the many church edicts against singing and dancing at that time. Poizat further elaborates the danger of this pleasure, however, by associating it with the ambiguous pleasure of the mystical trance in which ecstasy is both devout and suspect. That is, mystical pleasure escapes the logic of regulatory control because of its ambivalent nature. As Poizat puts it, the mystic is destined either to sanctity or to the stake: "La crainte des débordements, des déchaînements de jouissance mystique est toujours présente et les grands mystiques ont tous été à un moment ou à un autre suspects de satanisme: ils ont tous dû faire la preuve de l'origine divine de leur trance" (74) [The fear of the overflowing, the unleashing of mystical pleasure is always present, and the great mystics have all been at one moment or another, suspected of Satanism: they all had to prove the divine origin of their trance (my trans.)]. The sense of fluidity and of the crossing of borders recalls both Kramer's notion of modern desire as liquid and *Carmen*'s greatest moments of affective pressure. In the example of the mystic, however, the fluid unleashing leads to a problematic association of pleasure and morality. As Lacan's presentation of Saint Theresa supposes, it is the undesignated nature of mystical affectivity which causes alarm. In relation to the question of opera listening Poizat's association of the overflowing of musical and mystical pleasure is noteworthy because it links the liquidity of the swimming Nietzsche assigns to the Wagner effect with Lacan's intimation of the erasure of the source of mystical affectivity (one feels it without knowing anything about it or knows it without acknowledging any knowledge of it). In other words, it links the pleasure of opera listening to the passive inculcating of ideology.

The threat to authority occasioned by music's production of lyric ecstasy is at the heart of the *Carmen* narrative. Clearly, Carmen becomes associated with song, as her name suggests she should, and with *jouissance*, or an excess of intensity, while speech remains associated with José, with the military, and with a more general sense of policing and of authority. Susan McClary makes the point, for example, that José only sings, in the original comic-opera form, when driven to do so by uncontrollable emotional intensity (in response to his memory of his mother or to Carmen [*Bizet*, 46, 80]). She also notes that at moments of intense affective pressure (the "Habañera" scene, the "Flower Song" scene, and the "Duet-Finale") *Carmen*'s songs do not always remain firmly contained within the constraints of the formal set-piece structure typical of comic-opera form but, rather, flow over the borders into scenes that should traditionally be separated by applause (McClary 77, 95, 110). As these examples suggest, although all operas may be subject to the regulation of pleasure, *Carmen* tells the story of this regulation.

Perhaps more important, if grand opera, according to Poizat's history, is a form of telling which can elicit, at least fleetingly or intermittently, an imaginary subject effect that is indeed akin to that of a mystical trance, its capacity to mold ideological effects and to figure cultural identifications unconsciously becomes exceptional. Catherine Clément concurs, arguing that grand opera serves precisely this function by blurring the intelligibility of words and of intrigue in favor of musical pleasure. In relation to this blurring characteristic of grand opera in general and of Wagner's "continuous music" in particular, Bizet's comic-opera, along with other hybrid forms, like its precursor in Mozart's *Singspiel* or its antecedent in Schoenberg's *Sprechgesang*, may be said to double their forms of telling in order to separate what Clément calls the "double scène inséparable" of conscious and unconscious forces in operatic discourse (44). One result is to draw our attention both to what occasions and to what results from an otherwise characteristic blurring of narrative intelligibility. This distinction between grand opera and the *opéra-comique* adjusted by Bizet is the difference between what Clément sees as a form of music drama which encourages the values of a dominant ideology unconsciously, by using pleasure in the service of the maintenance of homogeneous social values, and a form of music drama which repeatedly questions its own complicity in that hegemonic use of pleasure. In other words, whereas music and song blur sentiments, formal borders, and moral values, speech binds and controls the movement of music, helping the terms of the drama or the plot enactment to remain intelligible. Similarly, whereas grand or Wagnerian opera homogenizes discourses (even to the point of cultivating a mode of opera criticism that focused exclusively, until recently, on the coherence or unity of musical composition [Abbate and Parker, 23]), Bizet's comic-opera draws attention to the heterogeneity of the operatic text and to the way in which textual and cultural homogeneity are nothing more than ideological effects.

The comic-opera's shifting between ways of telling and, in the case of *Carmen,* the explicitly self-conscious representation of that shifting in a narrative of *jouissance* and *maîtrise* also force listeners to shift between ways of listening: perceptual anticipation, imagined or fantasized futurities (the self-forgetting of ecstatic pleasure), are staved off or slowed by remembrance or recall of the literary model (a kind of self-control or mastery). In other words, in the same way that ways of telling are taken up by the narrative in *Carmen,* narrative tensions are taken up in the opera's regulation of listening pleasures: anticipation and recall. The result is a listening discomfort, an agitation, typically associated with the comic-opera form. Rousseau spoke of the "shocking and ridiculous mixture" of dialogue and song evidenced by this form (Poizat 84); Wayne Koestenbaum speaks of it as a "queer marriage" (176–97). I prefer to call it an oppositional, or bohemian, subject effect that, in a manner akin to Mérimée's *Carmen,* offers listeners an oscillating position between identification and resistance, swimming and dancing, pleasure and mastery.

In relation to the case of Wagner this means simply that, in place of a textual fabric made of continuous music, *Carmen* substitutes the more ruptured quality of music interrupted by theatrical declamation to submit our attention to the jarring effect of two separate textual registers. This jarring is not to be underestimated. Indeed, *Carmen'*s opening performances were scandalous—whether the excuses be the representation of workers onstage, *Carmen'*s unbridled sexuality, or Wagnerian sound.

But, after the inclusion of Ernest Guiraud's recitativos, designed to smooth out or smooth over, to homogenize, the disruptive quality of the original comic-opera form and turn it into a grand opera, the opera gained worldwide acceptance. The acceptance and even acclaim of the "tamed" form of *Carmen* in relation to the effect of scandal associated with its opening performances emphasize the extent to which its original "untamed" form was jarring or disturbing to its listeners. I shall further speculate that the perturbation of musical pleasure by dramatic intelligibility causes something akin to the *Verfremdungseffekt,* an analytic distance from the performance of pleasurable excess which allows the listener, unlike José, to identify that pleasure as a *performance* of excess. Such distance may also induce an imaginary identification, along the lines of Emma Bovary's, with the capacity of performers to display that excess, further emphasizing the imaginary or representational nature of the excess itself. Rather than becoming the subject of opera's excess, then, we are conscious of how opera encourages and regulates excess.[32]

The "Bohemian Song"

Each of *Carmen*'s songs is, in some way, about *jouissance* and *maîtrise,* or the relation of desire to the blurring of both intelligibility and the boundaries of identity. The "Bohemian Song" that opens *Carmen*'s second act, however, offers a self-conscious look at this blurring by marking itself loudly as a performance within the performance of *Carmen* and by staging the effects of this performance on its musical readers. As an important example of operatic self-reflexivity, it is not surprising that the "Bohemian Song" is also an ideal example of bohemian narrative in that it plays textuality against narrativity, thereby undermining the purely ideological coherency of operatic narrative. In this way the "Bohemian Song" also offers a *mise en abyme* of the musical writing logic of *Carmen* which I have been trying to describe.

In *Unsung Voices* Carolyn Abbate derides the assumption among opera critics and listeners that narrative songs merely further an enacted plot and that music is narrative when it mimes this dramatic *emplotment* (19–20, 72). On the contrary, a narrative song usually tells the opera's story in compressed or disguised form (69); it is, therefore, a rather rare moment that takes place outside of or arrests the flow of dramatic plot enactment (68). Such songs are antithetical to the "monaural" use of recitative to further plot and in which music serves, and must not violate, intelligibility (68–69). The more "reflexive" function of narrative songs generally interferes with the forward progress of musical narration, creating a point of tension which actually marks itself or calls attention to itself because of its apparent musical simplicity.

In the "Bohemian Song," as in Abbate's example of Lakmé's "Bell Song," the repetitive structure of a strophic song with a nonnarrative refrain is at odds with the forward movement of a narrative concerned with progressive inebriation and amplification. According to Abbate, this type of formal tension between progress and repetition "forces the reader-listener to fix on the meaning of the words and not their sound" in a trajectory opposite that of syntactically complicated, self-reflexive poetry, in which we concentrate on the "music" of the words rather than on their discursive meaning (71). In the "Bohemian Song" this tension between progress and repetition is further emphasized because of a dramatic distinction between the tonal return of the choral refrain and the unsettling flamenco sound of Carmen's chromatic descents. According to Abbate, the use of such repetitive form in a narrative song "forces us to deal explicitly with ourselves as listening subjects," since it underscores the song's status as a musical performance that others enjoy. It mirrors the activities we, as spectators, hear, see, and enact, and it puts the process of performance—musical enunciation, composition, and affective response—in the foreground (85).

Adapting Lucien Dällenbach's notion of the tendency of a *mise en abyme* toward "semantic compression and dilation," or reduction and elaboration, Abbate looks at the subject effect produced by such narrative songs on the opera reader: "In the case of performed arts, we need to stress the *oscillation* involved in understanding such moments. One moves between comprehending the reflexivity (the 'story within the story') as a miniature résumé of the whole, and the whole as a projection through greater expanses of time of a pregnant microcosm. Acknowledging this restlessness will remind us of opera's temporalness and acoustics" (68). The listener is restless before a narrative song, then, because she or he is pulled between two ways of reading, one that focuses on the logic of the song's story in relation to its musical form and sound, another that requires imagining the larger whole of the opera itself. With this double reading strategy in mind, let us begin by considering the "logic" of the telling of the "Bohemian Song" itself and then consider the ways in which it may sum up or reach out to the larger whole of the opera's structure.

The scene of the "Bohemian Song" is set in Lillas Pastia's tavern, as promised by the end of Carmen's "Seguidilla" and by the closing refrain of the first act, "L'Amour est enfant de Bohême," sung in accompaniment to the escape from her military escort. If the entr'acte just preceding the song evokes the military strains of a melody that will be reprised during José's offstage monologue later in the act, "Dragon d'Alcala" (Oeser 202), as the curtain rises, we hear the descending tetrachord progressions characteristic of flamenco dance (McClary 90–91). From within, but in contrast to, the military framework of both the act and the opera as a whole, we are invited to imagine a popular locale (rather than the red velours of the Opéra Comique's interior) in which guitar strumming, tambourines, and Gypsy *sistra* might be sounding. In this sort of locale the conventions of opera listening are suspended in favor of the liberated responses of spectators who become directly involved physiologically in the rhythms of music: at a flamenco performance in Seville, in an etching by Davillier and Doré, or in a Parisian cabaret.[33]

Reviewing the original performance of *Carmen* for *Le Gaulois* on 3 March 1875, François Oswald describes the scene:

Nous voici maintenant dans le *patio* d'une *posada* dont toutes les fenêtres flambent joyeusement et qui retentit du bruit des chansons et des guitares. Cette cour intérieure, éclairée d'un côté par les reflets pâles de la lune et de l'autre par les rouges lueurs des lanternes suspendues, produit un effet superbe. Tout autour circule un balcon curieusement ouvragé, et à travers les aloès et les lauriers-roses, plantés en pleine terre, dansent et se tordent les bohémiennes aux costumes éclatants, pour la plus grande joie des officiers en goguette. C'est dans cette édifiante société que nous retrouvons Carmen.

[We now find ourselves on the *patio* of a *posada* whose windows are illuminated joyously and in which the sound of songs and guitars reverberates. This interior courtyard, lit up, on one side, by the pale reflections of the moon and, on the other, by the red gleaming of suspended lanterns, produces a superb effect. All around a curiously wrought iron balcony circulates, and among the aloes and oleanders planted right in the ground the bohemian women clothed in brightly colored costumes dance and twist, for the great pleasure of the officers out on a spree. It is in this edifying society that we meet Carmen. (my trans.)]

In this remotely Spanish, faintly immoral setting bathed in the flaming red light of cabaret lanterns, strikingly colored costumes accompany the noise of songs and guitars and the scents of fresh flowers. The protocol of the scene supposes an atmosphere foreign, in other words, to that of the Salle Favart in Paris, one that may not stage, precisely, the *taudis*, or slums, into which Mérimée's Carmen leads her officers (as "Bénédict," reviewing for *Le Figaro*, pointed out) but one that reiterates, visually, the shock of that difference. This reiteration is important in light of the numerous criticisms of Meilhac and Halévy's tendency to water down the *Carmen* of Mérimée, since it suggests that the visual and aural effects of the performance did continue to create an environment equally, if differently, unsettling. The unsettling quality of this "foreignness" may explain why the first spectators, all artists, journalists, and musicians, found themselves "légèrement dépaysés" [slightly disoriented], as Oswald writes, according applause that "se ressentaient d'une indécision bien naturelle" [was imbued with a very natural indecisiveness].[34]

Within this "popular" locale Oswald's description presents us with a performance space in which Carmen and José's lieutenant, Zuniga, are spectators to the Gypsies dancing. According to the original libretto: "Deux Bohémiens râclent de la guitare dans un coin de la taverne et deux Bohémiennes, au milieu de la scène, dansent. —Carmen est assise regardant danser les Bohémiennes, le lieutenant lui parle bas, mais elle ne fait aucune attention à lui. Elle se lève tout à coup et se met à chanter (32)" [Two Bohemians strum guitars in one corner of the tavern and two Bohemian women, at the center of the stage, are dancing. —Carmen is seated watching the Bohemian women dance, the lieutenant speaks to her softly, but she pays no attention to him. She rises suddenly and begins to sing]. In this scene Zuniga's words are no match for the seductiveness of the music and dance. As a spectator to the performance of her Gypsy cohorts, Carmen is drawn, suddenly and spontaneously, into the performance space. She then begins to sing, and the dancing stops. Though her sung performance replaces the dance performance, her narrative describes it:

> Les tringles des sistres tintaient
> Avec un éclat métallique,
> Et sur cette étrange musique
> Les zingarellas se levaient.
> Tambours de Basque allaient leur train,
> Et les guitares forcenées
> Grinçaient sous des mains obstinées,
> Même chanson, même refrain,
> La la la la la la.
> *Sur ce refrain, les Bohémiennes dansent.*
> *Mercédès et Frasquita reprennent avec Carmen*
> *le: La la la la la la.* (32)

> [The rods on the *sistra* jingled
> With metallic brilliance,
> And at the sound of this strange music
> The *zingarella* stood up.
> Basque tambourines played along
> And wild guitars
> Winced under obstinate hands,
> Same song, same refrain.
> La la la la la la.
> *On this refrain, the Bohemian women dance.*
> *Mercédès and Frasquita reprise with Carmen*
> *the: La la la la la la.*]

Evoking the sounds of instruments we can only imagine—tambourines, *sistra*, and guitars, which are probably not part of the orchestra—the narrative concentrates on the effects of these sounds on spectator-listeners. The effects of these sounds are only partial and ephemeral but highly sensual: metallic brilliance, frenzied and wincing guitars, obstinate hands. Since this narrative describes a scene in the past tense, we can only suppose that it is this "strange music" that had caused the bohemian women to dance in the first place. As they have now stopped dancing, the song's narrative underscores the fact that Carmen is describing the scene from the point of view of a knowledgeable spectator for others who may be unfamiliar with this kind of music and, therefore, find it "strange." Then, in a phenomenon akin to Emma Bovary's growing disinterest in a story line in favor of attention to performance and performers, as the song continues, the narrative becomes more obscure—"same song, same refrain"—while its effects become more pronounced.

During the refrain the effects of this music on its listeners are enacted before our eyes as the Gypsy women do what Carmen says: they dance and sing. In this way the "La la la la la la" that disrupts the narrative also dramatizes it by signifying a compulsive behavior that, as words become repetitive and useless, repeats Carmen's own apparently spontaneous reaction at the start. In other words, the progressive interaction with the music—the feeling of being compelled to participate, or to pass from the status of a listener to that of a performer—is both enacted and talked about. It parallels the actual spectator's own mental enacting of an ethnic folk music we cannot really hear in the orchestra, inducing us to participate, like the Gypsy-performers, through our capacity to resonate, internally, with imaginary sound. In this way the first stanza offers a staging of what is often called a "scene of induction."

In the second stanza of the song Carmen tells of more explicitly fragmented material effects, as visual and physical images repeat their musical referents:

Les anneaux de cuivre et d'argent
Reluisaient sur les peaux bistrées;
D'orange et de rouge zébrées
Les étoffes flottaient au vent;
La danse au chant se mariait,
D'abord indécise et timide,

Plus vive ensuite et plus rapide
Cela montait, montait, montait!
La la la la la la. (32–33)

[The rings of copper and of silver
Gleamed on the tawny skins;
Striped with orange and red
The fabrics floated in the wind;
Dance and song were joined in marriage
First indecisively and timidly,
But then, becoming more lively and more rapid,
It (the mixture) mounted more and more!
La la la la la la.]

The sounds described in the first stanza blur into the colors and textures described in this one. The metallic brilliance of the *sistra* is repeated in the shining glitter of the dancers' copper and silver rings, the strumming of obstinate hands is replaced by the tawny skins of dancing bodies striped in exotic red and orange costumes, and frenzied music gives way to floating fabrics. The blurring described by these transformations of sound effects into visual effects is matched by the amplification of orchestral sound and the gradual speeding up of tempi (in the original score, an "andantino *quasi* allegretto" becomes progressively "più animato," with the value of the quarter note rising from 100 to 126 to 138 to 152 [Oeser 130–37]) and by Carmen's description of this more amplified blurring as an as yet undesignated *cela* bursting forth from a marriage of song and dance and mounting more and more intensely. Whereas the first stanza described the sounds that compelled Carmen to stand and sing and did not correspond to what we hear in the audience, this one describes the scene that begins during the refrain, "La la la." The dance of the Gypsy women "marries" her song, while our sonic environment "marries" the visual tumult of their movement, with Carmen acting as a narrator on the sidelines who leads us through this performance and progressive participation. As the *La la la* stops the narrative, it also asks us to rethink it, pitting the textual function of narrative song against the story recounted in it. At the same time, our sonic environment, the music we are imagining in the *posada* of our choosing, blends with our acoustic environment, the real sounds of the orchestra and voices, in that same *La la la la la la.*

Before giving way *tutta forza* to an orchestral postlude that will repeat this mounting mixture, or blend, Carmen analyzes what has just gone on, continuing to help us understand the pleasures of performance and their relation to music listening:

Les Bohémiens à tour de bras,
De leurs instruments faisaient rage,
Et cet éblouissant tapage,
Ensorcelait les zingaras!
Sous le rhythme de la chanson,
Ardentes, folles, enfiévrées,
Elles se laissaient, enivrées,
Emporter par le tourbillon!
La la la la la la.
Mouvement de danse très rapide, très violent. (33)

[The Bohemians, with flying arms,
Raged with their instruments,
And this overwhelming din,
Bewitched the *zingaras!*
Under the effect of the rhythm of the song,
Ardent, crazed, and feverish,
They (the Bohemian women) let themselves, drunken,
Be carried off by the whirlwind!
La la la la la la.
Very rapid and very violent dance movement.]

Charmed by the wild, blinding din, the *éblouissant tapage,* of the guitar players, the bohemian women become ardent, crazed, and feverish and are carried off into a state of rhythmic ecstasy. A state akin to that of Lacan's mystical *jouissance,* in that it is the product of a type of sound that blinds its participants, it differs from Lacan's in that, in addition to being an expression of unconscious affectivity, it is also a highly calculated motor response, an endless turning and whipping of perfect form which balances centrifugal and centripetal forces as in a pirouette or a tornado.

In other words, in its evocation of the pleasure of musical listening among dancers, this stanza describes the activity of performance as a passage from real sound to mental rhythms that reiterate it and from there to physical movements that reenact it. Kinesthetic energy, or the bodily know-how of dancers, overtakes conscious responsiveness to verbal or narrative logics both in the sounds and in the words we hear in the "Bohemian Song." (In this song the repetitive use of *z* and *s* sounds further highlights the erasure of verbal logic.)

The evocation of this kinesthetic response in the center of an *opéra-comique* serves to highlight the affectivity of music listening. Therefore, although the strangeness of the music and the foreignness of the setting encourage spectators to distance themselves from the pleasure being described—to analyze it, in other words—the witnessing of other spectators who do identify may offer us the imaginary satisfaction not of identifying with the enactment of ecstasy or with a loss of self-awareness (as among the Gypsies portrayed) but, rather, with the power of the performers to blend themselves into the *éblouissant tapage*. We identify with their capacity to reproduce mentally the musical precision, or mastery, of that tapping. This capacity to listen to music in a masterful enough way to blend oneself into it recalls Emma Bovary's flowing among "unseizable and unceasing thoughts" and the ways in which attention to the libretto helped her draw clear distinctions between herself and the characters portrayed only to blend herself subsequently with the music. Ultimately, as the "Bohemian Song" foregrounds the phenomenon of performance and of musical enunciation in its distinction from verbal utterance, it also links the affective response of performers to that of spectators, who are always potentially performing as they listen.

In this context of dance performance it is noteworthy that Wagner explicitly removed dance performances from his operas and that Bizet highlights them explicitly by forming them into an integral part of the dramatic plot. To deny the dancing body, as in Wagner's music dramas or in Lacan's *jouissance*, is to sublimate physical expression to some higher authority, some metaphysical voice that exists beyond individual physiology. To foreground the body, as in the "Bohemian Song," is to highlight the ways in which mental rhythms guide the physical impulses of both performers and spectators. Moreover, as Susan McClary writes, the question of dance in *Carmen* is central to the concerns of the bourgeois imagination: "*Carmen* can be read as an indictment of the bourgeois fear of the body or as a moral lesson about the consequences of succumbing to the pleasures of the flesh. But in either case, Bizet does not have Carmen dance to gratify the ballet-loving Parisian public: her swinging hips—which are alien to ballet—are a crucial issue in the opera" (56). As a crucial issue in the opera, the insistence on the question of the dancing body emphasizes Carmen's identity as a performer. For McClary, Carmen's stage persona creates a "basic ambiguity in her dramatic construction: when she sings, does she express herself, or is she just performing a number?" (75). But the ambiguity of Carmen's personal identity also offers a microcosm of the concerns of the *Carmen* narrative.

McClary is right, therefore, to underscore the ambiguity of bourgeois reactions to the body in general—this is clearly one of the ways in which Bizet alters the configuration of the moral duplicity of Mérimée's novella—and to suggest that Carmen's form of dance is particularly concerned with the physical, participatory aspects of folk art rather than with the metaphysical aspirations of ballet performance. Moreover, by borrowing the traditional narrative excuse for dancing so characteristic of classical balletic form—the setting up onstage of someone to watch a dance performance from within the logic of a larger dramatic plot enactment (as opposed to the typical balletic entr'acte)—Bizet also brings to our attention the capacity of the performing arts to forge an imagined community of ideal spectators.

This insistence on the question of the performance community that flamenco performing arts always strive to create (see chap. 4) may also be a gesture of self-distinction insofar as it is clearly opposed to the different kind of community apparently sought by Wagner. Indeed, in relation to what Theodor Adorno refers to as Wagner's "intoxicating brew," that "form of 'oceanic regression'" which functions by blurring "the dividing lines between the different arts," Bizet (with Meilhac and Halévy) embeds this song within a series of identifications so as to underline the relation of music drama to the potential politics of a pleasurable effect based on identification, self-forgetfulness, and the blinding loss of conscious control.[35] As a result, whereas Wagner had hoped to revive the lost energies of folk art to strengthen the bonds of a national community blind to the political "figuring" at work in its aesthetic products, this song stages a folk art that foregrounds a similarly undefined religiosity (something like the kind of spiritual *duende* sought by flamenco performers) in order to create a potentially diverse ethnic community among its spectators. Not only does the song allow a crossing of identity boundaries by both performers and spectators and the members of the two opposing social and cultural milieus that structure the *Carmen* narrative—soldiers and Gypsies, bourgeois and bohemians—but the environment created is a place in which the antibourgeois yet bourgeois parasitic capitalism, the border-crossing enterprise of Gypsy contraband, can occur.

Followed immediately by the disruptive sound of spoken dialogue that refers to respecting the borders of the law, it is clear that the Gypsies use their performance space to create a social atmosphere conducive to carrying on business as usual:

> PASTIA: Il commence à se faire tard . . . et je suis, plus que personne,
> obligé d'observer les règlements.
>
> LE LIEUTENANT: . . . C'est parce que ton auberge est le rendez-vous
> ordinaire de tous les contrebandiers de la province.
>
> PASTIA: Que ce soit pour cette raison ou pour une autre, je suis
> obligé de prendre garde. (33–34)

> [PASTIA: It is getting late . . . and I, more than anyone, am obliged
> to observe the regulations.
>
> THE LIEUTENANT: . . . It is because your tavern is the typical meeting place for all of the smugglers of the province.
>
> PASTIA: Whether it is for this reason or another, I am obliged to
> beware.]

If Pastia, like Carmen before him, evades the questions posed by the regulatory authority, his responses highlight the capacity of the Gypsy community to counter the effects of a dominant legal system while moving within its boundaries. It is striking that the symbolic phrase "Beware!" *(Prendre garde!)* has been appropriated by Pastia from out of the vocabulary of the regulatory authority he addresses. The shifting of this and

other repeated symbolic phrases between the worlds of the bohemians
and the bourgeois emphasizes the fact that clandestine affiliations in Pastia's tavern provide an "intercultural" environment.
In light of this blending of listeners with performers and bourgeois
soldiers with bohemians, it is also significant that the "Bohemian Song"
was considered an ethnographic moment in the opera, a moment that
sets itself up in parallel to the responses of Mérimée's ethnographer to
the scenes of Gypsy life he encounters while traveling. F. de Lagenevais,
writing in *La Revue des Deux Mondes* on 15 March 1875, seizes upon the
ways in which the opera's mise-en-scène as well as its direct citations of
Mérimée's dialogues remind us of this ethnographic parallel:

> Poètes, peintres et musiciens, tout le monde se préoccupe au-
> jourd'hui d'ethnologie; rien d'étonnant que cette curiosité d'infor-
> mation gagne et s'étende jusqu'aux moindres détails de la mise en
> scène; on cherche le vrai, on *fait nature*. Allez voir ce second acte de
> *Carmen*, c'est à se croire en Espagne: décor, costumes, le ton, le
> geste, l'air du visage, tout y est. . . . Ajoutons que dans l'originalité
> de cette mise en scène une juste part revient à M. Bizet, et que la
> couleur locale, comme il l'a comprise au début de son second acte,
> dénote aussi bien l'archéologue que le musicien. Sur un fond *vieil-
> Orient* de sons monotones et sourds tendu derrière la coulisse, la gent
> bohème brode ses arabesques et se dessine le chant militaire dans
> le lointain; vous diriez la civilisation picaresque de l'Espagne mod-
> erne émergeant de ses origines judaïques, arabes, égyptiennes, que
> sais-je? (480)

[Poets, painters and musicians, everyone is preoccupied today by
ethnology; it is not surprising that this curiosity about information
takes over and extends into the details of stage design; one seeks
the true, one *acts natural*. Go see that second act of *Carmen;* you will
believe yourself in Spain: sets, costumes, the tone, the gestures, the
quality of the faces, all is there. . . . Let us add that in the originality
of this stage setting, Mr. Bizet has had a large part, and that the local
color, as he has understood it at the opening of his second act,
denotes the archaeologist as well as the musician. On an *old Orient*
background of monotone and deaf sounds stretched behind the

wings, the bohemian gentry embroiders its arabesques and sketches
military chants in the distance; you might call it the picaresque civilization of modern Spain emerging from its Jewish, Arab, Egyptian
origins, what do I know?]

In a slightly cynical appraisal of the ethnological veracity of Bizet's styl-
ish mise-en-scène for *Carmen*'s second act, Lagenevais reveals the complicity of Bizet's archaeological imagination with the colonial project.
This complicity allows bourgeois sensibilities to confuse, in the name of
"the true," or of "acting natural," the Orient, Spain, bohemians, Gypsies, Jews, Arabs, and Egyptians. He also associates the "naturalistic"
stage sets of Bizet's second act, however, with the emergence of a modern Spanish bourgeoisie that is culturally diverse, or at least willing to
acknowledge itself as made up of ethnically mixed heritages.

In the context of a national art form accused of using Wagnerian
techniques to disturb both the conventions of listening in the Salle Favart and the cultural values associated with comic-opera as a genre, such
remarks suggest that, while participating in the ethnographic project
of the late nineteenth century known as Orientalism, the opera is also
staging relations between operatic practices and the ideology of colonial
expansion this project sustains. Awareness of the complicity does not
necessarily diminish the association of racial or ethnic diversity with a
dangerous and unacknowledged linking of race, religion, geography, or
morality, but, rather than promoting a generalized condemnation of
what McClary calls the "dreaded other" (56–57), Bizet's transposition of
a popularized flamenco art tradition may encourage a reconsideration
of the colonial/archaeological/naturalist project itself. At the very least,
Lagenevais's reading of Bizet's ethnographic imagination appears attentive to ethnic tolerance and intolerance. The "old Orient" background
that stretches behind the wings, for example, is a reference to Bizet's
entr'acte music, and the sketching of military songs "in the distance"
indicates that Lagenevais has been forced to see from the bohemian point
of view. It is from this point of view that Lagenevais imagines the emergence of a modern Spanish bourgeoisie; it is curious that, one hundred
and eight years later, Carlos Saura also considers *Carmen* from this point
of view.

Lagenevais's reference to Bizet as an archaeologist is further reminiscent of Mérimée's narrator cum archaeologist cum ethnographer, who told us the story in the first place. This reference underscores the fact that the four acts of Bizet's opera closely parallel the four chapters of Mérimée's novella: (1) the bourgeois-bohemian conflict; (2) Carmen's world; (3) José's story, his jealousy, his violence, and his life with the bohemians; (4) the return of the scholarly tone of the narrative opening, designed to offer both closure and moral ambiguity. In this parallel configuration the "Bohemian Song" not only supposes Carmen's world; it also echoes the opening of Mérimée's second chapter, in which the theoretically distant narrating ethnographer finds himself compelled to describe his first encounter with Gypsy women. Both scenes turn around the word *tapage*, the idea of the blinding din that marks a confusion of sound and vision or of acoustic and sonic environments.

In the novella, as I noted in chapter 2, the narrator views Gypsy bathers from afar and transforms their devilish *tapage* into the chiaroscuro contours of a poeticized vision of Diana and her nymphs. Having thus framed and stilled the scene, he then identifies with the desirous impulses of Actaeon, who, like José, ultimately causes his own destruction. It is as if the *tapage* blinds him in that this silent, reflective moment blurs any real cultural awareness of the reality of those women, who have become, instead, mere players in his own personal fantasy. And, like Actaeon, the narrator does end up "acting out" his fantasy vision in his subsequent relations with Carmen, thus identifying *avant la lettre* with the protagonist of the story, Don José. This capacity to introject images from afar and to make of them imaginary performances that one ultimately ends up realizing, is transposed in the opera into the effect of Bohemia on José and the effect of the "Bohemian Song" on its listeners.

Bizet's echoing of the original *Carmen,* and especially of those troubled moments in the story when distinctions between the protagonist and the narrator are most confused, has the effect of recalling the literary source of *Carmen* and of asking us to "listen" beyond the scene that we see. This idea of listening to Mérimée's text while watching an "ethnographic moment" in the opera in turn recalls Abbate's notion that, when listening to the *mise en abyme* of a narrative song, we listen both inside and outside, paying better attention to the words because of the structure of the strophic song but also constantly expanding our thoughts beyond the song to the designs of the larger composition. Mérimée's novella is one example of the larger intertextual "outside" to which we listen in the "Bohemian Song." This particular outside is repeatedly called to our attention throughout, of course, because of the comic-opera's direct citations of Mérimée's text. In the original libretto these citations were often quite lengthy.

In addition to direct citations of whole scenes and passages from Mérimée's text, however, Jean-Louis Martinoty argues that in *Carmen* there is an intentional exploitation of specific words or expressions, *mot-symboles* [word-symbols], which are continually repeated in such a way as to highlight the values of the different worlds of the *Carmen* narrative. According to Martinoty, Meilhac and Halévy are perfectly conscious of these textual echoes and their capacity to forge a network of themes which differs from the Wagnerian web of leitmotivs because it relies on the repetition of words. Along with the *prendre garde* I already noted and the *suivre là-bas* or *ailleurs* studied by Martinoty (106), *ensorceller* or *charme*, *oiseau*, and *tapage* are notable examples. This type of reference differs from that of direct citation in that citations are used to map the structure of the opera onto the structure of the novella and to put the opera listener in a position akin to that of Mérimée's narrator, whereas the use of word-symbols helps us to read a "hidden" and symbolic narrative in the larger whole of the opera itself. The case of *tapage* is of particular interest for my purposes because, in referring to the here and now of the Gypsy performance space, it recalls the literary source of *Carmen* and, in so doing, reveals a symbolic narrative hidden in *Carmen* related to violence, confusion, disorder, and blinding noise. With a view to uncovering this narrative in the opera, its repeated use is worth tracing.

The first use of the word *tapage* occurs prior to the "Bohemian Song" in a moment in the opera in which bohemian life becomes associated with the frightening image of an angry mob, in the knifing scene that takes place in the tobacco manufactory. As part of a spoken dialogue in scenes 8 and 9 of the first act, the word recurs twice, reminding us why there is a military presence in this community. First, Zuniga orders José: "Prenez, José, deux hommes avec vous, et voyez là-dedans qui cause ce tapage" (22) [José, take two men with you, and see who is causing that din inside]. Then, while the women working there are maintained at a distance by a row of dragoons, José explains to Zuniga, "J'ai d'abord trouvé trois cents femmes, criant, hurlant, gesticulant, faisant un tapage à ne pas entendre Dieu tonner" (24) [I first found three hundred women, screaming, gesticulating, creating a din loud enough to silence God's thunder]. Clearly associated with the unruly behavior and popular energies of bohemians, workers, and women, *tapage* takes on the further sense, in José's words, of a devilish silencing of the Word, or authority of God. Recalled in the "Bohemian Song" in act 2, the now symbolic word resonates with these previous associations.

When the word *tapage* next occurs, in Escamillo's celebrated "Toreador Song" at the end of act 2, it describes the response of spectators to the performance of bullfighters. Viewed from the perspective of this narrative song, *tapage* harks back to the infernal noise-making of the bohemian women and forward to the more controlled and socially sanctioned noise-making of the crowd attending the bullfight at the end of the opera. That is, while recalling Gypsy performance, it also anticipates the future of the operatic narrative and its invitation to join the more controlled mob. Escamillo's inference, in fact, is that all spectators hover on the edge of wild and uncontrolled intoxication but that, within the constraints of the *cirque*, or arena, such behavior may be channeled into a condoned release of affective energies.

Escamillo sings:

Les spectateurs perdent la tête
S'interpellent à grands fracas;
Apostrophes, cris et tapage
Poussés jusques à la fureur,
Car c'est la fête du courage,
C'est la fête des gens de coeur.
     Toréador, en garde, etc. (38)

[The spectators lose their heads
Calling to each other noisily;
Apostrophes, screams, and a blinding din
Pushed to the point of furor,
Because it is the festival of courage,

It is the festival of brave folks.
Toreador, beware, etc.]

Losing their heads as they repeat the *tapage* of the bohemian dancers, the spectators of the bullfight participate in a socially sanctioned expression of Bohemia's enthusiastic energies. In this setting one need not be a Gypsy dancer to join in, for bohemian pleasures are extended to all men and women of courage. More important, in its realizing of textual echoes and anticipations, or Martinoty's word-symbol thematics, the repetitions of *tapage* trace a progressive accumulation of associated meanings that tell one kind of *Carmen* story. From the unruly behavior of angry workers, to their need for authoritarian restraint, to their capacity to fascinate and seduce (in the *éblouissant tapage* of the "Bohemian Song"), and, finally, to the containing of that unrestrained but contagious behavior in the pseudomilitary theatrical setting of the bullring, this sliding of meanings stages the dominant moral lesson of Mérimée's *Carmen:* we must control the dangerous movements of workers, foreigners, bohemians, and popular energies in general. But, in the specific context of the opera, this sliding of meanings from worker unrest and bohemian behavior to bourgeois social control and the sanctioned release of affective energies by popular art also suggest that popular national art forms—the bullfight but also the opera—may represent one important way to contain such energies. We have, then, another example of a bohemian space created in and by the dominant bourgeois culture: a well-regulated din.

As the example of *tapage* implies, listening to the "Bohemian Song" *as readers* from within the words of the narrative song to scenes and moments beyond the song, we hear one *Carmen* story. Listening *as spectators,* however, to the song's nonnarrative refrain, "La la la la la" (most always sung in *Carmen* as "Tra lalalala"), we hear a different *Carmen* story. That is, whereas the words of the narrative song evoke José's values and the moral lessons that issue forth from the dominant social milieu, behind or beyond the nonsignifying vocables of its refrain we hear a subtle accumulation of meanings associated with Carmen and the social values of her milieu. The repetitive refrains of *tra lalalala* not only signify, then, the ways in which the progress of the operatic narrative is retarded by the pleasures of song and dance as they overtake those of conscious behavior and speech; they also juxtapose, in performance, new terms for the narrative by taking on meanings from each of the stanzas they follow. After each stanza, respectively, *tra lalalala* takes on new associations: (1) with seduction and/or the induction to listen; (2) with physical affectivity and/or the kinesthetic reiteration of sound; and (3) with *jouissance* and/or an abandonment to musical intoxication. In this association of meanings *tra lalalala* shows how empty vocables signifying nothing but song and pleasure may, following a logic similar to that of Martinoty's word-symbols, also take on meanings from the larger context of the song's narrative to denote an acceleration of affectivity. And, because they only mean or contribute to narrative sense-making by way of purely musical associations, the nonnarrative vocables in the "Bohemian Song" suggest that operatic narrative is itself a purely imaginary linking of complementary visual and aural senses that progress and take on an air of narrative logic by blurring intelligibility and substituting, or shifting, meanings, surreptitiously.

Curiously, although narrative song may represent the musical moment most rife with narrative clues, it is also the one most likely to mask its own intelligibility because of the physical demands required by the production of such vocal sound (Poizat 67–69). In this instance, whereas the "story" of the "Bohemian Song" may be unintelligible as we listen, it is also taken up or represented in sounds we do hear. We are more likely to remember the "catchy" *tra lalalala* of the refrain and note its recurrence than to hear the words of the song. Since the "Bohemian Song" talks about this very phenomenon at the same time that it participates in it, however, it is the musical thematics of keywords and nonnarrative vocables, especially as they are repeated, which help us to establish narrative values by supplementing them with sonic associations.

In the case of *tra lalalala*, at the same time that the refrains take on meanings from their immediate context, they also function, beyond the song, as a vocal motive associated with Carmen's opposition to the status quo of military dominance and social control. In fact, as in the "Bohemian Song," Carmen repeats this motive, within the larger structure of the opera, on three occasions. Her first use of *tra lalalala* is a way of responding to Zuniga's authority immediately following the knifing scene. This *tra lalalala* marks her refusal to speak:

ZUNIGA: Avez-vous quelque chose à répondre? Parlez, j'attends!
CARMEN: *(fredonnant)* Tra lalalalalala, coupe-moi, brule-moi, je ne
te dirai rien! . . .
ZUNIGA: Ce ne sont pas des chansons que je te demande, c'est une
réponse. (Oeser 98)

[ZUNIGA: Have you something to answer? Speak, I'm waiting!
CARMEN: *(humming)* Tra lalalalalala, cut me, burn me, I will tell
you nothing! . . .
ZUNIGA: I am not asking for songs, but for an answer!]

In this scene verbal responses anxiously surround Carmen's willful denial of authority, as Zuniga's spoken dialogue loudly counters Carmen's
melodic pride in a kind of verbal-musical jousting.

Carmen repeats the motive again at the end of her "Seguidilla," where
it takes on the force of her seductive seeking of pleasure in drink and
dance. In this scene it is designed to rouse José's affective response and
reprises in answer to his question "Carmen, je suis comme un homme ivre
. . . si je me livre, ta promesse, tu la tiendras?" [Carmen, I am like a
drunken man (an echo from Mérimée) . . . if I surrender, will you keep
your promise?]. Carmen answers: "Oui. Nous danserons la Séguedille et
boirons du Manzanilla. . . . tra la la la la la la la la" (Oeser 119–21) [Yes,
we shall dance the Seguidilla and drink Manzanilla. . . . Tra la la la la la la
la la]. Finally, after its association in the "Bohemian Song" with abandonment to the self-indulgence of musical intoxication, Carmen repeats
it, one last time, as an accompaniment to her private dance for José. In
this last scene her motive prompts José to tell his own story of intoxication as he pulls the *fleur de cassie* from his jacket and begins his "Flower
Song."

Across these four repetitions of *tra lalalala* one can see that the "Bohemian Song" compresses or offers a microcosm of Carmen's behavior
and values by revealing the way in which seduction, physical affectivity
and abandonment to intoxication are mapped onto the larger structural
composition of the comic-opera itself. It is notable, in this context, that
the knifing scene followed directly by the verbal-musical joust between
Carmen and Zuniga as well as the "Seguidilla" and the scene of the
"Flower Song" are all moments when the dramatic force of the opera

breaks through the conventional restraints, or borders, of the comic-opera form (McClary, *Bizet*, 50, 85–89, 95), calling our attention to a more general concern in the opera with the ways in which formal pressures are challenged by musical ingenuity. In the last of these scenes, just prior to José's "Flower Song," the vocal motive that has become quite clearly associated with Carmen's disregard for dominant bourgeois values confronts the repetition of another vocal motive, the mock bugle sound of "Taratata." In relation to the bohemian pleasures of Carmen's *tra lalalala*, the "Taratata" motive comes to signify José's acceptance of bourgeois values. A motive that, by its very nature, already signifies military duty (and is accurately accompanied by trumpets and piccolos), *taratata* is first heard in the children's chorus that mimics the changing of the guards near the opening of the opera. In this opening scene *taratata* signifies a mode of play which links military protocol to familial and patriarchal protocol by evoking a *dressage*, or physical and mental formation of values, common to both the military and to the raising of children:

> Ta ra ta ta, ta ra ta ta;
> Nous marchons la tête haute
> Comme de petits soldats, . . .
> Les épaules en arrière
> Et la poitrine en dehors. (8–9)
>
> [Ta ra ta ta, ta ra ta ta;
> We march with heads held high
> Like little soldiers, . . .
> Shoulders back, chest out.]

In addition to associating the motive with the mimicking of military protocol, the children also use it to recall a military marking of time characteristic of resistance to melodic blurring: "Une . . . deux . . . marquant le pas" (8) [One . . . two . . . marking the steps]. It is significant in this light that the sense of self-control, or *maîtrise*, evoked in the chorus gives way to a dialogue between José and Zuniga in which José speaks of his own youth, his childish inability to control his temper, and his being obliged to join the army, given his tendency toward violent behavior, because he was unable to seek a career in the church (12).

When the *taratata* motive is recalled in Carmen's and José's love scene, it is specifically mapped onto José's need for bodily control, his resistance to intoxication, and his concern with conforming to social propriety and military and familial duty (52–54). Carmen waxes ironical about these needs by disregarding the motive's semantic associations and adapting its purely semiotic value—its musical sounds, even 4/4 rhythm, and diatonic tonal space—to her performance of "tra lalalala" (see McClary, *Bizet*, 95). José, on the other hand, pleads with her to respect the semantic associations of the motive. As always, he wants things to make verbal and rhythmic sense. But the protagonists also mimic each other, exchanging the *tra lalalala* for the *taratata* and creating an acoustic example of the bohemian/bourgeois system.

Though *tra lalalala* and *taratata* are only nonsensical and conventional operatic vocables, it is clear that in *Carmen* they are effectively constructed to take on the tensions of the double discourses, dominant and oppositional, which regulate the social politics of Mérimée's narrative. Whereas *tra lalalala* looks forward, through the force of its repetitions, to the inebriating pleasures of *jouissance*, to apparent transgressions of protocol, and to bohemian liberties, *taratata* looks backward, signaling a return to bourgeois order, to familial, catholic, and military responsibilities, and to *dressage*, or *maîtrise*, in the children's chorus. More pointedly, Carmen's desire for movement, change, and pleasure associates the values of community (or even of the Commune) with the chromatic descents of flamenco performance but also with the "low" art forms that characterize the pleasures of Parisian nightlife (cabaret songs and drunken dances) and with the popular sovereignty of an indeterminate, elusive, and potentially destructive sense of liberty. The reactionary force of José's recollections, on the other hand, associates the church, the military, and the family with social control, reminiscence, repetition, restoration, and with a nostalgia for social control and imperial sovereignty. As Jerrold Seigel's *Bohemian Paris* reminds us, however, both sets of associations describe bourgeois values, and the intensity of their conflict or opposition, dramatized by the events of the 1871 Parisian insurrection known as the Commune, is related less to their actual distinctiveness than to the difficulty individuals encountered attempting to reconcile them. Despite conservative reviews of *Carmen*'s opening performances which critiqued the staging of working-class women and prostitutes, in other words, the essential conflict of *Carmen*, like that of the Commune, seems related to the very ambiguity of bourgeois values themselves.

The tension between the two discourses is emblematized in the ambiguous image of *tapage*, which can be understood as both a rhythmic, controlled tapping and an unrestrained noise. These two senses come together in Carmen's accommodation of *tra lalalala* to *taratata* in her seduction of José and, again, in the bullring in act 4. This means that for the reader of the opera *tapage* can reveal one of the ways its dramatic logic meets or marries its musical logic, insofar as a dramatic impulse heading toward closure and the control of unruly behavior parallels a musical impulse toward an unending, undesignated tapping of rhythms (or castanets and heels). In this way a narrative about the progressive dangers of inebriation, one kind of *tapage*, is complemented by a textual performance of the pleasures of inebriation (particularly through rhythm or dance), another kind of *tapage*. It is this more general tension that reverberates in the "Bohemian Song"'s confrontation of textual repetition and narrative progression.

Though the vocal motives *tra lalalala* and *taratata* are not heard beyond act 2, their senses echo throughout the opera to its end. The force of *taratata*, for example, is taken up by the sounds of a quasimilitary celebration march at the opening of act 4, blending its meanings into those associated with the festival of courage which frames the opera. The force of *tra lalalala* is taken up by a line that leads into act 3, with Carmen's final invitation to José to escape into the unstructured freedoms of the bohemian lifestyle: "Là-bas là-bas dans la montagne" [Over there, there, in the mountain]. Insofar as *tra lalalala* only signifies by virtue of its octosyllabic rhythm and its repetitive phoneme, the motive is as if heard again in the long a sounds of: "Là-bas là-bas dans la montagne" (55–56).

Whereas act 3 largely plays these undesignated bohemian pleasures against José's reactionary values—turning, as we shall see, on the double directions of *là-bas* [over there]—the conflict is resolved ultimately, if not very satisfyingly, in the opera's closing scene. In that scene the celebration framework of the opera finds closure musically and visually in two opposing versions of inebriation: that of the crowd and that of José. The first, orchestral and choral, signifies those activities taking place inside the arena; the second is played out in the uncompromising final duet between José and Carmen in front of the closed velum outside the arena. As if questioning both the violence of closure itself and what should be a satisfying return to order of "endless melody," one expression of inebriation, or *tapage,* is murderous and disturbing, the other channeled into a popular pastime.

Resounding Duplicities

The opposing pressures of the ambiguous narrative discourses purveyed by the vocal motives *tra lalalala* and *taratata* are emblematic both of the formal tensions of comic-opera divided into songs and words and of the double discourses of the operatic narrative pulled between *jouissance* and *maîtrise.* Yet the vocal motives do not alone carry the impetus of Carmen's musical logic. Indeed, these pressures are taken up within each of the materials of expression available to the comic-opera form, resounding and reappearing vocally, as we have seen, but also orchestrally, visually, and verbally, in a gesture that can be called "textual self-referencing." By this I mean that each of the materials of expression of the comic-opera form sets up motivic correspondences that reiterate *Carmen*'s narrative duplicity. This repetitive self-referencing has two notable effects: first, it interrupts the forward thrust of the narrative of José's accelerating intoxication, in much the same way that the refrains of the "Bohemian Song" interrupt the forward progress of the sung narrative; second, Carmen's and José's two value systems are sustained within all kinds of operatic signifying systems, thereby highlighting the heterogeneous materiality of opera itself and its capacity to channel an imaginary logic of narrative continuity.

As Susan McClary has shown, the narrative dichotomy, adapted from Mérimée (and which I have associated with *tra lalalala* and *taratata*), is repeated at an orchestral level by way of a distinction between, on one hand, diatonic melodies and tonal music suggestive of both "metaphysical transcendence" and postponed but inevitable gratification and, on the other hand, a chromatic slippage suggestive of a "threat" to the maintenance of authority posed by bodily pleasures (*Feminine Endings*, 56–57). This distinction takes on a narrative value of temporalness in two structurally decisive motives that originate in the opera's ambiguous prelude: the chromatic halftone descent of Carmen's exotic fate motive and the diatonic refrain of Escamillo's "Toreador Song." While repeatedly evoking an unsettling confrontation between the two social worlds that structure the *Carmen* narrative, the diatonic and chromatic impulses meet most dramatically at an equivocal ending, which sets up an almost unbearable tension for the listener. As McClary explains it, "The opera terminates with a gesture that provides satisfaction on some levels (the resolution of dissonance, the purging of chromaticism, the return to diatonicism), while it also betrays its essential impotence (the final key is arbitrary, the thematic terrain belongs to the droll, exotic people who were supposed to remain in their place as a sideshow)" (63). The opera reaches closure, orchestrally, then, by returning to the military celebration motive that opens the prelude, but the closure remains "impotent," partial, unresolved, or ambiguous due to both the disturbing effect of the knifing onstage and José's bitter triumph noted by so many of the original musical reviewers.[36]

This orchestral tension between tonal closure and chromatic slippage is repeated verbally through the use of those symbolic words, like *tapage*, which Martinoty describes as ambiguous gestures whose meanings can signify one set of values or the other. Particularly striking, in this respect, are *là-bas* (and its coordinates *suivre* and *en route*) and *prendre garde* and *en garde*, which structure act 3. *Là-bas* [over there] initially evokes the undesignated destination characteristic of the liberties of bohemian life, as in Carmen's "Là-bas, là-bas, tu me suivras" [Over there, there, you will follow me], just before Zuniga's return to the tavern at the end of act 2 (56). But the bohemians link this destination to the attention motif *prends garde!* [Take care! or Beware!] at the opening chorus of act 3: "La fortune est là-bas, là-bas / Mais prends garde pendant la route" (60) [Fortune is over there, there / But beware along the route!]. Whereas *là-bas* supposes an indefinite nomadic movement and inevitable crossing of borders, *prends garde* recalls the limits of the law and of other frontiers. (These are reiterated as well in a play of *en route* and *halte* [75].) Curiously, however, when José and Micaela take up the verbal motives in act 3, *là-bas* reiterates the defined destination it signified in act 1, Mother's village back home (17, 62, 76), while *prends garde* reverts to the meaning Carmen initially assigned to it in her "Habañera": the almost military discipline needed to resist the violent impulses of desire. This is the meaning that finally becomes quite ominous in José's "Prends garde à toi, Carmen . . . je suis las de souffrir" (75) [Beware, Carmen . . . I am tired of suffering]. In this way, in the course of the opera's unfolding, the associations of unlimited movement and transgression have been twisted into opposing poles and as if switched back into their initial positions, moving verbally toward that uneasy closure that the orchestral motives also channel.

This "bohemian" switching and twisting of words and their associations is echoed forcefully, in the final act, in the transformation of *là-bas* into the *à bas* [down with] of a choral reaction to the *alguaŗils* [judges], representatives of the law, as they enter the arena. "L'alguazil à vilaine face, A bas! à bas! à bas! à bas!" (81) [Down with the judge and his ugly face, Down! Down! Down! Down!] repeats and denigrates the sound of the bohemian's previous insistence on *là-bas*. At the same time, Frasquita's warning that Don José is hiding in the crowd, "Prends garde" (83), the refrain of Escamillo's and José's ensemble, "Mettez-vous en garde!" (73, 74), and the pertinent reprisal of Escamillo's "Toréador, en garde" (78, 87) all resist the compelling rush toward the violence of closure. The duplicity of these terms and their capacity to signal a shifting between the values of the bohemians and those of the dominant social order recall Nietzsche's emphasis on the unresolved dramatic ambiguity of José's closing line, "C'est moi qui l'ai tuée! Ah! Carmen! ma Carmen adorée" (Nietzsche, *Case*, 159) [It is I who killed her! Oh Carmen! my adored Carmen].

This same tension is sustained, visually, through a thematics of enclosure and escape. Enclosures, or circles, permeate the libretto's description of mise-en-scènes, once again dramatizing the relationship between maintaining, or marking, borders and transgressing them. Outside of the literal imprisonment of Carmen, of José, or even of Zuniga there is a repeated gesture toward circling characters who do not want to be captured. Though these circles, or limits, are always accompanied by flights that enable the operatic narrative to progress, gestures toward futurity, or escape and progress, are in each case halted by the visual representation of restraint. The result of this interaction is a visual thematics of enclosure/escape or resistance/movement which reiterates a structural logic of musical acceleration and spoken deterrence to progress, a verbal logic of unlimited movement and legal limitations, and an orchestral logic of chromatic transgression, or disturbing "impotence" and closure.

Shortly after the overture that frames the opera orchestrally, for example, Micaela appears onstage in search of Don José. The dragoons surround her, calling her a little bird and beckoning her to stay, but she escapes, singing, "Je reviendrai" (5) [I'll return]. This visual representation of restraint, or encircling, from which Micaela escapes is reprised when Carmen enters the scene to sing of another kind of bird in her "Habañera," the bird image becoming a symbol of escape and liberty. Though Carmen, too, is surrounded by men, she breaks through the ring to address José and reprise the song (a slightly different version of "Je reviendrai"). Likewise, when Zuniga investigates the knifing in the tobacco manufactory, he is surrounded by the workers and uses military force to limit their intrusion. The working women encircle Zuniga again when Carmen escapes at the end of the act, reprising her "Habañera."

In the third act real prisons and circles are replaced by José's internalized, only metaphorical, imprisonment: his need to choose between two versions of *là-bas*.[37] It is significant in this respect that the scenes of this act were originally set in a semicircle, or *cirque*, circumscribed by the surrounding rocky terrain and that this mountainous, interim terrain of the Pyrenees offered a visual suggestion both of a height and of a kind of in-between, or no-man's-land, from which either *là-bas* might be selected (60). At this point in the drama, in other words, the setting tells us that José could go either direction. But during the final duet, set in front of "les murailles de vieilles arènes" [the walls of the old arena], the story of Carmen and José comes to a close as the opposing energies of imprisonment and escape, or of borders and transgressions, find their ultimate union in the activities we do not see but can only imagine because they are enclosed inside an arena: "L'entrée du cirque est fermé par un long vélum" (79) [The entrance into the circus is closed by a long awning].[38]

This textual self-referencing of the vocal, verbal, visual, and orchestral tensions by way of which movement and resistance become associated, respectively, with bohemian energy and with military control and/ or social protocol highlights the capacity of operatic form to adapt the moral values of literary narrative to the stage by producing signifying systems that extend beyond or move between the logics of words. Moreover, by self-consciously reinforcing the destabilizing effects of the separation of speech and song vocally, verbally, orchestrally, and visually, *Carmen* may also separate what Clément refers to as grand opera's staging of "la double scène inséparable" [the inseparable double scene] of conscious and unconscious thinking by forcing spectators to oscillate between two kinds of reading strategies: narrative and textual or dramatic and musical. The contradictory exigencies of these doubled reading strategies exemplify the primary way in which *Carmen* discloses the reliance of operatic listening on the kind of double reading strategy we have already considered in Flaubert's *Madame Bovary*.

In a manner akin to Emma Bovary's oscillation between narrative analysis and identification, in fact, this tendency to "see" double is reiterated both by Carolyn Abbate's notion of restlessness among spectators listening to a narrative song and by Susan McClary's sense of equivocation and unbearable tension produced among listeners at the end of the opera. In other words, a certain undecidedness—which, incidentally, Freud saw as necessary to the very sustenance of intellectual thought itself—hovers over the comic-opera *Carmen*. This same phenomenon of double contradictory imperatives that must somehow rely one upon the other has been described by Nietzsche as Apollonian and Dionysian and, more generally, by Stendhal, in *Racine et Shakespeare*, as two interdependent types of theatrical pleasure: epic and dramatic.[39] Whereas *epic pleasure* suggests a spectator's capacity to appreciate the technique of performers and dramatists, *dramatic pleasure* supposes our capacity to lose track of space and time, during brief moments of heightened emotional response. One is a social and public response, the other an emotional and private, or psychic, response, but each relies upon the other a bit like Terdiman's discourses and counter-discourses or Seigel's bohemians and bourgeois. In his specific attention to the listener of opera Michel Poizat also evokes this idea of duplicity when he insists that each listener is always pulled between two affective extremes: the judging of voices and of individual performances (a mode of cultural critique, or *maîtrise,* so popular among opera spectators) and the giving way to the ecstasy of pure voice which forces us to close our eyes and to forget any distinction between the person of the opera singer and ourselves (56, 59–60). In each case it is a question of marking borders, consciously, and (or thereby) of transgressing them, unconsciously, by way of momentary identifications.

The "Carmen Effect"

The relation between this kind of double reading response and the duplicity of the *Carmen* narrative is amply illustrated, for our purposes, by Catherine Clément's presentation of the opera in *L'Opéra ou la défaite des femmes.*[40] As one example among others, Clément's reading demonstrates the ways in which the confrontation of narrative and textual functions in the opera encourages a "bohemian effect" of creative rereadings—remakes that do not seek merely to reiterate or restage narrative values but to rethink and literally rearrange, re-present, or rewrite them. This creative restaging of *Carmen* is the work of a new and original critical writing style that allows Clément to be drawn progressively into the imaginary scene of her own memories. This progressive involvement is figured in her writing through subtle shifts in address which situate Clément's voice in the positions of a playwright, a narrator, a spectator, and an actress. As is always the case in bohemian narrative, her persona finds itself both inside and outside the theater of her writer's mind.

Like most readers of *Carmen,* Clément may be said to read Mérimée's novella covertly at the same time that she proposes an overt reading of Bizet's opera. The covert reading presupposes that Mérimée's story lingers on in the minds of most French spectators of the opera as indeed it did in the minds of the spectators who first attended *Carmen*'s opening in 1875. As Ernst Reyer points out in the "Feuilleton du *Journal des débats*" of 11 March 1875, everyone had read it except for young girls, and "ceux qui ne l'ont pas lue la liront après avoir vu jouer la pièce, il ne faut pas en douter" [those who have not read it will read it after having seen the play, there is no doubt about it (my trans.)]. More important, the covert reading of Mérimée's novella inscribed into Clément's presentation of Bizet's opera also offers a model for the kind of identification the opera appears to encourage in its readers. The model for this process of identification is underscored, in Clément's writing, by her use, on one hand, of a narrative voice dependent upon textual borders and, on the other, of repetitive, even obsessive, refrains to represent the mobility of the subjective presence behind that voice of the opera's reader. Due to this writing style, Clément's telling has the musical quality of a narrative song interrupted by nonnarrative refrains.

Clément's covert reading of Mérimée's novella shows us that it is not what the reading consists of that matters but, rather, how that previous reading operates to help structure the response of spectators to the textual strategies of the opera. As in the case of Carlos Saura's *Carmen*, Clément's telling repeats the formal attributes of Mérimée's narrator. The *Carmen* story is told twice, as it is in Mérimée. The first time it is related dispassionately, as if it were almost irrelevant to Clément's presentation; the second time it is related very personally, in a series of interrupted, staccatolike, nonlinear memories. But the textuality of the *Carmen* story is likewise taken up in Clément's stylistic marking off of an imaginary stage space designed to foreground the mobility of the writer's voice in and around it. As in Mérimée's, the tone of the opening of Clément's essay is analytical, or critical: *Carmen* has become an object of study and, in that respect, is kept at a scholarly distance just like the scenes of Gypsy life in Mérimée's novella. In addition, Clément offers a footnote to Meilhac and Halévy (95–96) in an effort to further secure her objectivity. This scholarly distance is soon followed, however, by a précis in italics made to look like the program notes one might find in any opera's libretto which presents a résumé of the narrative. The change in typescript signals the presence of someone else's writing, allowing Clément to become a reader along with us and to refresh her own memories as we do just prior to a performance. While the précis gives us the sense that the show is about to begin, it puts Clément herself in the ambiguous position of being both a spectator to and a performer, or writer, of the *Carmen* tale.

In the following paragraph the narrative of the précis is neatly displaced, along with the location of the speaking subject. Clément's scholarly voice becomes theatricalized and takes on the staccato style of dramatic stage directions to create a new précis permeated with the present tense of the verb *to be*. This verb ushers in the performance by calling its only virtual reality to mind:

> Jour de fête à Séville. Les arènes de la Maestranza sont joyeuses, très blanches; des décorations peintes en jaune doré dessinent sur les murs des arabesques baroques; les hautes portes rouges cloutées de noir sont grandes ouvertes, et les grilles noires aussi, qui enferment l'espace du cirque dans un collier ajouré. On vend, on achète, des gâteaux, des cigarettes. C'est bruissant, bousculé, c'est une fête bourdonnante et sans menace. (96)

> [Holiday in Seville. The bright white arenas of the Maestranza are joyous; decorations painted in golden yellow trace baroque arabesques on the walls; the tall red doors with their black nails are wide open, and so are the black iron gates, enclosing the amphitheater with a necklace of openwork. There is buying and selling: cakes, cigarettes. It is noisy and jostling, a humming, harmless festival. (Wing 49)]

At the outset Clément sets the stage for the end of the opera by substituting her own personal description of a present-day bullfighting experience for Meilhac and Halévy's "murs de vieilles arènes." Relying upon that ambiguous position of the librettist or playwright who is both creating a stage setting and imagining it to be already in existence, Clément sets, or fixes, the accoutrements of a bright white, golden yellow, red, and black stage space by writing from the perspective of an imaginary spectator. These colors, the movement of baroque lines, and the noisy, unruly *tapage* of a crowd emphasize the position of someone who is watching, an "*on*" [one, us] who is both personal and impersonal, singular and collective. This *on* is both inside the tumult ("bousculé") and describing the bright enclosure ("un collier ajouré") from afar. The style of this stage setting is in fact reminiscent of Gustave Flaubert's *La Tentation de Saint Antoine,* a book later footnoted by Clément (104) which appeared, in its final version, the same year as Bizet's *Carmen.*

This description and its establishing of the positions of a librettist or director and of an imaginary spectator is then interrupted, as in Flaubert's *Tentation,* by personal anecdotes that further confuse the roles of performers and spectators and accelerate a desire on the part of the speaking subject to secure a position outside the textual space of representation. Consequently, the dramatic stage indications return in a kind of jittery, obsessional, and repetitive mode, but this time more specifically to narrate and describe Carmen:

> Jour de fête à Séville. Prise dans la foule, Carmen est en costume de dame, elle, la Gitane. Donc, un peu pute, un peu juive, un peu arabe, tout à fait illégale, toujours dans les marges de la vie. . . . Vois Carmen en poupée: le peigne sévillan sur le chignon, le cliquetis des bijoux d'or en filigrane, les serpents mouvants des franges de son châle, et des volants partout. . . . Ce n'est pas la Tzigane. Mais, au travers d'une musique française . . . pointe toute l'histoire éteinte d'un peuple voyageur. Sache, sous les dentelles, écouter l'écho distordu de la vérité. . . . l'Inde . . . puis l'Egypte et l'Afrique maghrébine, jusqu'à l'Espagne. (96–97)

> [Holiday in Seville. Caught in the crowd, Carmen is all dressed up like a lady, Carmen the Gypsy. Therefore, somewhat whore, somewhat Jewess, somewhat Arab, entirely illegal, always on the margins of life. . . . Look at the Carmen doll: she wears a Sevillian comb on her chignon, her jewelry of filigreed gold jingles, the fringes of her shawl move like serpents, and there are flounces everywhere. . . . That is no Gypsy. But through this French music . . . the whole extinct history of a wandering people comes to light. Try to hear through all the lace the distorted echo of truth. . . . India . . . then Egypt and the Maghreb, all the way to Spain. (Wing 49)

Following the example of Mérimée's first-person narration, Clément's voice moves from the position of the librettist-spectator into that of a narrator. She describes the scene both dispassionately ("Jour de fête") and intimately ("Vois," "Sache écouter"), as she invites an implied reader to "see" and "know how to listen" along with her. As in Lagenevais's description of the stage set for act 2, the lumping of exotic others into one fluid perception highlights Carmen's slippery identity and links it to that of a nomadic people curiously both "over there" and right here in Paris. We are asked to look beyond Bizet's tamed-down, popculture distortion of Gypsy life, in other words, and to contemplate the judicial exclusion and illegal marginality of actual Gypsies and other immigrant peoples both then and now.

These references to seeing and knowing how to listen required of the imaginary interlocutor secure the parameters of the imaginary stage space in such a way as to allow Clément both to stay on the margins, maintaining an analytic distance relative to the distorted echo of ancient truths, and to participate by sharing the twisted echoes of her own intimate memories. The performance now appears to be in progress as she continues: "La première fois que j'ai vu Carmen, tout à l'heure, elle était cigarière. . . . Ainsi tu peux comprendre pourquoi elle chante à plein coeur la liberté" (97–98) [The first time that I saw Carmen, a moment ago, she was working in a cigarette factory. . . . So you can understand why she sings for all she is worth about freedom (Wing 50; modified)]. As the imaginary opera now begins to unfold in very personal leaps and bounds, Clément's narrative familiarity, *je,* permits itself an intimate address to the reader, *tu,* as well as a certain familiarity with the perspective of the characters in the opera.

This familiarity situates Clément among the women working in the tobacco manufactory: "Comment elle s'est retrouvée en tôle, je n'en sais trop rien. Les unes disaient que c'était elle qui avait porté les premiers coups, les autres la défendaient, et comme après tout ce n'est qu'une gitane, le capitaine l'a coffrée. Cela ne tire pas à conséquences, avec ces filles-là" (98) [How she ended up behind bars I really do not know. Some of the women said she hit first, others defended her, and because after all she is only a Gypsy, the captain locked her up. It is of no importance with those sorts of girls (Wing 50; modified)]. As if playing the role of one of the tobacco factory workers herself, Clément's voice and colloquial expressions ("en tôle," "coffrée") evoke the working-class persona of the woman who, though present, did not see what happened because she is not privy to the secret workings of power. This woman can, nonetheless, reiterate a dominant discourse that marginalizes both Gypsies and women, because such common notions "go without saying." Outside or inside the opera, in other words, the imprisonment of Gypsies is of little consequence.

While confusing the drama of the opera with a real attitude about

Gypsies still prevalent today, Clément also confuses or transgresses the boundaries that distinguish performers and characters, spectators and librettists, but also the bourgeoisie and those particular bohemians who belong to or identify with the working class. It is logical, then, that, as her memories of *Carmen* resurface, disrupting but also compelling the linear unfolding of the drama, the past-tense recollection of the story told by one of Carmen's intimates evokes a present-tense demonstration of Carmen's musical transgression.

These contradictory perspectives are flanked by two references to Carmen's "tra lalalala" scenes, the musical-verbal joust with Zuniga and the opening of the "Seguidilla" scene, in which Carmen seduces José in the hopes of being liberated. First: "Je m'en souviens bien, elle n'avait pas l'air étonnée d'être enfermée. Elle avait même l'air de s'y attendre, chantant rêveusement au lieu de répondre aux questions du capitaine" (99) [I clearly remember that she seemed not at all surprised at being locked up. She even seemed to expect it, singing dreamily instead of answering the captain's questions (Wing 50)]. Then: "Alors Carmen se dresse, et chante doucement la parole révoltée: 'Je ne te parle pas, je chante pour moi-même, et je pense: il n'est pas interdit de penser'" (99–100) [Then Carmen stands up and sweetly sings the rebellious words: "I am not talking to you, I am singing for myself, and I am thinking: it is not forbidden to think" (Wing 51; modified)]. Having associated Carmen's refusal to speak with musical and social transgression, it is not surprising to see Clément follow the logic of Carmen's first *tra lalalala* into the scene of the "Seguidilla" seduction and, from there, into the act 2 setting of the "Bohemian Song" in Lillas Pastia's tavern.

In Pastia's tavern an imaginary stage is once again evoked in the present tense to come alive before the eyes of a spectator-librettist-narrator-participant caught both inside and outside the imaginary scene. In her capacity as both performer and spectator Clément appears to mimic both Mérimée's narrator and the Carmen character, half-distanced from and half-identified with the events taking place in the narrative. Like Mérimée's narrator, Clément inhabits a whole collection of imaginary roles. Like Carmen, Clément's voice in this scene is characterized by what McClary calls "discursive perversity"—Carmen's capacity to speak in all musical languages without revealing herself (*Bizet*, 57). In this scene Clé-

ment mixes together all of the positions she has come to occupy thus far
in a performance of progressive inebriation which parallels that of the
"Bohemian Song":

Echappée—mystérieusement laissée en liberté—la voici dans cet
endroit gitan, nocturne, où elle et les siennes passent le temps. C'est
la taverne de son ami Lilas Pastias, sous les remparts. On n'y fait
rien; on attend. Et Carmen chante la miraculeuse chanson où les
mots français retrouvent, dans leur tintement, quelque chose de la
vie gitane. Ecoute ces étonnantes paroles: "Les tringles des sistres
tintaient. . . ." Les entends-tu, ces instruments venus d'Egypte, ces
hochets de métal qui tintent comme des tringles? Et sais-tu, selon
Plutarque, l'origine archaïque de cette musique? . . .

"Les tringles des sistres tintaient, avec un éclat métallique, et sur
cette étrange musique, les Zingarellas se levaient." Et le foyer gitan,
allumé en plein air, nomade, feux en forêt, lueurs éblouies dans la
nuit, devient dans la bouche d'or de Carmen l'Egyptienne une fête
d'Isis la nocturne. . . . peut-être t'en souviens-tu. (100–101)

[Escaped—mysteriously set free—we find her in this gypsyish, nocturnal place where she and her people spend their time. It is the
tavern of her friend Lilas Pastias, in the shadow of the ramparts.
Nobody is doing anything there; they wait. And Carmen sings
the marvelous song in which the French words somehow take on a
Gypsy ring. Listen to these astonishing words: *"Les tringles des
sistres tintaient."* The sistrum's rods were jingling. . . . Can you hear
them, these instruments from Egypt, these metal rattles jingling like
sistra? And do you know what, according to Plutarch, is the archaic
origin of this music? . . .

"The rods on the sistra jingled with a metallic brilliance, and at
the sound of this strange music the zingarellas stood up." And in the
golden mouth of Carmen the Egyptian, the Gypsy hall all lit up in
the open air,—nomadic, fires in the forest, a dazzling glow in the
night—becomes a celebration of the nocturnal Isis. . . . perhaps you
remember. (Wing 51; modified)]

It is striking that the "Bohemian Song" sets the scene of Clément's
most affective tumultuous *tapage*. It repeats, obsessively, the information

provided by the song (the nonnarrative refrain appears to have forced her attention to the words), and it elicits her most frenzied variety of vocal tones. (In its description of what spectators do it solicits an identification with the mental whirlwind of performers.) Moreover, by evoking the tenebrous side of *Carmen*'s power which resonates from beyond the limits of the narrative and despite the bright lights (that "collier ajouré") of the arena/stage, it also brings the newly theatricalized *Carmen* story to a doubled close. Twice we are back at a start that has ended so many times: "La voici aux portes des arènes, où elle n'entrera pas" (101–2) [Now we see her at the gates of the arena, where she will not enter (Wing 52)]; and "Des arènes bruissantes monte la rumeur du combat. Carmen est morte tout à coup. Je me souviens, elle dansait en chantant à mi-voix" (103–4) [The sound of the fight rises from the humming arena. Suddenly Carmen is dead. I remember, she danced while singing under her breath (Wing 53; modified)]. The repetition of a set indication that brings us back to the arena parallels the doubled précis that opened the presentation in the first place. Together these précis and indications form a framework for this imaginary theater which, like Bizet's opera and Mérimée's novella, finds only partial closure. Though Carmen is unavoidably marked as excluded, her murder is replayed twice. Instead of simply dying, she leaves behind the memory of her voice and movement as well as the revitalizing energy of the breath of Isis, a mythic memory silenced but still resonating.

Textually speaking, Clément's analysis uses narrative progression and musical reiteration as well as a thematics of imprisonment and escape to structure her essay. Carmen is *enfermée* and *echappée;* there are open doors and closed ones, limits and transgressions, interdictions and the "rebel word." In addition, these oscillating pressures come to be associated with the alternating lighting of the tavern's nocturnal glimmerings and the arena's bright white light (101) and with the two spaces of the performance—the actual space of the opera house and the fictive, or virtual, space of the arena (102). This linking of light and dark spaces with the actual and virtual spaces of performance suggests that, in its peculiarly alternating, oscillating, divided effects, the spaces of the *Carmen* opera are also divided between the scenes of conscious and unconscious thinking, whose light and dark associations transgress or slide between memory and desire in the creation of imaginary scenarios—or phantasms. In

relation to these, as Clément's rhapsodic style demonstrates, one is neither fully present nor fully absent. The voice of the writer is mobilized,
at times adopting a public distance that is variously creative, controlling,
or fluid in its descriptions, at times confused with the drama and the performers, at times enclosed in an intimate and private dialogue with another reader.

By virtue of this style we can say that Clément has identified not with
the Carmen character but, instead, with the Carmen position, that of a
performer who shakes up operatic and narrative conventions or who, in
Clément's words, "secoue, réveille, chante comme les sistres; c'est ce
qu'on appelle une femme remuante. Telle est bien sa fonction: déranger"
(101) [shakes, wakes up, sings like the *sistra;* this is what we call a rous-
ing woman. This is precisely her function: to disturb (my trans.)]. Despite any critique of her work or of her lack of attention to music, Clément has clearly had this "Carmen effect" in the world of opera theory.
One has only to acknowledge the debt paid to her by Nelly Furman,
David J. Levin, Susan McClary, and Michel Poizat. She shakes us up,
bothers us, and wakes us to new possibilities for operatic analysis.

Structurally speaking, it is important to point out that, although Clément rewrites the *Carmen* narrative by mimicking the work of Mérimée,
she also isolates from within it the moments, or scenes, marked in the
minds of listeners by Carmen's *tra lalalala.* Indeed, from her refusal to
speak (99) to her invitation to seduction (100) to the intoxicating energy
of her voice, which echoes a tingling of nocturnal *sistra* (100–101), to the
uniforms of the men who inevitably keep her from moving (102), Clément's reading structures itself according to the logic of the *tra lalalala,*
continually forcing the borders of any précis in the program notes. In
this way Clément is able to lead her readers beyond the opera's final closure, to the imaginary ethnographic moments of the bohemian world
that *Carmen* asks us to imagine.

This retracing of the scenes associated with *tra lalalala* invites a final
reconsideration of the work of the vocal motives in the opera. For, although the vocal motives, *tra lalalala* and *taratata* reiterate a discursive
tension adapted from Mérimée to structure the opera and to account,
undoubtedly, for the uncertain democracy of France's Third Republic,
their primary significance is the way in which they demonstrate how oth-

erwise meaningless and absolutely conventional operatic vocables progressively take on meanings by way of the ideological forces they represent: *taratata* evoking José's dominant bourgeois values, *tra lalalala* evoking Carmen's oppositional, or bohemian, bourgeois values. Though this narrative dichotomy is repeated throughout Bizet's opera visually, orchestrally, and verbally, as we have seen, in their peculiarly indeterminate quality of sounds that are not quite music and not quite speech, the operatic vocables also emblematize the constraints of a musical form caught between a verbal maintaining of borders and a musical blurring of them, between the power of words to distinguish between two value systems and the power of song to confuse them. In other words, the interplay of *tra lalalala* and *taratata* in *Carmen* suggests, like Clément's reading across them, that operatic narrative may be nothing more than the suggestive promotion of ideological effects channeled both by the blurring of intelligibility and by the complementary supplementing of meanings or of logics of association where there are none.

Slavoj Zizek points out, in *The Sublime Object of Ideology*, that a properly ideological subject effect is defined, precisely, as this supplementing of associative meanings about which we remain unaware, about which we say, "That goes without saying" (87). Given that the figuring of ideological values that "go without saying" may well pass through those fleeting moments of ecstasy, or *jouissance*, about which we also say, after Lacan's Saint Theresa, "I feel it but don't know anything about it," the capacity of opera to promote pleasurable effects in the service of ideological agendas may have less to do with unintelligibility itself than with the progressive dissolution of meaning under the effect of a certain kind of musical writing logic that escapes the logic of words. Michel Poizat concurs: "Or cet effet est d'autant plus fort, par contraste, lorsque l'intelligibilité est assurée comme il le faut partout où le compositeur a voulu, consciemment ou non, qu'elle soit respectée" (71) [This effect is all the stronger, by contrast, when intelligibility is assured, as is necessary in all those places in which the composer wanted, consciously or not, to respect it (my trans.)].

In the case of Bizet's *Carmen*, pleasurable moments whose affective source remains elusive, leaving their unwitting recipients open to ideological persuasion, may be heightened by the composer's attempts to make certain other meanings—the heterogeneity of the operatic text, the hypnotically inebriating effects of opera listening—perfectly clear. That is, by making dramatic dialogue into a semantically dominant purveyor of the ambiguous senses of Mérimée's narrative, Bizet may actually contribute to our love of *Carmen*. And the association of Carmen with song and with bohemian liberties may actually promote our capacity to identify not with Carmen and her values but, instead, with the person of the performer whom Carmen represents: the performer who can sing and dance excessively or, in Clément's case, metaphorically, by refusing the social conventions of verbal communication and shaking up the stylistic protocol of either bourgeois life or scholarly writing.

Ultimately, by playing textual functions (the repetition of nonnarrative refrains, the crossing of generic boundaries, interdisciplinary self-references) against the continuity of a narrative of progressive intoxication, *Carmen* appears to have a destabilizing effect on the blind intoxication of opera spectators through which cultural indoctrination, or political "figuring," takes place. In this context *Carmen* is as much about the ideological effects of operatic sound and its reliance upon the exigencies of an unheard narrative intelligibility as it is about bourgeois politics or the story of two lovers whose worlds never coincide. Retracing the textual ambiguity or anarchy faced by Mérimée's narrator and readers, Bizet's comic-opera *Carmen* forces our attentions to oscillate between two ways of thinking in order to stage the subliminal nature of operatic narrative itself and the ways in which it can manipulate and program the pleasures of song in a cosmopolitan Europe already under the spell of the Wagner effect.

⊱ 4 ⊰ Carmen

Choreofilm

THE YEARS 1983–84 formed the backdrop for four diverse film readaptations of *Carmen* by Peter Brook, Jean-Luc Godard, Francesco Rosi, and Carlos Saura. All of these films are self-conscious in their own unique ways about the nature of film adaptation, and all are concerned, at least tangentially, with exploring potential relations between the *Carmen* phenomenon and the cultural concerns of the European Community.[1] Among these readaptations Saura's *Carmen* distinguishes itself by virtue of the fact that it adapts both the *Carmen* story—that story of the lover who succumbs to the seductions of a Gypsy only to endanger his career and then kill off the source of his troubles—and the formal dynamics of its two *Carmen* models: Prosper Mérimée's novella of 1845 and Georges Bizet's comic-opera *Carmen* of 1875.[2] Just as Mérimée presents the *Carmen* narrative within an unsettling confrontation of literature and history and Bizet, within the jarring encounter of music and spoken dialogue proper to the comic-opera form, Saura films the choreographic preparation of Antonio Gades's Spanish dance version of *Carmen* to unmask the equally anarchical relations between theatrical dance and film. As a result, in the same way that Mérimée's hybrid narrative discloses the myth of an objective and scientific historiography and Bizet's, the secret politics of pleasure institutionalized in operatic form, Saura also replays the well-known narrative as a foil, but this time to foreground the complementary roles of narrative, of pleasure, and of music listening in the potential shaping, or shifting, of the cultural boundaries of Europeanness.[3]

Saura adapts Mérimée's doubled story and Bizet's doubled sounds to the specific concerns of a modern-day Spain just emerging from a transition from Franco's fascist regime into Felipe González's more tolerant, free market economy. Through this adaptation of earlier models Saura's film questions the ways in which the foreign identity of the cosmopolitan European has been imported by the greater majority of the Spanish populace at the expense of, or in opposition to, the image of a more culturally tolerant and regionally diverse Spain wrought from within the amalgam of Greek, Jewish, and Arab influences that characterize the specificity of Spain's national and cultural heritage. These ideologically opposed versions of Spanish culture are figured both in the narrative and in the form of Saura's film. While the Mérimée model lends its shape to the film's restaging of *Carmen*'s inquiry into the dominant cultural discourses of nineteenth-century narrative, the comic-opera form of Bizet's model inspires the film's tense interactions between film work and choreographic work and between acoustic and visual registers.

As in Mérimée's original *Carmen,* Don José's story is told twice, or doubled. Relations, in Mérimée's novella, between the narrator and his protagonist are transposed into relations between the director and his choreographer, while the cultural values at odds in Don José and Carmen's story are transposed into the ideological tensions that distinguish and ally a greater Spanish national identity and an Andalusian subregional Gypsy identity. Following Mérimée's model, these opposing identities are represented in the film narrative by the cultural misunderstandings that trouble José and Carmen (or Antonio Gades and his Carmen); by the different dance styles of the film's leading female protagonists, Carmen and Cristina (or Laura del Sol and Cristina Hoyos); and by the responses of the performing arts community to these misunderstandings.

Alongside the opposing pressures of Mérimée's model, however, Bizet's furnishes a formal set of oppositions that reiterate the concerns of the narrative in ways specific to film spectators. These include tense juxtapositions of European and flamenco performing arts traditions, of film narrative and dance performance, and of voice on (i.e., sound heard by characters in the film narrative) and voice off (i.e., sound heard by film spectators alone). Through the constant confrontation of these media, of their complementarity and their distinctiveness, Saura dramatizes the ideological nature of the dominance of a Spanish national identity, encouraged by Franco to identify with a whiter and purer Occidental Europe,[4] over the subregional Gypsy identity. In keeping with the bohemian quality of its models, Saura's *Carmen* moves oppositionally between the pressures of two cultural systems and two mental landscapes, one private or psychic, the other public or social.[5]

In *The Films of Carlos Saura: The Practice of Seeing* Marvin D'Lugo explains that, like many of his generation emerging from Spain's National Film School in the 1960s, Carlos Saura has a history of attempting to disclose, even within the constraints of censorship, the ways in which Franco's fascist regime has marked and defined the cultural codes of a Spanish national identity.[6] Studying "allegories of authorship" in Saura's entire oeuvre, D'Lugo is able to underscore how Saura's film techniques question the historical and political imprints that turn artists into agents of cultural institutions and constrain the very subjectivity of the Spanish *auteur*. As regards *Carmen,* however, D'Lugo does not account for the ways in which Saura's film demystifies the very notion of a unified authorial subjectivity by oscillating, continually, between two authorial intentions—that of the director and that of the choreographer—and by inviting the film spectator to rearrange the materials of expression available to choreographers and filmmakers. In light of this dismissal of the potentially oppositional force of a communal, or shared, effort at creative processing, I will suggest that, by exploring the film's adaptations of its nineteenth-century models, we foreground Saura's attention both to the ambiguous and dangerously malleable nature of cultural identity and to the communal sharing of the performing arts space as an ideal setting from which to imagine how cultural identities may adapt to new and real cultural communities unfettered by larger national boundaries.[7]

The Choreonarrative Frame

Just as Mérimée's *Carmen* opens with a historiographical frame for fiction and Bizet's with a festive, military frame for operatic narrative against which the whole of their structures must be "read," Saura's film opens with a unique choreonarrative frame designed to expose, at the outset, the peculiar musical and choreographic logic of its version of the *Carmen* narrative.[8] This choreonarrative frame precedes the credits sequence and immediately addresses distinctions in point of view between film and theatrical dance. By exploiting a remarkable absence of movement in both the image and the sound tracks, it forces us to remain conscious of our own sensorial mobility and the capacity of the film apparatus to limit or channel that mobility. There is a generous lack, in this opening segment, of what Claudia Gorbman calls "unheard melody," a generally abstract music that accompanies film acting as a narrative agent to aid the film spectator's imaginary involvement in the film.[9] As Gorbman explains it, this lack of extradiegetic music often works to enhance the realism or the immediacy of the scene before our eyes (18). In *Carmen*, however, it also encourages its observers to engage in two kinds of reading strategies— one that attends to the silent representational work of the camera, another that must attend to the noisy presentational work of dancers. The intensity of this distinction between the representational and the presentational is strikingly accentuated when, following the stillness, the distinctive twelve-beat rhythms of flamenco fingers and heels begin to emanate from the dancers and their theatrical space.

At the opening of this framing segment a classic high-angle shot of the backs of dancers gestures to itself as a perspective only possible from within a cinematic apparatus. Then, as if beckoned by the *tapage* of heels and fingers, the camera joins the forward traveling of the group of dancers, drawing attention to the movement of the camera, which will act like a toreador who variously encourages or resists the movements of choreography. At the same moment one man, Antonio Gades, distinguishes himself as he steps forward and turns to face the dancers.[10] As the dancers and the camera progress, however, the choreographer cedes to the bodies and their rhythms, hovering on the cinematic frame, stage right, and revealing that these dancers are rehearsing in front of a studio mirror.

Though we are caught, as spectators, within the constraints of the cinematic point of view, the reflection in the studio mirror also invites us to see from the idealized perspective of the imaginary audience represented by the mirror (see D'Lugo 206), since we see both the fronts and the backs of these dancers. Ironically or not, this shot of the dancers in their mirror situates us in our own "mirror stage," splitting our attention between the perspectives of imaginary and real audiences. This split perspective is then mimicked meaningfully by Gades, whose position on the edge, or boundary, of cinematic and theatrical frames will allow his point of view to shift unceasingly between that of a spectator to the performance of his own choreography and that of a dancer performing before an internal, mental mirror. This splitting of our perspective between the cinematic and the choreographic not only imitates Antonio's self-consciousness, however; it also contributes to a kind of Brechtian *Verfremdungseffekt,* or what Nietzsche referred to as an anti-Wagnerian "wariness" among spectators before the ideological persuasiveness of institutionalized forms of representation.[11]

Throughout the film the use of the studio mirror and its doubling of point of view recurs as a specular metaphor to remind us of our split perspectives and to insert us into those of Antonio's private theater. Consequently, alongside the narrative confusion of life and art suggested by the choreographer's own inescapable interweaving of an authorial, choreographic perspective and an imaginary, kinesthetic identification with José, the mirror itself links the duplicity of the dancing body—as both the subject and object of our desires—to the constant aestheticizing of Antonio's personal psychological conflicts.[12] Like the choreographer-dancer Gades, who finds himself both inside and outside of his creation, the dancer is at all times divided between the perfecting of physical technique kept in check by gazes into the mirror and the perfecting of an art form that relies upon an inner "vision" of drama, music, and lines, or engravings, in space. That is, the dancer's attention is always split between imagining her or his body as representation from the point of view of a spectator and figuring the presentation of the mind's inner stage, kinesthetically.

The studio mirror, as Saura himself points out, represents the social gaze of ideological restraints to which the look of the dancer's body must submit through years of refined technique (as noted by D'Lugo 199). As Carmen's dance teacher remarks later in the film, however, "Technique is only good when it is used as part of your art." As a dancer trains, in other words, the mirror furnishes an imaginary audience almost always displeased as it scrupulously marks the failure of the human body to conform, technically, to cultural expectations about the perfectibility of a mobilized statue.[13] This inevitable failure in turn inspires more "hard work." But, as dancers, Gypsies, and flamenco artists know well, it is the moment of performance which allows an intermittent forgetting of the "master narrative" of bodily control, a kind of liberation through mastery into the cultural community shared by the participants in the performance space. This is the kind of sharing that only rarely emerges in front of a mirror but which contributes to what Merce Cunningham has called the "aliveness" of performance.[14]

This elusive aliveness regulates Gades's attention to dance. As Gades reviews individual dancers in the choreonarrative frame in search of one to dance the role of Carmen, for example, the distinction between technique and aliveness—which dancer traces her movements in the mirror and which one "dances"?—largely determines both his rejection of the regular members of the company and his ultimate choice of his Carmen. Though some of the dancers may be physically or technically capable and appealing, they are dismissed pointedly as soon as they look into the mirror, this being the sign of their submission to social regulation. His gaze lingers only on those dancers who display that intensity of an inner look which all dancers have felt and known. In a direct quotation of Mérimée's narrator Gades's thoughts echo a theme of animality which his Carmen's particular look comes to emblematize: "Ojos de gitano, ojos de lobo dice un refrán español" [Gypsy eyes, wolf eyes, as a Spanish saying goes]. In the case of his Carmen, whether this exceptional aliveness surfaces because of or despite her weak technique, there is something about her dancing that remains out of the realm of technique and, therefore, out of Antonio's control.

This "look" beyond technique and beyond Antonio's control explains why glances in the mirror, paralleled in the film work by a play of shot-reverse-shot images of attentive faces, become a kind of leitmotiv throughout the film. As a leitmotiv, these glances repeatedly foreground the distinction between "aliveness," in which internal tensions are projected outward, and a "going through the motions" of dance steps and combinations. Moreover, this projecting outward of internal tensions that contribute to the aliveness of dancers reminds us that, whereas classical dance always makes the individual subservient to technique, or subsumes personal psychological expression, the traditional flamenco performance arts always extol the externalizing of internal conflicts in which the human community must come to recognize itself (see Deval 30).

Rereading *Carmen*

As in a literary incipit, a classical theatrical expository scene, or an operatic prelude, the opening image of dancers confronting their own mirror reflections as others in the choreonarrative frame presents a *mise en abyme*, or microcosm, of both the film narrative and the formal aesthetic realization of those narrative concerns.[15] For the duration of the film this relation of the dancer to her or his own virtual image exemplifies Antonio's own internal psychological conflict: Is he a dancer or an "author," an object or a subject, a protagonist or a composer? Is he narrating Mérimée's José or playing that role?

Although there is never really any solution to the personal conflict, it is mapped onto a parallel confrontation, within the film narrative, between the ballet's two principal dancers, Carmen and Cristina. Carmen is the young, irresponsible, and technically less accomplished dancer, who, working nights in the underbelly of Seville in a flamenco nightspot, follows the unwritten laws of the Gypsy community and its flamenco traditions. She learned to dance and sing watching her parents. Cristina, on the contrary, is the more mature, more technically masterful classical dancer, who, as Antonio's dance mistress and leading dancer, is identified, by way of her technique, with that purified Spanish national identity encouraged, by Franco, to align itself with Europe rather than with Spain's regional and ethnic diversity. According to an apologetic Antonio, she is somehow too "old" to play Carmen. In this way the principal dancers in the film play one version of an "old" Europe against another "new" Europe, as Gades's personal conflict becomes a more general cultural identity crisis. Put otherwise, though the conflict is a private one, occasioned primarily by Gades's choreographic desire to insert the folk power of flamenco into the constraints of European art forms and to reclaim the "Spanishness" of a *Carmen* co-opted by Mérimée and other nineteenth-century travelers, it works itself out artistically, in the roles of the two dancers, and then communally, in the staging of the first scene from the new *Carmen* ballet, the *tabacalera.*

This *tabacalera*, or tobacco factory scene, is representative of the film's interweaving of psychic and social pressures, in that it not only resolves psychological conflicts posed by the film narrative; it also makes the concerns of the individual into a cultural or social issue in which the entire fictional community participates. That is, from within the conflict of the divided Antonio to that of the two dancers and their two aesthetic principles, we, too, continue to be implicated by way of our participation in the perspectives of the two audiences, of film and of dance.

The *tabacalera* scene is a choreographic version of the tobacco fight chorus from Bizet's opera which plays during the credits sequence, to which I shall return, immediately following the choreonarrative frame. In its visual reenactment of Bizet's operatic sounds it recalls the opening image of conflict suggested visually by the studio mirror while being reworked acoustically into the sounds and rhythms of a flamenco *cante.* The two groups of women initially figured by way of the studio mirror "come to life" in this scene as two groups of women taking sides in the dispute between la Manuelita and la Carmencita. From the perspective of the film spectator, however, the performers and their roles become confused, insofar as the choreographed Manuelita-Carmencita conflict also replays and resolves the fictional Carmen-Cristina conflict set up by the film narrative. Following the model of flamenco performance, the women dance and sing the conflict into a social issue of interest to the entire fictional community. Consequently, while portraying the conflict as the exclusive adaptation of Antonio's own choreographic version of Bizet's operatic representation of conflict, the *tabacalera* also functions as the representation of the Gypsy community united through its judgment of and identification with its performing spokeswomen.

The already layered representation of internal conflict in the *tabacalera* is further complicated by the filming of the scene. As the camera movements during this scene continue to repeat their problematic relation to the filming of dance, the delineation of camera movement and body movement, of audience and dancers, or of dancers and singers is rendered almost impossible. The camera swoops and swerves with and against the bodies it would record, either identifying its own rhythms against theirs, mixing in with their intensity, or remaining still at eye level, as the dancers move to and fro. These variously allied or distinguished camera movements remind us of the camera's privileged and uniquely visual distance from the sweat and the spirit of performance aliveness. We come nonetheless to recognize by way of this scene that the *cantaor* [flamenco singer] whose personal conflict will be embodied in and resolved by the performance community is at once Antonio and, behind him, Gades and, behind him, Saura himself.

Antonio's identity crisis and his progressive attempts to resolve it by interweaving his private obsessions into his social performances are as central to the film's elaborate structure as José's and the narrator's are to those of the novella and the opera. In fact, the cinematic composition reiterates both the structure of Mérimée's doubled narrative and the reverse pattern of Bizet's opera in its attempt to weave the private into the social. This becomes evident in the second half of the film, once Carmen and Antonio begin their love affair. Following the reversing of the operatic narrative in which first the women (Micaela and Carmen) and then the men (Zuniga and José) are imprisoned or encircled, the conflict of the two dancers (Carmen and Cristina), extended to their larger community in the *tabacalera* scene, is taken over by the conflict of the men (Antonio, Carmen's husband, and Escamillo) and their community.

Similarly, following Mérimée's representation of progressive involvement in the Carmen lure—first the narrator, then José, more and more intensely, find themselves ready to kill for her—Antonio's insatiable desire for Carmen leads to two duels, one between Antonio, the choreographer, and Carmen's "real-life" husband and a second between Antonio, the dancer, and the dancer playing Escamillo. Yet, as in the case of the *tabacalera* scene, as each of these narrative conflicts finds aesthetic solutions in dance performances that in turn reshape the real lives of the dancers, the impulse of the so-called classic Hollywood film to unfold according to a nineteenth-century readerly logic of exposition-middle-end is woven into a comic-opera logic of dialogues and songs which will itself be contained or restructured into a flamenco logic of tension-release-tension (Deval 11). This layered, "bohemian" twisting ultimately provides the film with its unique structural design.

In the twisting of this larger structural design Antonio's creativity gets the better of him. That is, although his artistic goal, like that of the real Antonio Gades, is to insert the folk power of flamenco into the constraints of European art forms, the flamenco style of his creation ends up controlling him as if from the inside out. In fact, if the film opens with a flamenco and theatrical frame suggesting, as D'Lugo argues, that Saura will depict a growing awareness on the part of the artist of the social and historical constraints that bind what appears to be a personal creative vision, it closes in an unresolved duplicity about life and art, inner sensibilities and outer constraints, theater and film, the psychic and the social. As many readers of the film have pointed out, it is never clear if Carmen's murder, at the end of the film, is real or represented, part of only one of the narratives or both.[16] As a result, the intensity contained within the artist aimed at re-presenting his own inner vision outwardly on the stage as a communal concern contaminates the serene boundaries of the filmic container for the dance, mimicking the flamenco experience of tension-release-tension designed, for both spectators and performers, to exorcise or externalize and share the *duende,* or "soul," within (Deval 11).

In light of the film's greater structural design, it is not surprising that the film narrative recalls its nineteenth-century "realist" models while, at the same time, displacing their discourses and counter-discourses both culturally and historically onto the twentieth-century realms of New Spanish Cinema and modern flamenco dance. That is, whereas the opera stands in opposition to a representational theater art form bound by the constraints of the ingrained conventions of the comic-opera form—happy endings in marriage, tonal closure, delayed-action plots, surprise and resolution[17]—the film and the dance experience exposed within it react to an antirepresentational, self-referential period in European cinema and Spanish dance. In cinema I am thinking of the self-aware techniques of Rossellini, Buñuel, and the directors of the French New Wave influenced by Hitchcock; in dance I have in mind the resistance of flamenco traditionalists to its progressive concert hall theatricalization and its concomitant Hispanicization of Gypsy culture (see Deval 46–47). In other words, in the same way that post-postmodern dance (e.g., Yvonne Rainer or Twyla Tharp) reacts to the self-referential nature of dance events that are only about dancing (e.g., Merce Cunningham and John Cage) by privileging narrative because of its capacity to unmask the use of the body as a setting for ideological regulation (Foster 259 n. 3), Saura and Gades narrativize the traditional forms of flamenco music and dance so as to strip away European illusions about Spain, Spanishness, and the values of flamenco while at the same time appealing, commercially, to the greater European imagination (Deval 47). *Carmen* remains Saura's most recognized and most commercially successful film outside of Spain (D'Lugo 224).

Even though the European imagination wrongly equates Spain with Andalusia, Andalusia with flamenco, and flamenco with Gypsies, the greater part of Spain sides with Europe against Andalusia. As if colonized by the mentality of outsiders toward Spain (an act of colonization nurtured by texts such as *Carmen*), Spaniards react to Andalusia and to its flamenco traditions with the same Cartesian and technological disdain typical of the rest of Europe and, for that matter, of the Occidental world (Deval 12, 23). In this light Saura's appropriation of traditional flamenco art forms into the shapes and sounds of a classic European narrative has the effect of disrupting presuppositions purveyed by that narrative while representing both a general European and a Spanish national ambivalence about Gypsies and the history of flamenco.

In Saura's film flamenco and Gypsies function as a counterdiscursive track that pits itself against a discourse of Spanish nationalism nurtured by Franco and identified with a greater European and Occidental identity. The tension between these two tracks remains remarkably similar to the tension represented by the doubled identity of Mérimée's narrating historian: the tourist who romanticizes Gypsies and bandits, feeling himself to be culturally identified with them merely because he shares their bread, and the ethnographer who reinforces negative stereotypes about them, "scientifically," as if from the outside of their culture. In Saura's film the choreographer, Antonio, shares this unconscious ambivalence in that he wants to identify with certain Gypsy traits: liberty, endogamy, revolt, an openness of sexual expression, and a more general, nonspecific intensity, or aliveness, in dancing, but he remains assimilated into a sense

of "Castilian" self-distinction and ethnic separateness.[18] Within the anarchical force of the film's counterdiscursive elements, therefore, and like
its model borrowed from Mérimée, the film remains ambiguous by reinforcing Spanish attitudes about Gypsy stereotypes while, at the same
time, complicating the origin of that very representation.

In a further effort to render its two ideologically distinct discursive
positions problematic, Saura's film reappropriates, as does Bizet's opera,
the strategies by which Mérimée's novella marks representation as a
dichotomous political battlefield of revolutionary hopefulness and subsequent disillusionment. Produced at the very end of Spain's *transición* (1976–83), the film's artistic vision of this period of relative liberation remains ambivalent. For the choreographer Carmen represents the
nineteenth-century bohemian à la Murger who seeks a certain freedom of
expression but does not understand fully that Rousseauian relation of
personal freedom to personal constraint or obligation, of rights to responsibilities (whether to a love relation or to her own dance technique).
Indeed, we might call Carmen an ethically malleable "dissenter" in that
her goal is to question authority (following the Gypsy stereotype) but not
necessarily to confront or change it. On the contrary, she acts without any
sense of the bourgeois intellectual's "raised consciousness," and her principles might best be described as the kind of "knack" Ross Chambers
evokes to account for an individual's accommodation to circumstances as
necessary, from within a given system (*Room*, 10). In other words, as Carmen herself helps us to move nomadically or oppositionally, as in the
image of the dissenter, between the constraints of two social landscapes,
the *Carmen* film repeats her suggestive oscillation formally.

Formal aspects of the film reenact Carmen's oscillation between two
social landscapes by way of tense confrontations between European and
flamenco performing arts traditions. The first confrontation is announced
loudly in an abrupt cut from the choreonarrative frame and its intradiegetic flamenco rhythms to the credits sequence and its extradiegetic
operatic sounds. In this sequence the credits and title, "CARMEN: INSPI-
RADA EN LA NOVELA DE PROSPER MÉRIMÉE," are projected across
engravings taken from Charles Davillier and Gustave Doré's 1862 *Tour
du monde* engravings of Gypsy life and performance, the same engravings that influenced Bizet's adaptation of Mérimée's story (Martinoty

100–101). They are accompanied by the crashing sounds of Bizet's choral music for the tobacco fight scene, into which an insistently repetitive operatic version of Antonio's personal conflict is keyed: "Oui, c'est la Carmencita! Non, non! Ce n'est pas elle!" [Yes, it's la Carmencita! No, no, it is not she!] and, near the end of the segment, Zuniga's resounding "Eloignez-moi toutes ces femmes-là!" [Clear away all of these women!]. It is, of course, this very scene that is Hispanicized in both aural and visual terms in the flamenco contours of the *tabacalera*. And, while that later choreographic reworking of the fight chorus from Bizet's opera features the swooping, swerving, and stopping of Saura's camera to create an effect of conflict, of bullfighting, or of battle and to externalize Antonio's internal tensions in the flamenco manner, it also figures a melding of operatic and flamenco impulses in the film.

This melding of the impulses of European and flamenco traditions suggests that the solutions offered by art to the conflicts of individual psychologies might well find parallel solutions in the only potential ethnic mixing of an only potential European cultural community, but this suggestion of cultural melding, or mixing, only comes to the fore because of the film's initial laying out of stark distinctions between the shapes and sounds of the different art forms. At the outset, it should be recalled, the accent on the presentational mode of flamenco dancers and rhythms in the choreonarrative frame contrasts dramatically with the representational mode of the film's credits sequence, with its *montage* of nineteenth-century engravings and *mixage* of Bizet's choral score.

The *montage* and *mixage* of nineteenth-century influences projected during the credits sequence serves as a reminder that film as a twentieth-century art form has its nineteenth-century antecedents in opera and engraving. But, like the *tabacalera* scene in which the tensions of operatic narrative and music are woven into flamenco song and dance, its jarring distinction from the sounds of flamenco rhythms in the choreonarrative frame reminds us that Spanishness itself is only tentatively carved out between a nineteenth-century Europeanness with which Spain identifies and the amalgam of cultural and regional heritages that make Spain into something of an ideal model for an ethnically diverse and culturally tolerant twentieth-century Europe. It is between these two concepts of European identity, moreover, that Antonio, Saura, and the film spectator will oscillate, as Bizet's opera music locates itself (a little like Flaubert's free indirect discourse) both outside the film's diegetic sound space and inside the choreographer's creative mental processing.

Listening to *Carmen*

One obvious way in which Saura's film dramatizes its paradoxical relation to its operatic model is its tendency to displace Bizet's leitmotivs in favor of its own series of leitmotivs, the result being an effort to link the actual film spectator to the actual director. By relying primarily upon music taken from Bizet's dance numbers (the "Seguidilla" and the "Habañera"), from his crowd or choral scenes, and from his entr'actes, the film constructs its own personal system of leitmotivs so as to offer film spectators both literal and figurative insight into the creative processing of choreographic thought as well as the power to compose our own private *mixages.* This insight and power is literal insofar as we are invited, by way of the leitmotivs, to identify with Antonio or to slip inside his thoughts and to see from the inside out. But, figuratively, the film also exploits the echoing of operatic themes—a little like ballet pantomimes of the early nineteenth century[19]—to teach us to read the silent expressions of body movements, glances in the mirror, and cinematic editing by relying upon our past knowledge about and associations with *Carmen.*

Bizet's leitmotivs are often used in the film as an image of pure drama or melodrama, "unheard melodies" that heighten the dramatic tension of the film narrative. For example, Carmen enters a prison presumably to visit her husband interred there, and, as we read the word *Peligro* [Danger] blazoned across the prison bars, we hear the chromatic sound of what is often called Carmen's "fate motive" creating a general sense of ominous foreboding. Yet this foreboding remains ironically unrelated, I would argue, to either Antonio's conflicts or the real concerns of the film narrative. In the film, in fact, Bizet's motives are severed from their original operatic function of weaving a sense of narrative continuity, of continuous motion if not diegetic logic. Whereas the opera maintains this continuity because the motives appear to be keyed into one another— the orchestral motives of military celebration and chromatic tension parallel the visual motives of enclosure and tentative escape, the vocal motives of *taratata* and *tra lalalala*, and the verbal motives of *Prends garde!* and *là-bas*—the motives in Saura's film remain disparate or disjointed. Instead of continuity, they offer only confused signals that ultimately signal only confusion. The visual motive of glances in the mirror, for example, finds a parallel in the verbal cue to Carmen's "wolf eyes" but always in such a way as to evoke her essential duplicity, or unreadability: Is she "alive" or self-conscious?

Bizet's orchestral motives are likewise rendered ironic in that they recall the operatic narrative while highlighting confusions between the film's narratives. The chromatic sound of Carmen's motive accompanying the word *Peligro*, for example, indecisively suggests both Carmen's fear and fear of Carmen. When it sounds again, prior to the murder, it dramatizes a confusion regarding which narrative is reaching a fearful close and signals fear of our own confusion. The festive military strains of the toreador motive cross similar boundaries, indicating, at one moment, the playful pleasures of a cast party and, at another, a Spanish dance hall scene located, with complete uncertainty, neither fully inside nor fully outside the *Carmen* ballet. Indeed, the narrative purpose of the motive is rendered ironic by its designation of moments in which narratives and points of view are blurred. In the same way the dance music of Bizet's entr'acte to act 3 sounds throughout the film as a more curious linking of the opera to Saura's re-Hispanicization in this film. In its evocation of a kind of generalized tenderness or respite from conflict, it is equally capable of connoting between-rehearsal relaxation, the temporary resolution of Antonio's psychological conflicts, the dishonest exploitation by Carmen of an illusion of tenderness, or a willful seduction and use of feminine wiles for personal gain. It sounds when, within the ballet, Carmen seduces José as she is being dragged off to prison, softening his military and conformist exterior. It sounds again when they first meet outside of the setting of the rehearsal hall the evening Carmen arrives at Antonio's studio. This repetition of the motive compels us to draw relations between these narrative and choreographic seductions, further rendering Carmen's real intentions indecipherable.

In this latter scene of choreographed seduction, during which Antonio cedes to Carmen's tenderness as he takes her off to prison, the confusion between intradiegetic sensibilities and extradiegetic sound occasioned by the recurring of the leitmotiv provokes a similar confusion between Antonio's inner thoughts and those of José, the character he plays. It is not surprising, therefore, that this blurring of the two narratives is laid across the equally blurred moment, in Bizet's opera, when the nonverbal vocal motif, *taratata,* blends into Carmen's performance of *tra lalalala.* In its reiteration of a bohemian fusing of opposing values, in fact, this scene dramatizes the fact that motives that should contribute to narrative sense merely convey empty signs of narrative motion as they dissociate expectations and memories and dislodge our desire for narrative completion or closure.

If Saura constructs his own web of leitmotivs through, notably, the repeated use of the third entr'acte to symbolize Antonio's progressive involvement with Carmen, the play of the leitmotiv in emotionally distinct scenes suggests its capacity to evoke psychological permutation rather than narrative wholeness. These leitmotivs are particularly useful, then, not in smoothing over disparities between materials of expression by creating links between themes but, rather, in underscoring their fundamental incompatibility. Moreover, as signposts designed to indicate moments of cinematic blurring, during which the otherwise distinct realms of both the two narratives and the two sound spaces become simply inseparable, they draw our attention away from the narrative and toward the maneuvering of the film work itself. It is this same blurring technique that helps to link the actual spectator to the actual director by inserting that spectator into the position of the choreographer, Gades.

The film underscores its own capacity to blur intra- and extradiegetic signs by distinguishing markedly between the two sound spaces in its initial expository scenes and by further delineating, within the intradiegetic space of Antonio's narrative of conflict, another more private space lodged between the inside and the outside of Antonio's thoughts. In other words, Antonio's mind is constructed like the two-way mirror at the far end of his studio; it, too, underscores his dramatic oscillations between the representational and the presentational. Within the diegesis he speaks or dances thoughts for the other characters in the film, but within that inner mental space, an "inner intradiegetic" space, he speaks and dances only for himself and us, often citing Mérimée's text from memory. The advantage of this layering of cinematographic sound spaces is the degree of participation it encourages on the part of the film spectator, who is discreetly inserted into the creative confusions of the choreographer's attention to both his life and his art. As Freud once said of the pleasure we experience viewing tragedy, the more secure a distinction between imagination and reality, or in this case representation and presentation, the more likely the spectator will be to smooth over or confuse those distinctions on the basis of his own phantasmatic capacity to fill in gaps. Conversely, the more blurred those distinctions, the more likely we are to remain aware of ourselves engaged in the activity of viewing a film. The studio mirror helps secure such distinctions because of its capacity both to reflect the performance space and to separate public rehearsal from private practice (behind the mirror). The smoothing over or reconciling of the concerns associated with the separate spaces is left, however, to the unique sensibility of the film's readers, since neither the resolving of Antonio's psychological conflicts nor the marriage of flamenco and European art forms is ever fully realized. We become intensely aware of our own desire to smooth over, to resolve, to realign incongruities, and of our own unsettled place, clearly allied with that of Antonio's *Carmen*, between cultural and aesthetic options.

Saura helps us to understand this relation of the film spectator to representations of the two culturally distinct arts of the theater at issue in *Carmen* by showing us that, as a choreographer, Antonio is always also necessarily a spectator, who must progressively fill in precisely these kinds of gaps. Marvin D'Lugo comments on the most striking of these scenes, when, immediately following Carmen's unexpected departure from their first night of love, Antonio finds himself alone before his own private studio mirror. In place of his own reflection Antonio sees an image of Carmen appearing before him in the clichéd "getup" of the commodified *españolades* of the Spanish dancer: mantilla, comb, lace. Though this scene may well offer evidence for what D'Lugo refers to as Antonio's inculcation of a Spanish identity formed outside of Spain (and of his desire to indoctrinate Carmen into that identity through the containing of her aliveness by way of attention to her dance technique), it also shows us the choreographer's capacity to enliven a completely blank space of representation (an empty mirror replaces the more typical white page) with individual fantasy elaborations before which he is constituted as an imaginary spectator. The scene is as useful, in other words, as a demonstration of the images Antonio has introjected from his culture as it is as a demonstration of his capacity to project those images outward and, thereby, to examine them critically or reform them into an aesthetic vision.

In this same mirror scene Antonio is depressed by Carmen's departure and unable, we presume, to think beyond clichés of women or of Spanish dancers. The process of representation is therefore not only marked by the internalizing of the stamp of exterior social and cultural images or identities but also by the simultaneous externalizing, or performing, of the stamp of private scenarios or elaborations and the capacity of the choreographer momentarily to believe in and interact with purely phantasmatic projections. Artistic representation is thereby figured as a process of mobile and circular exchanges between the outer and inner representations of dancers and their mirrors, choreographers and their dancers, or spectators and their attention to or reading of performers. Through Saura's invitation to become intermittent dance spectators before his film, we are also invited to replay Gades's processing of imaginary representations, which is why, at the end of the film, we renew the search for our own private Carmen.

Saura's film attends as much to this process of conscious-unconscious exchange, in my estimation, as it does to the channeling of artistic will by the unconscious pressures of a particular social, historical, or cultural milieu. Important ways in which the film stages this kind of tension between conscious and unconscious representations include the disparity of leitmotivs, the presenting of Antonio as a spectator with whom we are enjoined to identify because his mind is constructed like a theater or two-way mirror, the initial delineation and progressive confusion of sound spaces inside and outside the film narrative as well as inside and outside Antonio's thoughts, and the reiteration of this progressive confusion of sound spaces through a similarly progressive interaction of the camera's representational eye with the character's psychological obsessions. The camera eye questions its own omniscient indifference from the start through its marking of a distinction between film and theatrical perspectives, but it plays openly and continually with its intermittent distance from and identification with José's/Antonio's desires.

The mobility of this variously distanced, variously identified cinematographic eye is dramatized strikingly by its paradoxical relation to choreographed scenes such as the *tabacalera*. Yet the progressive inability of the camera's eye to remain objective (i.e., to tell Antonio's story instead of its own) is quite clearly represented in the center of the film, when Carmen comes to Antonio's studio at night to consummate, finally, her play of suggestive glances. As she insists that Antonio slow down and allow time to create a mood of love, the camera responds, perhaps better than Antonio himself, with a slow pan across Carmen's legs and face, preparing the sexual intensity of their forthcoming love relations. In the camera's eye it is Carmen who is to be consumed voyeuristically. Antonio, on the other hand, imitates José, in that he pays less attention to Carmen than to his own anxious emotions. In a gesture of erotic self-expression he decides to present himself formally by performing an intense *farruca* for Carmen's pleasure. The *farruca*, as its adjectival form suggests, signifies a defiant, bold, or cocky attitude. In Antonio's eye, in other words, it is he who is there to be consumed. This preparation for sexual intimacy is thereby rendered decidedly misleading, or at the very least bohemian, in that the camera leads us to believe that Carmen is the love object, while the performance of the *farruca* leads us to believe that it is Antonio. As the camera is seduced by Carmen the woman, Carmen is seduced by Antonio the dancer, who, like José, appears not to want her but, instead, to be self-absorbed and alive. As Antonio externalizes interior self-sufficiency and aliveness through his performance of the *farruca*, the camera is at odds with the inner strength of the performance as it succumbs to the traditional gesture of a pan across female body parts.

The camera's visual repeating of Antonio's oscillation between indifference to his love object (when dancing) and confusion with it (when choreographing) is reiterated, for the benefit of the film spectator, through a similar oscillation between extra- and intradiegetic sound spaces. At the beginning of the film these spaces are decidedly separate: the extradiegetic space shared by the director and the film spectators alone is initially reserved for the music of Bizet's opera. This music contrasts starkly, in its first appearance during the rolling of the credits and title, with the intradiegetic sound space of the film's choreonarrative frame, shared by the characters and associated uniquely with Spanish guitar, flamenco heels and fingers, and dancing bodies in rehearsal. As Tom Conley has suggested in his study of verbal cues in film, the appearance of the credits and title demand that we further distance ourselves from imaginary involvement in the film by asking us to read rather than to listen.[20] In this light it is by running the credits over Davillier and Doré's nineteenth-century *Tour du monde* engravings of flamenco performers and performances that the credits sequence and its music take on all of the power of that romanticized European version of Gypsies and Spanishness which encourages Mérimée's historian to be charmed by bandits and prostitutes and which causes us all to associate wrongly Gypsies with Andalusia and Andalusia with Spain.

Insofar as Meilhac, Halévy, and Bizet could only have created their version of a lighthearted Spanishness by re-presenting those same engravings in their libretto and score (Martinoty 100–102), another opposition is set up between that false Spanish cultural identity exported by foreign travelers but imported by a Spanish culture hungry to identify with a greater Europe, on one hand, and, on the other, a "truer" or newer Spanish culture represented by the efforts of the Castilian-identified Saura, Gades, and Paco de Lucia to appropriate the heterogeneity of the flamenco tradition (those sounds, heels, and fingers of the choreonarrative frame) within their more classic, or "colonized," Spanish art forms. Moreover, those engravings, however dated they appear by contrast to the realist effects of the film, also signify the inability to get outside of the engravings of generations of cultural consciousness, so that any true Spanish culture must forge itself a future in relation to these French representations of its past.

As long as a distinction is maintained between extradiegetic opera music and its association with the mental engravings of Mérimée's text and intradiegetic flamenco sounds and the kinesthetic response of moving bodies, a distinction is also maintained between Antonio's Castilian, or European, identification and his flamenco, or Gypsy, culture. Such clear distinctions allow us, as spectators, to remain comfortably outside of the cultural and artistic concerns of representation. Exchanges between these sound spaces jolt the spectator into reconsidering Spanishness itself, however, by encouraging our participation in the creation of an imaginary film of the *Carmen* ballet. That is, these exchanges confuse

distinctions between film work and choreography, between representation and presentation, between European and flamenco performing arts
traditions, by offering us the raw materials of expression which Antonio
attempts to weave together in his modern ballet: Bizet's opera music,
flamenco guitar rhythms, Mérimée's narrative, Spanish dance technique,
and flamenco aliveness. The film work insures the jolting of these exchanges by drawing attention to its own capacity to blur sound effects at
the same moments that it furnishes us with those raw materials Gades
hopes to combine in his ballet.

The important result of the jolting effect occasioned by exchanges
between sound tracks is that the movements between the inner and outer
representations of private identity I evoked in the context of our identification with Antonio as spectator to himself are repeated on the outside
of the film, so to speak, in our identifications with Antonio the choreographer. When I say "on the outside of the film," I mean that, just as
Antonio reserves a private mental sound space (that inner intradiegetic
space) within the filmic space of the diegesis, we are reserved a mental
sound space within the extradiegetic world (an outer extradiegetic space)
which is only partially shared with the director. By accessing this outermost spectator space, the film repeats the mobile exchanges across
Antonio's mirror which link and differentiate between outer and inner
representations, or engravings, as if on the outside of the film. Such exchanges are reminiscent of the functioning of the arrows in Lacan's
poinçon (< >) to illustrate the mobility of identifications in unconscious
fantasy scenarios. They occur at three levels in the film—narrative,
acoustic, and cinematographic:

Narrative (from Mérimée):
Antonio, choreographer < mirror > Antonio, dancer

Acoustic (from Bizet):
extradiegetic space   <   proscenium > intradiegetic space
                              arch
(of Paco, Gades, Carmen)   (of Don José, "Carmen")

Cinematographic (from Saura):
outer, extradiegetic space < screen   >   inner, intradiegetic space

It is through the distinction and confusion of these doubled spaces of representation that the film manages to stage a specular version of flamenco's logic of tension-release-tension.

The twisting in and out of Antonio's inner conflict, of the two Carmen stories, and of the film's two sound worlds access the outermost spectator space we ourselves occupy by offering us, as I have already suggested, the not yet constructed elements that choreographers use in the amalgams that are their finished artworks. In Saura's film, rather than showing us only finished scenes from *Carmen* as choreographed by Gades, in other words, we are also offered the raw materials of expression with which Gades himself must grapple in his choreography. These occasions given over to the spectator's capacity for the creative interweaving of raw materials, or "floating signifiers," each take place, ironically, at the onset of what I have characterized as a "cinematic blurring" of the five discrete tracks of cinematic expression: voice (on and off), sound (on and off), and image tracks. The availability of floating signifiers, together with the blurring of the cinematographic materials of expression, signal both an interrogation into the discursive and counterdiscursive logics of the film narrative—the interactions of European and Gypsy identities—and an oppositional exposition of the aliveness of performance or of the power of choreographic expression to move between these discourses. It is as if the various associations set up during the film's initial sequences with different materials of expression (choreographic and cinematographic visual images and operatic and flamenco leitmotivs) were clearly distinguished from the start precisely so that we might internalize them in the same way Antonio does. As a result, we are put in the position of repeating Antonio's creative processing and his externalizing of a flamenco *duende* at the precise moments that extra-, intra-, outer extra-, and inner intradiegetic sound spaces blur.

Following the flamenco logic of tension-release-tension which structures the *Carmen* film, it is not surprising to find the two most important scenes open to the spectator's creative processing near the opening and the closing of the film, respectively. During these two scenes of tension (surrounding the relatively brief sense of release provided by scenes of sexual intimacy), we are acutely aware of the jolting effect of disconnected materials of expression. The first scene, to which I shall return, follows directly upon the credits sequence; the second occurs near the end, during the choreographed duel between Antonio and Carmen's husband, a figure who is not a professional dancer, much less a member of the company. In this second scene there is never any way to know if the duel represents part of the *Carmen* ballet or a fantasy scenario Antonio acts out internally. Moreover, a play of shadows aggrandizes and further dematerializes the figures so that dance seems an appropriate way to attend to unspoken psychological duels. The first scene is of particular importance, however, because it sets the stage for Antonio's desire to seek the ideal "Carmen" as it readies the spectator for participation in the choreography of the *Carmen* ballet from the start.

This first scene coincides with the first moment in the film in which the characters in the film narrative actually hear Bizet's music, that music initially reserved for the spectators to the credits sequence. As Antonio symbolically threads a reel-to-reel tape of the opera, music once heard exclusively as extradiegetic background to the credits sequence now becomes the focus of the film's diegetic concerns; Antonio is working on a new *Carmen* ballet and confronting an obvious conflict between European opera and flamenco rhythms. This conflict is so loud, so to speak, that it manages to disrupt the attention of the performers within the diegetic space. At the same time, however, it is also "loud" enough to disrupt our attention by taking up, within the film narrative, the values associated, respectively, with the choreonarrative flamenco frame and the operatic Europeanness of the credits sequence. As Paco de Lucia and a female singer begin a traditional flamenco *cante*, Antonio threads the reel-to-reel tape of Bizet's "Seguidilla." Simultaneously, a shot-reverse-shot links Paco's *rasgueado*, or percussive right hand, to Antonio's right hand, as it gently attempts to capture the sense of Bizet's music by tapping out *sevillanas*, a ternary rhythm associated with a superficial and tardive "flamenquization" of dance and song (Deval 76). This shot-reverse-shot sequence restates both the image of the reel-to-reel mechanically and the choreographer's attempt to unite two cultural impulses symbolically. The sound of an operatic voice singing the "Seguidilla" interrupts the attention of the *cantaor*, however, revealing the dominance of the European musical discourse and its individual vocal bravura over the flamenco intensity of a communal passion expressed in flamenco dance and song.

Knowing that it is Antonio (and not the singer) who is the real *cantaor,* in the sense that it is his conflict to be externalized in the *Carmen* ballet and he who relies upon the creative assistance of this musician, Paco calms the disrupted moment by proposing a version of Bizet's "Seguidilla" reworked into the more dance-worthy rhythm of the *buleria.* The *buleria* is a festive and more purely flamenco form nonetheless reminiscent, formally, of burlesque pleasantry, or mockery (*buleria,* from *burla* [Deval 71]). It is already associated in the listener's mind with the sounds of the "Seguidilla" and its closing *tra lalalala* vocal motive.

In this context it is significant that the *buleria* connotes, at once, the notions of burlesque pleasantry, of a technically demanding rhythm, and of improvisation. In fact, Paco's introduction of this rhythm seems at first ironic about the inability of Bizet's music to accommodate dance movements because of the very difficulty of the task. But it soon encourages Antonio to engage Cristina in a dance improvisation. Almost unbeknownst to us, we, as spectators, are then beckoned to follow Antonio's dance improvisation with our own version of a choreographic improvisation as we, too, agree to associate Bizet's "Seguidilla" and Paco's *buleria* and to put together the unconnected materials of expression of Antonio's new ballet. Distinctions between these materials are dramatically marked. First, Antonio asks Cristina to work the dancers—their arms and posture (a particular mark of flamenco as influenced by Eastern dance)—in the rhythms of the *buleria.* Then he asks Paco to continue to work on his Spanish guitar version of the "Seguidilla." The two work separately. Yet, as Antonio watches and listens to these not yet associated sounds and movements hovering, as earlier, on the stage-right edge of cinematic and theatrical frames, we also hear the sound of Mérimée's text in Spanish; it is the narrator's description of Carmen (622), in the voice of Antonio, playing inside Antonio's thoughts: "Sus ojos tenían una expresión voluptuosa y hosca al mismo tiempo que no he vuelto a encontrar en ninguna mirada humana. Ojos de gitano, ojos de lobo dice un refrán español" [Her eyes had, at the same time, a voluptuous yet wild expression that I have never encountered again in any human gaze. Gypsy eyes, wolf eyes, as a Spanish saying goes]. This expression of the uniquely untamed animal Carmen is associated with an ideal vision of a dancer to play Carmen, since this dancer has not yet been found. More important, however, these words evoke the energetic intensity of a deflected desire provoked by a personal mental image of Mérimée's description—an uncontrollable sexual intensity to be sublimated and redirected into the creation of a ballet.

At the very same moment that Antonio thinks of Mérimée's text, we hear the operatic version of the "Seguidilla" and its closing *tra lalalala* invitation to be seduced into dancing. The strains of this aria are apparently playing inside Antonio's head: "Vous arrivez au bon moment! . . . car avec mon nouvel amant . . . j'irai danser la Séguedille et boire du Manzanilla. . . . tra lalalala" [You have come at the right time, because with my new lover I shall dance the Seguidilla and drink Manzanilla. . . . tra lalalala]. Cinematographically, this moment is blurred, insofar as the location of this music is uncertain. The extradiegetic sound space occupied until now by Bizet's score has been pulled into the diegesis by way of the image of the reel-to-reel and, then, into an inner intradiegetic space that signifies Antonio's own private soundstage. To work through this elaborate confusion of sound spaces and to create logic out of the otherwise heterogeneous mise-en-scène (of the dancing bodies and their flamenco arm combinations, the *buleria*, the operatic aria, and Mérimée's text), the inner intradiegetic space of Antonio's thoughts is almost imperceptibly transformed into an outer extradiegetic space for the spectator's own personal creative amalgam, or blurring. Perhaps despite him, his *duende* has been literally ex-pressed.

During this initial occasion given over to the spectator's capacity for the creative composing of what I have called floating signifiers, while the representational work of the camera and the presentational work of dancers remain necessarily distinct, flamenco and European sounds blur, or move between, the values associated with these two spaces. In other words, Antonio's own efforts to meld flamenco and the European performing arts traditions flow out over the constraints of the film narrative, imposing an almost unbearable desire to realign those materials and their floating senses. As spectators to the film, we are now situated, in other words, in the position of Bizet's José, who cannot bear the uncertainty of confused musical messages. Once these blurring effects begin to occur, we are no longer able to remain seated in a fixed and stable subjectivity outside of the film. On the contrary, like José, Antonio, Mérimée's nar-

rator, or Saura the director, we have become involved in the characteristic exchange of identities on which the aliveness of the performing arts
relies.

Ultimately, this solicitation of the film spectator seems designed to
help us maintain a watchful distance from the powerful unconscious effects of film on the formation of national and cultural identities. Like
Bizet's *Carmen,* it seeks to impose a conscious "wariness" and a sense of
moral agitation among its participants by way of its own tactical ambivalence and staging of self-conscious critique. Moreover, like Antonio,
whose aesthetic solutions to real psychological conflicts result in a still
unfinished *Carmen* ballet, Saura's gesturing to the film spectator reminds
us that attention to the very real conflicts—monetary, political, agricultural, and social—shared by the members of the European Economic
Community has yet to account for the diverse ethnic and cultural heritages of Europeans. Yet, because the film also marks the communal sharing of the performing arts space as an ideal setting from which to imagine new cultural affinities, it invites us to consider how the performing
arts experience and its creation of a performance-specific audience / community can help us to adapt, both mentally and kinesthetically, to the
sharing of an identity no longer defined by traditional group and class
formations. On the contrary, like the Gypsy communities represented in
the ballet or the informal gatherings of the cast of the ballet represented
in the film, such an identity resembles that of Bohemia, an assemblage of
slippery and mobile social affiliations which nurtures a certain political
plasticity and remains otherwise unfettered by larger national boundaries.

In the final analysis, by way of its exploration of the other which
constantly redefines and displaces both our art forms and our sense of
self, the *Carmen* experience recontextualized by this film intermixes regional and national artistic expressions, French and Spanish cultural heritages, and, because of its general commercial success, the worlds of the
Mediterranean and of a "greater" Europe. In so doing, it begins to etch
out tentative new ways of thinking up a European *cultural* community
and of sustaining the aliveness of the modern middle class which Carmen continues to fuel.

Notes

Introduction: Reading *Carmen*

1. Various lists of *Carmen* films and performances can be found in Jacqueline Ollier's "Carmen d'hier et d'aujourd'hui," *Corps Ecrit: L'Opéra* 20 (Dec. 1986): 115–16; and Susan McClary's *Georges Bizet: Carmen* (New York: Cambridge Univ. Press, 1992), 130–31. McClary describes the porno film *Carmen Baby* and the lesbian subculture's *Kamikaze Hearts*. The Gypsy Folklore Society announced its version, featuring "real Gypsies" in its annual newsletter. I have also been attentive, however, over the past four or five years, to versions of *Carmen* proliferating both in France and the United States much too numerous to reference. Hereafter I shall refer to McClary's handbook as *Bizet*.

2. In addition to the discussions of *Carmen* I shall recall shortly, the notion of the modern myth can be found in several essays of the *Cahiers Eïdolon, Carmen*, special issue (Oct. 1984), in Daniel Guichard, "Mérimée, *Carmen* (Chapitre III)," *L'Ecole des Lettres* 77, no. 15 (June 1986); Philippe Berthier and Kurt Ringger, eds., *Littérature et opéra. Colloque de Cérisy, 1985* (Grenoble: Presses Universitaires de Grenoble, 1987); and the forthcoming book by Mary Blackwood Collier, *La Carmen essentielle et sa réalisation au spectacle* (New York: Peter Lang).

3. Mérimée readapted an earlier translation of Pushkin's epic poem in 1852. It was originally published in 1827 and may well be the origin of the story of the Gypsy woman for whom loving is fatal, even if Mérimée himself always maintained that the origin of the anecdote was Eugénie de Montijo. Though it does not feature the ambiguous narrative structure of the novella, it could be argued

that the use of the epic poem in the early nineteenth century is indeed an effort to hybridize, a little on the order of the prose poem. On Mérimée's claims, see Henri Martineau's preface to the Pléïade edition of Mérimée's works: Prosper Mérimée, *Romans et nouvelles* (Paris: Gallimard, 1951), xxviii. On Mérimée's relation to Pushkin's story, see Robert L. Füglister, "Baudelaire et le thème des bohémiens," *Etudes Baudelairiennes II* (Neuchâtel, Switz.: La Baconnière, 1971), 122.

4. Benedict Anderson, *Imagined Communities* (1983; rpt., London: Verso, 1993), 1–7, 37–46. See also Nancy Armstrong and Leonard Tennenhouse's use of Anderson's discussion in *The Imaginary Puritan: Literature, Intellectual Labor, and the Origins of Personal Life* (Berkeley: Univ. of California Press, 1992).

5. Jerrold Seigel, *Bohemian Paris: Culture, Politics, and the Boundaries of Bourgeois Life, 1830–1930* (New York: Viking Penguin, 1986). Seigel's excellent discussion of Bohemia forms the framework for my discussion of the phenomenon in chapter 1. I do, however, take issue with Seigel's fundamental notion that Bohemia was always defined by its opposition to the bourgeoisie. As my occasional references to the example of George Sand's *La Dernière Aldini* will suggest, Bohemia's most enduring characteristic is to be oppositional but not always to the bourgeoisie. As political regimes change, so do the enemies of Bohemia, so, too, the definitions of Bohemia itself.

6. Lest one sense that the "culture wars" have no direct relation to the nineteenth-century bohemians, it is important to understand them as an effect of reading, that is, in response to theoretical expressions of "cultural politics" coming out of May '68 in Paris. On this Tom Bishop writes: "That we fight 'French Culture Wars' today is the clearest sign that the French penetrated American intelligentsia in an unprecedented manner, providing striking models of reflection and analysis as well as legitimate targets for conservative culture critics" ("I Love You, Moi Non Plus," *SubStance* 76–77 [1995]: 23).

7. See, in particular, Jeremy Tambling, *Opera, Ideology, and Film* (New York: St. Martin's Press, 1987) 25–29; see also Christian W. Thomsen, "Peter Brooks 'La Tragédie de Carmen' und Carlos Sauras 'Carmen'-Film: Zwei Experimenten in zeitgenössischer Theater- und Film-Ästhetik," *Studien zur Ästhetik des Gegenwartstheaters* (Winter 1985): 150–69; Denis Bertrand, "Les Migrations de Carmen," *Le Français dans le Monde* 181 (Nov.–Dec. 1983): 103–8; and McClary, *Bizet*.

8. Hayden White, *Metahistory: The Historical Imagination in Nineteenth-Century Europe* (Baltimore: Johns Hopkins Univ. Press, 1973).

9. Mérimée, *Romans et nouvelles*, 611, 621. All further references to Mérimée's *Carmen* will be to this edition.

10. Jane F. Fulcher, *The Nation's Image: French Grand Opera as Politics and Politicized Art* (New York: Cambridge Univ. Press, 1987).

11. Antonio Attisani, as quoted by Gautam Dasgupta, in his essay "Italian Theater in the New Europe: Notes on Santarcangelo dei Teatri XXII," *Performing Arts Journal* 44 (May 1993): 68.

12. George Sand, *La Dernière Aldini. Vie d'artistes* (Paris: Presses de la Cité, 1992), 129–254. On this idealized pan-European utopia, the hero of the novel, Lélio, exclaims: "Mais les temps sont venus où l'inspiration divine n'est plus arrêtée aux frontières des Etats par la couleur des uniformes et la bigarrure des bannières. Il y a dans l'air je ne sais quels anges ou quels sylphes, messagers invisibles du progrès, qui nous apportent l'harmonie et la poésie de tous les points de l'horizon. Ne nous enterrons pas sous nos ruines; mais que notre génie étende ses ailes et ouvre ses bras pour épouser tous les génies contemporains par-dessus les cimes des Alpes" (133) [But the time has come when divine inspiration is no longer stopped at the borders of States by the color of uniforms and the garish mix of banners. There are in the air I know not what kinds of angels or sylphs, invisible messengers of progress, who bring us harmony and poetry from all points of the horizon. Let us not bury ourselves beneath our ruins; rather, let our genius stretch its wings and open its arms to encompass all contemporary geniuses beyond the heights of the Alps (my trans.)].

13. Jacqueline Ollier describes reaction to the tale in the *Revue des Deux Mondes* in her essay "Carmen d'hier et d'aujourd'hui," 114. Peter Robinson lists the various articles appearing in the same issue of the *Revue des Deux Mondes* as *Carmen* in "Mérimée's *Carmen*," a piece that introduces McClary's *Bizet* (1).

14. On the European Community's (EC) sense of itself as pulled between the superpowers, see Wallerstein's *Geopolitics* but also the opening remarks of Robert Lafont in his *Nous, peuple européen* (Paris: Editions Kimé, 1991).

15. John Pomfret, "Exodus in Europe," *Washington Post National Weekly Edition*, 2–8 Aug. 1993, 7. Pomfret also notes that, "for 40 years, immigration policy was a battlefield of the Cold War" (6).

16. Derek W. Urwin, *The Community of Europe: A History of European Integration since 1945* (London: Longman, 1991), 165, 180, 208–10.

17. See McClary's discussion of the current *Carmen* feminism in her book *Bizet* (123–29). See also her foreword, "The Undoing of Opera: Toward a Feminist Criticism of Music," in Catherine Clément's *Opera, or the Undoing of Women*, trans. Betsy Wing (Minneapolis: Univ. of Minnesota Press, 1988), ix–xviii. It is noteworthy that in the field of musicology, according to McClary's 1988 foreword, "the voices calling for a feminist criticism are those of well-established men" (ix).

18. One exception is David Wills, who covers race, gender, class, and the EC

by suggesting that Carmen may be an image of Margaret Thatcher ("Carmen: Sound/Effect," *Cinema Journal* 25, no.4 [1986]: 33–43). On this issue, see my chapter 4 on Saura's *Carmen* and especially n. 1.

19. McClary's work on *Carmen* appears in both her Cambridge Opera Handbook and in her *Feminine Endings: Music, Gender, and Sexuality* (Minneapolis: Univ. of Minnesota Press, 1991). See also Mina Curtiss, *Bizet and His World* (New York: Knopf, 1958); Winton Dean, *Bizet* (London: J. M. Dent, 1975); and Catherine Clément, *L'Opéra ou la défaite des femmes* (Paris: Grasset, 1979) (trans. in 1988; see n. 17).

20. Wayne Koestenbaum, *The Queen's Throat: Opera, Homosexuality and the Mystery of Desire* (New York: Poseidon Press, 1993), 176–97. With regard to Godard's relation to Bizet, it is worth noting that, in an interview about *Carmen* in the *Cahiers du Cinéma*, Godard declares quite dramatically, and in total refusal of any influence whatsoever of the Mérimée model, *"Carmen,* c'est la musique!" (*Jean-Luc Godard par Jean-Luc Godard*, ed. Alain Bergala [Paris: *Cahiers du Cinéma* /Editions de l'Etoile, 1985]).

21. See Sherrie Fleshman, "Transitions in Narrative Distancing in the Short Stories of Balzac, Mérimée, and Flaubert" (Ph.D. diss., University of Oregon, 1994), in which the use of landscapes as a *mise en abyme* of the whole of a story's dynamics is discussed.

22. In *La Carmen essentielle*, Mary Blackwood Collier apparently studies several representations of *Carmen.* Though I have not yet seen this book, I base my remarks on Collier's essay "Carmen: Femme Fatale or Modern Myth?" (presented at the Eighteenth Annual Colloquium on Literature and Film, West Virginia University, Sept. 1993); and on my meeting with the author.

23. Nelly Furman, "The Languages of Love in *Carmen,*" *Reading Opera*, ed. Arthur Groos and Roger Parker (Princeton: Princeton Univ. Press, 1988), 168–83. Furman is also working on a larger comparative *Carmen* project, but I have not yet seen it.

24. For more on the significance of Clément's very personal reading of the *Carmen* story, see my essay "The Carmen Effect" in chapter 3. Due largely to the emphasis in my discussion on a textual analysis of Clément's French prose, all references to that book are to the original French edition (94–104). Anderson's *Carmen* video appeared as part of her 1993 tour, *A Conversation with Laurie Anderson.*

25. These critics will include Carolyn Abbate, Nancy Armstrong, Roland Barthes, Charles Baudelaire, Ross Chambers, Jacques Derrida, Marvin D'Lugo, Gustave Flaubert, Susan Foster, Jane Fulcher, Théophile Gautier, Claudia Gorbman, Fredric Jameson, Julia Kristeva, Philippe Lacoue-Labarthe, Susan

McClary, Friedrich Nietzsche, Michel Poizat, Arthur Rimbaud, Richard Terdiman, and Hayden White.

Chapter 1   The Imaginary Scenarios of Bohemia

1. Immanuel Wallerstein, *Geopolitics and Geoculture* (Cambridge: Univ. of Cambridge Press, 1991), 70–72. The citation in the epigraph is from Charles Baudelaire, "Vocations," *Oeuvres complètes* (Paris: Gallimard, 1975), 334. All further references to Baudelaire's writings in this chapter will be to this edition and will be indicated by "OC." All translations are my own, unless otherwise indicated. They are intended to be literal rather than poetically meaningful. As always, something is lost.

2. In *Bohemian Paris* Jerrold Seigel refers to the groups organized around Mazzini in the early 1830s and points out that the "Young Hegelians" was "a name that recalled Hegel's description of youth as a phase in the life cycle characterized by the impulse to 'make war on the world'" (20). Of 1848 he notes, "The wave of revolution spread throughout the Continent, to Italy . . . Germany, and Central Europe, even threatening for a moment to wash up on the shores of England" (59).

3. Continually reproducing itself in various antisystemic "movements" and in lifestyles and art forms that may be largely associated with those of the bohemians themselves, of the Surrealists, of the Beats, of the Yippies, of the Hippies, of the Punks, and even to some extent in the "revolutionary" behaviors of the Tel Quel group in Paris, Bohemia renews its dependence on revolutionary ruminations and euphorias to dramatize cultural responses to what Ross Chambers refers to as the symbolic gap in sovereignty left by the decapitation of Louis XVI in 1793, a kind of delayed series of responses to the repression of the symbolic "regime" and the equally repressive counterreaction known as "the Terror." See Chambers, "Poetry in the Asiatic Mode," *Yale French Studies* 74 (1988): 98–99; and *Room for Maneuver: Reading (the) Oppositional (in) Narrative* (Chicago: Univ. of Chicago Press, 1991), 242.

4. See Linda Orr, *Headless History: Nineteenth-Century French Historiography of the Revolution* (Ithaca: Cornell Univ. Press, 1990). Orr argues that a postrevolutionary society must create its own legitimacy from out of a "headless" collective social body, since it can no longer rely on the person of the king. She also points out that terms to name this phenomenon of communalism have ranged from the literal (*socialism, democracy, communism*) to the more metaphoric (*le peuple, public opinion, la chose sociale,* and even *bourgeois*) (23). It is the latter that interests me here.

5. See Jacques Derrida's essay "The Other Heading: Memories, Responses,

and Responsibilities," *The Other Heading: Reflections on Today's Europe*, trans. Pascale-Anne Brault and Michael B. Naas (Bloomington: Indiana Univ. Press, 1992), 29, as one example, popular in this country, of fears among leftist liberals of the universalizing agenda of the European Union, formerly the European Economic Community (EC) and the terms in which it subtly organizes cultural enterprises as a potentially hegemonic "whitewashing" of differences. Note as well that it is not only the symbolic regime that gains currency in this view of the new community but also the symbolic Revolution, a countercultural event that, as Linda Orr demonstrates, could only ever be grasped metaphorically (*Headless Revolution*, 23). See also Gianni Vattimo, *La Fine della modernità* (Milan: Garzanti, 1985) (trans. as *The End of Modernity* [Baltimore: Johns Hopkins Univ. Press, 1988]); and Theodore Zeldin, *The French* (London: Collins, 1983), 513.

6. As Tom Bishop has recently asserted with regard to Franco-American intellectual relations, "That we fight 'French Culture Wars' today is the clearest sign that the French penetrated American intelligentsia in an unprecedented manner, providing striking models of reflection and analysis as well as legitimate targets for conservative culture critics" ("I Love You, Moi Non Plus," *France's Identity Crises*, special issue, *SubStance* 76–77 [1995]: 23). For information on London's bohemians, I am grateful to have been able to read and hear April Bullock's essay "Looking for Mr. Fitzball: The Origins of Bohemian London" (MS).

7. I borrow this notion, respectfully, from a discussion, to which I shall return, in Walter Benjamin's *Charles Baudelaire: A Lyric Poet in the Era of High Capitalism*, trans. Harry Zohn (London: NLB, 1973).

8. Seigel, *Bohemian Paris*, 3–13. Seigel's valuable study will form a constant point of reference for my remarks on Bohemia, even though his specific focus on Murger as the symbolic starting point of nineteenth-century Bohemia shifts away from the image of a social utopia promised by earlier conceptions of a bourgeois society such as we shall see shortly in the work of George Sand.

9. Jean-Louis Martinoty studies the influence of Davillier and Doré's *Tour du monde* engravings (1874) on Georges Bizet's conception of Carmen and her world. In "De la Réalité au réalisme," *L'Avant-Scène Opéra* 26 (Mar.–Apr. 1980): 100–101.

10. In "Baudelaire et le thème des bohémiens" Robert L. Füglister explains that Borrow's work was partially translated into French between 1836 and 1874 and was almost single-handedly responsible for awakening interest in the real life of Gypsies (123–24). Prosper Mérimée refers to Borrow's book *The Zincali, An Account of the Gypsies of Spain* (1841) at the end of *Carmen*.

11. On the subject of travel narratives Richard Terdiman points out, "If the dominant discourse was the speech and writing of a France resolutely middle

class, self-absorbed, and certain of its self-sufficiency, then in our period one of the most prominent and most influential of the counter-discourses mobilized to subvert it was what we might term the discourse of *everywhere else*" (*Discourse/Counter-Discourse: The Theory and Practice of Symbolic Resistance in Nineteenth-Century France* [Ithaca: Cornell Univ. Press, 1985], 277). As he goes on to argue in the case of Gustave Flaubert's *Voyage en Orient*, however, going to the Orient inevitably meant finding there exactly what one set out to see (232). Referring then to Said's acknowledgment of real counterdiscursivity in Flaubert, Terdiman further explains: "But at the same time *Orientalism* suggests how these dreams of escape and of renewal presuppose the quite concrete political domination of the territory ideologically invested as the 'elsewhere' of romantic imagination. These dreams, and these texts, silently inscribe that domination in a manner which stresses them from within, and threatens to empty them completely" (231).

12. Seigel discusses Murger's various writings on Bohemia at length (*Bohemian Paris*, 31–58); I am interested in the multitude of theatrical versions that novel reflected and further encouraged. It is worth noting, in this context, that Murger's efforts, in 1849, echoed Gautier's, in 1844, to define and thereby circumscribe the kind of Parisian bohemian he is interested in promoting.

13. Théophile Gautier, *Histoire de l'art dramatique en France depuis vingt-cinq ans*, 6 vols. (Leipzig: Hetzel, 1858–59), 2: 106–7. Seigel mentions the play and its association of Gypsies with "new specters rising from the shadows of urban life" but not Gautier's critique of it (23).

14. It is notable that that revolution resulted in a political version of Bohemia's own tactical ambivalence with the dissatisfying establishment of Louis Philippe's "bourgeois monarchy," a tactical ambivalence that, by 1844, was already producing its own spontaneous regeneration, since, according to Seigel, that monarchy faced its strongest opposition in the bourgeoisie of 1848 (*Bohemian Paris*, 7–8).

15. Robert Füglister refers to this kind of bohemian community as a *Schicksalsgemeinschaft*, a "community forged by destiny" ("Baudelaire," 141).

16. Living in Eugene, Oregon, one of the largest remaining bastions of Hippies and countercultural radicals in the United States today, one is struck by those bohemian artists who recognize the advantages of mainstreaming their wares. It is clear, however, that this ambivalence is at the heart of bohemian behavior. In Eugene, for example, the Bohemia represented by the Grateful Dead "heads" always appeared to exist in reaction to mass consumerism but brought a tremendous economic influx to town when the band was scheduled to perform. This income in turn provoked further ambivalent response. Though ultimately scrapped, the scheduling of the Grateful Dead at Bill Clinton's pres-

idential inauguration also comments forcefully on bourgeois cultural ambivalence toward Bohemia. Cultural ambivalence may also explain why the Bohemia of the Sunset Strip in the Los Angeles of the 1960s could exist in reaction to the crass commercialism of, say, the Playboy Club, while Hugh Hefner helped to finance the efforts and lifestyle of "free love" war resister bus trips. I am grateful to many of these remaining Hippies for various of these insights.

17. This vision of Bohemia, as an antidote to the nefarious effects of "civilization," is expressed in Gautier's introduction to Mérimée's *Carmen* in *La Presse* (20 June 1853) and reproduced in *Emaux et Camées* (Paris: Minard, 1968), 141.

18. See Beryl Schlossman, *The Orient of Style* (Durham, N.C.: Duke Univ. Press, 1991).

19. Ross Chambers studies one exemplary model of this shifting in "Au lecteur," in his essay "Asiatic Mode" (103).

20. Margaret Miner, "Dionysos parmi les bohémiens, un parcours baudelairien," *Europe* 760–61 (Aug.–Sept. 1992): 52.

21. Jean-Luc Steinmetz points out that it is the relationships between writing and voice, in particular, that form the major thrust of Rimbaud's legacy to the Surrealists, themselves interested in finding an interior voice that would assume and carry out the dictates of the Unconscious. He also argues that Rimbaud's project to "disorder senses" relates to a passage from writing to speech, from meanings to the actual physical sensations of the plurivocality of identity. See his essay "Le Chant traverse l'identité," *La Poésie et ses raisons* (Paris: José Corti, 1990), 15, 17–18, 28–29.

22. Füglister points out that Baudelaire and Rimbaud were the most effective bohemians to imprint an image of Bohemia onto that of the misunderstood artist ("Baudelaire," 104). This provides only a partial explanation for the kind of influence Rimbaud in particular has had. Indeed, I am arguing that there are stylistic exigencies expressed in bohemian narratives that nurture new and creative writing experiments.

23. Despite the fact that Claude Pichois has shown the uncertainty of dates in the completion of lyric and prose versions of "La Chevelure," for example (OC 1321), most critics of the prose poems who preceded Barbara Johnson have read the prose as finding its point of departure in the lyric verse (see Johnson, *Défigurations du langage poétique: la seconde révolution baudelairienne* [Paris: Flammarion, 1979], 148–49). Johnson discloses this traditional tendency to accord primacy to lyric verse.

24. As this citation suggests, Johnson accentuates the necessary shuttling between versions required by the "rewrites," refusing the traditional tendency to accord primacy to lyric verse. Another example of this comparative shuttling can be seen in the recent work of Dominique Combe (*Poésie et récit: une rhé-*

torique des genres [Paris: José Corti, 1989], 96–98). I, too, am interested in the shuttling, though my reading of "L'Invitation au voyage" will suggest that Baudelaire's prose is a commentary on the way in which his own lyric verse participates in and is inevitably determined by what Richard Terdiman has called the dominant discourses of bourgeois ideology that prose poems are intended to expose. Yet, whereas Terdiman argues that the prose poems are unable to "denaturalize the self-evidence of the dominant" by excluding it, precisely because "the contaminating presence they had sought to contain irresistibly bleeds back into their own substance" (*Discourse/Counter-Discourse*, 280), I will suggest that the required shuttling between forms of the same narrative forces our attention to the bleeding and to the necessary commodification of the poetic project itself. In other words, for Terdiman, "the paradox of any social distinction is that the heterogeneity sought is determined by that which it excluded: situated thus, one never gets outside" (278). For me one form never wholly excludes the other but constantly recalls its heterogeneous "other." Or, as Johnson writes, "Or, inclure l'exclusion, c'est effacer ou problématiser la limite même qui distingue l'intérieur de l'extérieur; c'est interroger *ses propres limites*, sa propre extériorité— intérieure à la poésie" (160) [Well, to include the exclusion is to erase or to complicate the very limit that distinguishes the interior from the exterior; it is to interrogate *its own limits*, its own exteriority—inside poetry (my trans.)]. Another kind of opponent to the powerful argument Terdiman makes is Nathaniel Wing, who looks at the ways the writings of Baudelaire, Flaubert, Rimbaud, and Mallarmé "powerfully disrupt the imaginary representations which sustain bourgeois power" (*The Limits of Narrative: Essays on Baudelaire, Flaubert, Rimbaud, and Mallarmé* [London: Cambridge Univ. Press, 1986], 147 n. 5).

25. Terdiman, *Discourse/Counter-Discourse*, 264–65. Terdiman sees the elitism of the avant-garde poets, specifically Mallarmé's celebrated obscurity, as one of the main reasons their work has no real oppositional force. Marie Maclean, *Narrative as Performance: The Baudelairean Experiment* (London: Routledge, 1988), 48–49. Both Nathaniel Wing (*Limits of Narrative*) and Leo Bersani (*Baudelaire and Freud* [Berkeley: Univ. of California Press, 1977], 125–36) are also interested in what Wing calls the "dysfunctional" universe of the prose poems, but neither confronts the question of address opened by Vincent Kaufmann's book on Mallarmé, *Le Livre et ses adresses (Mallarmé, Ponge, Valéry, Blanchot)* (Paris: Méridiens Klincksieck, 1986).

26. In this respect Terdiman's work follows the lines of that of Julia Kristeva on Lautréamont and Mallarmé and her association of the prose poem with the anarchism of the avant-garde. See Kristeva, *La Révolution du langage poétique: l'avant-garde à la fin du XIXe siècle: Lautréamont et Mallarmé* (Paris: Seuil, 1974).

Citing Kristeva, Terdiman gives a good sense of my notion of a bohemian aesthetic: "It is true that . . . Baudelaire, Nerval or Rimbaud . . . still remain tied to the requirements of estheticism [*l'exigence esthétique*], and their negativity appears rather as an anarchic and individualist revolt than as an *attempt at social intervention*" (Terdiman, *Discourse/Counter-Discourse*, 265; see also 272; and Kristeva, *La Révolution*, 617).

27. Johnson remarks with respect to the ongoing influence of this shuttling: "L'influence des poèmes en prose sur la poésie post-baudelairienne est indéniable. . . . Les *Fleurs du mal*, par contre, semblent exercer une influence de plus en plus faible sur la créativité poétique actuelle" (*Défigurations*, 14) [The influence of the prose poems on post-Baudelarian poetry is undeniable. . . . The *Flowers of Evil*, on the other hand, seem to exert a more and more feeble influence on poetic creativity at present (my trans.)].

28. Seigel also sees these two roles as related in the same way as the bohemian and the bourgeois, but he does not consider stylistic issues related to them. See his discussion in *Bohemian Paris*, 97–124.

29. On Sartre's preoccupation with Baudelaire's moral complicity with bourgeois culture, see his book *Baudelaire* (Paris: Gallimard, 1947).

30. See Suzanne Bernard, *Le Poème en prose de Baudelaire à nos jours* (Paris: Nizet, 1959), 14–15; and Combe's recent discussion of it (*Poésie et récit*, 92–93).

31. As Johnson insists, following Suzanne Bernard, "le code de la poésie n'est donc pas seulement un ensemble d'éléments considérés comme 'poétiques,' mais aussi une exclusion, une dénégation, un refoulement actif de tout ce qui appartient à d'autres codes" [the code of poetry is not only an ensemble of elements considered "poetic" but also an exclusion, a denial, an active repressing of anything that belongs to other codes (my trans.)]. Conversely, the prose makes explicit not only "ce qui est exclu, mais l'acte même d'exclure" [all that is excluded, but the act of exclusion itself].

In addition, I would argue that the prose further compromises this image of the rarefied purity of poetry by dramatizing the commodification of art as an unconscious ideological support system. For example, the narrator of Baudelaire's "Invitation" exclaims: "Qu'ils cherchent, qu'ils cherchent encore . . . ces alchimistes de l'horticulture! Qu'ils proposent des prix de soixante et de cent mille florins. . . . Moi, j'ai trouvé ma *tulipe noire* et mon *dahlia bleu!*" (OC 303) [Let them search and continue to search . . . these alchemists of horticulture! Let them propose prices of sixty or of a hundred thousand florins. . . . I myself have found my *black tulip* and my *blue dahlia!* (my trans.)]. With this exasperated exclamation the narrator insists upon the exceptional nature of poetic or imaginary flowers in relation to those of horticulturists, who might, in the manner of Huysmans's Des Esseintes, realize any number of expensive and slightly

"Oriental" hybrid stems which literally confound distinctions between poetic purity and exchange value. But he also displays the inevitability of relations between art and commodity, since the tulip and the dahlia are references, as Johnson points out, to the already clichéd popular writings of Alexandre Dumas and Pierre Dupont (140). Like these flowers, Baudelaire's own also face eventual commodification.

32. Arthur Rimbaud, *Oeuvres complètes* (Paris: Gallimard, 1951). All further references to Rimbaud's writings will be to this edition and will be indicated by "OC." All translations are my own, unless otherwise indicated.

33. *La Poésie eclatée* (Paris: Presses Universitaires de France, 1980).

34. In *The Emergence of Social Space: Rimbaud and the Paris Commune* (Minneapolis: Univ. of Minnesota Press, 1988) Kristin Ross speaks of "social space" in ways that resemble what I refer to as the "imaginary scenarios of Bohemia." For Ross social space is a way of thinking, a "social imaginary," which parallels political and social realities. In the case of Rimbaud the transformation of social space taking place during the Commune is worked out analogously in the literary event that is Rimbaud's *Saison en enfer*. Terdiman goes one step further in his characterization of this kind of social/literary parallel in a discussion of Mallarmé that he also sees as relevant to Rimbaud: "For the first time in the incipient capitalist period the experience of historical change permitted conceptualizing the role played by the structures of social life in the formation of consciousness" (292). Rather than a mere parallel, then, the structures of social life are more interventionist, actually shaping the social imaginary unconsciously, one presumes.

35. On the question of the *récit* and its relation to genre as they were defined during the late nineteenth century, see also Combe, *Poésie et récit*. For Combe it is the refusal of the *récit* which inaugurated an entirely new *rhétorique des genres* at the end of the century, even though it is not itself a genre, and it enters into both verse and prose, literary or not (31–34).

36. Jean-Luc Steinmetz (*La Poésie*) also reads Rimbaud's later prose against his 1871 project.

37. Baudelaire himself had already considered the question of the musicality of lyric voice in the context of Wagner's poetic dramas and the potential community formed by way of the "analogous thoughts" that certain modes of representation produce in the minds of different listeners—himself, Liszt, and Wagner. See his article "*Tannhaüser* à Paris"; and my discussion of it in chapter 3; as well as Richard Sieburth, "Symbolist Poets Publish *La revue wagnérienne;* The Music of the Future," in *A New History of French Literature*, ed. Denis Hollier (Cambridge: Harvard Univ. Press, 1989), 789–98.

38. The translations of Rimbaud's writing in the following discussion are

those of Wallace Fowlie in *Rimbaud: Complete Works, Selected Letters* (Chicago: Univ. of Chicago Press, 1966). All page numbers refer to this edition.

39. Terdiman's (*Discourse/Counter-Discourse*) discussion of Baudelaire suggests that, whereas Baudelaire refers to the modern city in terms of destruction and reconstruction, Rimbaud reproduces the shards of that activity, forcing the reader to de- and reconstruct anew with each reading. According to Ross (*Emergence of Social Space*) Rimbaud's constant renewal of de- and reconstruction is the expression of the social imaginary, the staging of a poetic reality and identity that parallel the political and social reality of the Commune (see n. 35). On the question of Baudelaire's musicality, it is quite possible that the "music" of the *Spleen* poems forms a direct response to the swallowing up of the poet's lyric voice which Baudelaire sensed in Wagner's dramas. I shall return to this question in chapter 3.

40. See Robert Hunter, *A Box of Rain, Lyrics, 1965–1993* (New York: Penguin, 1993); *Kerouac and the Beats: A Primary Sourcebook*, ed. Arthur and Kit Knight (New York: Paragon House, 1988); and Hank Harrison, *The Dead Book: A Social History of the Grateful Dead* (New York: Links Books, 1973). It is worth noting in this context that Ginsberg situates himself very squarely between "the old Dylan Thomas, Hart Crane, Baudelaire, Rimbaud tradition," on one hand, and, on the other, "younger kids like Dylan" (Knight, *Kerouac*, 245). Moreover, on the question of a community sought by these followers of the old tradition, Ginsberg adds:

> That perception in Kerouac, which he awakened in me, is very similar to the substance of the Bodhisattva vow. Then there's the problem that if you calculate too much esthetically in terms of careers and in role-playing, you obviously can make mistakes. . . . So it then comes back to dependence on spontaneous mind for inspiration and trust in the heart as the teacher, as the guru, poetically and cosmo-socially, and playing it by ear. . . . the public role is a poem for everybody, not just the poet, everybody invents their existence and their theater except poets are aware of doing it, sometimes—and maybe are even able to cut through it and show the backstage of the theater; in other words, show that it is theater rather than try to hypnotize other people. (246)

41. Nancy Armstrong, *Desire and Domestic Fiction: A Political History of the Novel* (New York: Oxford Univ. Press, 1987), 3–27. See also *The Imaginary Puritan*, in which Armstrong and Leonard Tennenhouse pay specific attention to the role of print capitalism in the origins of the modern Anglo-American middle class. Following Benedict Anderson's lead, they argue that the emergence of print vernacular in America literally forged new communities that

flowed back into Britain to forge a middle-class sense of community.

42. "The Narrativization of Real Events," in *On Narrative*, ed. W. J. T. Mitchell (Chicago: Univ. of Chicago Press, 1980), 249–50. See also his article "The Value of Narrativity in the Representation of Reality," 1–23, in the same volume. I shall return to these texts in chapter 2.

43. Susan Stewart, "The State of Cultural Theory and the Future of Literary Form," *Profession* (1993): 12–15.

44. To explain the emergence of these double discourses Terdiman argues that, after 1848, when the surreptitious nature of symbolic opposition becomes more and more necessary, everything in the nineteenth century really does come down to a binary exposition of the opposition of the workers and the bourgeoisie, with 1848 and 1871 representing two anomalous events that express the intense heterogeneity of positions within that exposition (*Discourse/Counter-Discourse*, 280–81). He further acknowledges that, as a consequence of these doubled discourses, everything written at that time, but read from our contemporary perspective, does necessarily take on the quality of a protostructuralist account (whether, as Terdiman suggests, because of our post-Freudian sense of a doubled subjectivity or, as Wallerstein would suggest, because of our post-Yalta balance of power sensibilities). Terdiman does not acknowledge, however, that the space of choice opened by counterdiscursivity in narrative may lend expression, within bourgeois art itself, to a multitude of individualities and, indeed, of subjective legitimacies or sovereignties best served—both nurtured and allowed to dissipate—within the confines of the structure provided by opposing discourses. In its continual energizing and deflecting of political enthusiasms, Bohemia, then and now, is a place in which to offer this legitimacy to the many who seek to exist between the definitions of strictly political tensions.

45. The following discussion of the book offers a very abbreviated version of Chambers's own introduction to the original conception of oppositionality.

Chapter 2 *Carmen:* Novella

1. This description is quoted and translated by Linda Orr in "The Revenge of Literature," *New Literary History* 18 (1986–87): 5. It originally appeared in association with the names of Jules Michelet, Guizot, Thierry, Barante, Mignet, and Sismondi in Charles Louandre's "Statistique littéraire de la production intellectuelle en France depuis quinze ans," *Revue des Deux Mondes* 20 (1847): 426.

2. Most critical work on Mérimée looks at his exploitation of the frame narrative and its capacity to interrogate relations between narrators and protagonists. Much of it focuses on *La Vénus d'Ille*. Consider, for example, Frank Paul

Bowman, "Narrator and Myth in Mérimée's 'Vénus d'Ille,'" *French Forum* 33 (1960): 475–82; Marie E. Ramsland, "Inspiration avec un sourire ironique: 'La Vénus d'Ille' de Mérimée," *Essays in French Literature* 23 (Nov. 1986): 19–28; Anthony E. Pilkington, "Narrator and Supernatural in Mérimée's 'La Vénus d'Ille,'" *Nineteenth Century French Studies* 4, nos. 1–2 (1975–76): 24–30; Ross Chambers, "Violence du récit: Boccace, Mérimée, Cortázar," *Canadian Review of Comparative Literature* 13, no. 2 (1986): 159–86; and, on *Carmen*, Gillian Horrocks, "A Semiotic Study of *Carmen*," *Nottingham French Studies* 25, no. 2 (1986): 60–72; P. W. M. Cogman, "The Narrators of Mérimée's *Carmen*," *Nottingham French Studies* 27, no. 2 (1988): 1–12.

3. In *Metahistory: The Historical Imagination in Nineteenth-Century Europe* (Baltimore: Johns Hopkins Univ. Press, 1973) White notes that the discipline of history was founded at the Sorbonne in 1812 and that it was followed by the growing popularity of historical societies such as the Ecole des Chartres founded in 1821 as well as the financial support of the government during the 1830s (136). On the question of the historian in *Carmen*, see Denis Bertrand, "Les Migrations de Carmen," *Le Français dans le Monde* 181 (1983): 103–8. On the inevitable link between the storyteller and the historian, see also Catherine Velay-Vallantin's *L'Histoire des contes* (Paris: Fayard, 1992) and, in particular, her study of historical reconstruction in *La Vénus* (11–41, 135–84).

4. With these questions I am invoking two important discussions by White to which I shall later refer, "The Value of Narrativity in the Representation of Reality," in Mitchell, *On Narrative*, 1–23; and *The Content of the Form: Narrative Discourse and Historical Representation* (Baltimore: Johns Hopkins Univ. Press, 1987).

5. "Epic and Novel," in *The Dialogic Imagination*, ed. Michael Holquist, trans. Caryl Emerson and Michael Holquist (Austin: Univ. of Texas Press, 1981), 39.

6. One might even argue that *Carmen*'s fourth chapter was added in 1847 as a moral evaluation to make the historical value of the tale more evident and to tame down the alluring appeal of the socially and politically radical, if fictitious, bohemians.

7. According to Bakhtin, this "polyglossia," as one basic characteristic of the novel, among others, is powerfully affected by Europe's entrance into a period of international and interlingual contacts, a period when having "national languages coexisting but closed and deaf to each other, comes to an end" ("Epic and Novel," 11–12).

8. On the question of existential history, see Fredric Jameson, *Ideologies of Theory*, 2 vols. (Minneapolis: Univ. of Minnesota Press, 1988), 2:154–56. See also Linda Orr's review article of Stephen Bann's *Clothing for Cleo*. Also, though

this is not the place to discuss the empirical pursuits of the so-called realist fiction, clearly, the latter's conception coincided with concerns to represent the same mutability of the present and of those who observe it.

9. Parts of the following discussion appear in my article "Prosper Mérimée Is Thinking the Revolution," in *The French Revolution of 1789 and Its Impact*, ed. Gail M. Schwab and John R. Jeanneney (Westport, Conn.: Greenwood Press, 1995), 135–45.

10. This same discussion of the rhetorical rules of nineteenth-century historical narrative appears in "Figuring the Nature of Times Deceased," a paper distributed and discussed at a University of Oregon faculty seminar in 1988 (12).

11. See chapter 1; and Seigel, *Bohemian Paris*, 23–24.

12. This and all further translations of passages from *Carmen* are my own.

13. Caesar is, of course, an important opening image in that, besides being a noted historian and general, the Roman emperor was the figure espoused by Napoléon I's empire to signify France's emergence out of the "dark ages" of the Revolution and to recall the necessity of an ever-expanding European empire, an empire expanding far enough, in 1830, to establish the first French colony in Morocco. Moreover, Caesar is an ambivalent figure who triumphed both against the republicans, the Senate in Rome, and against Pompeii, the first consul in Rome. He, too, played "double or nothing."

14. The veracity of the chronicle is further complicated by Mérimée's own reference to the famous bandit José-Maria, or "El Tempranito." It appears in a letter written in 1830 from Madrid, "Lettre sur les voleurs en Espagne," *Revue de Paris* (August 1832).

15. This scene plays an important role in Bizet's opera in the form of the "Bohemian Song" that opens act 2. See chapter 3.

16. This transformation recalls Michel Foucault's argument about the repressed and therefore celebrated sexuality of the Victorians in *The History of Sexuality* (1980).

17. See Lacan, *Ecrits* (Paris: Seuil, 1966), 412; and *Encore, Le Seminaire, livre XX* (Paris: Seuil, 1975), 172; as well as discussions of this phenomenon by Mikkel Borch-Jacobsen in his *Lacan: le maître absolu* (Paris: Flammarion, 1990), 235–43; and by Malcolm Bowie in *Freud, Proust and Lacan: Theory as Fiction* (Cambridge: Cambridge Univ. Press, 1987), 166–78.

It is significant to read in Mérimée's Diana and Actaeon the story of what Borch-Jacobsen describes as "the *subject* of desire . . . who is devoid of sexuality—as is his "object"—because this subject is none other than itself insofar as it differs from itself and desires itself such as it cannot be" (240–41; my trans.). Such a conception of the desiring subject or subject of desire helps explain the narrator's identification with a "bad reading" of Don José. Borch-Jacobsen also reminds us that the subject of desire differs from the "me" of the "Stade du miroir," who sees itself in the other, insofar as it is only constituted in speech as the subject who speaks to the other (*Lacan*, 95–97). For Borch-Jacobsen, Klossowski's *Bain de Diane* (1956) is a decisive factor in Lacan's setting up of the phallus as the absent organ of sexual pleasure. Behind Lacan's Actaeon, however, Bowie would rather see those of Bruno and Petrarch, as he insists that, in Lacan's use of it, the Ovidian parable is a metaphor for the desiring mind seeking its own death. As Bowie writes: "The mind, by allowing its passion to pursue certain goals at all—Laura, the beauty of the Divine, the unconscious—conduces to its own ruin; the imagery of all three writers fuses the sexual and intellectual modes of desire into a unitary portrait of mind as enthusiastic, rapacious and self-consuming in all its pursuits" (*Freud, Proust and Lacan*, 169). Bowie's commentary is useful to my discussion of Mérimée's use of the parable insofar as the notion of the desiring mind pursuing its own death underlines Mérimée's insistence upon the destructive force of the bourgeois imagination as self-generated rather than caused by Gypsies, women, or bohemians.

18. The work of textual echoes also influences the structuring of Bizet's opera, as we shall see in chapter 3.

19. Seigel (*Bohemian Paris*, 403) also writes, "Those who built the image of Bohemia self-consciously recalled the Romantics of the 1830s, but in terms that transformed the real Romantic estrangement into an idealization of bourgeois youth." On this new poetic Bohemia, see also Henry Murger, *Scènes de la vie de Bohème* (1851; reprint, Paris: Editions d'Aujourd'hui, 1979), 5–10.

Chapter 3   *Carmen: Opéra-comique*

1. Carolyn Abbate, *Unsung Voices: Opera and Musical Narrative in the Nineteenth Century* (Princeton: Princeton Univ. Press, 1991), 19–20, 72. This book presents the only systematic attempt to answer the questions posed—rather than just the presumptions channeled—by the notion of operatic narrative. It is a brilliant exposé of the problems, and I will refer to it frequently. David J. Levin's *Opera through Other Eyes* also offers a collection of insightful essays on the problems posed by operatic narrative. I regret not having been able to consult these essays prior to the final preparation of my manuscript.

2. This distinction between narrative conceived as an act of telling versus an "effect" of bringing to life before our very eyes is at the heart of the polemic presented in *On Narrative*, essays by speech act theorists and poststructuralists, including Mary Louise Pratt and Hayden White.

3. It is not my intention to enter into a discussion of the phenomenology of

operatic listening. This work has been pursued in very exciting and creative ways by Peter Kivy in *Osmin's Rage: Philosophical Reflections on Opera, Drama, and Text* (Princeton: Princeton Univ. Press, 1988). In that book the question of anticipation and recollection in opera listening is associated, provocatively, with prophecy and ecstasy (3–6, 15), terms that help support those of Michel Poizat, *jouissance* and *maîtrise*, considered later in this chapter.

4. Carolyn Abbate and Roger Parker, *Analyzing Opera: Verdi and Wagner* (Berkeley: Univ. of California Press, 1989), 3, 24. The introduction to this book offers a very clear exposition of the present state of the musicological affairs of opera.

5. The "principle of nationality" that transformed the political allegiances of Europe between 1830 and the 1870s was a Mazzinian phase of nationalism starkly distinguished from the politically conservative shift during the last two decades of the century for which the term *nationalism* was invented and to which ethnicity and language became central. See Eric J. Hobsbawm, *Nations and Nationalism since 1780: Programme, Myth, Reality* (Cambridge: Cambridge Univ. Press, 1990), 101–5.

6. As Abbate and Parker point out in *Analyzing Opera*, "For opera is not music alone; it lives in association with poetry and dramatic action, an association that has made it idiosyncratic and special, certainly different in fundamental ways from instrumental music" (3). Or later: "Of course, any writer who, like Schenker, chooses to regard opera as music alone is seeing only one of the three primary colors. 'Analyzing opera' should mean not only 'analyzing music,' but simultaneously engaging, with equal sophistication, the poetry and the drama" (4). Though I shall certainly not engage in musical analysis with "equal sophistication," I am interested in the problem of operatic narrative precisely because it moves beyond or through questions posed by specific disciplines (and the demands of disciplinary expertise which are necessarily defined by them). I shall consider the problem in terms of the only theoretical object that is an operatic *text*, in other words, and not in terms of the disciplines and interdisciplinarity posed by opera, as do musicologists.

7. The librettos of realist operas in general tend to talk about their own inner mechanics in a self-reflexive commentary that resembles, according to Peter Conrad, that of other forms of nineteenth-century fiction. Far from respecting the verisimilitude of which they boast, the characters in these operas behave unrealistically, says Conrad, by singing about "art for art's sake," about the concerns of their own professions as artists. As Conrad points out, Tosca sings about singing (although most heroines of realist operas probably do), Adriana sings about dramatic interpretation, Michonnet about stage management, Andrea Chénier about poetic inspiration, Escamillo about the art of bullfighting (*Ro-*

mantic Opera and Literary Form [Berkeley: Univ. of California Press, 1977], 136–39). Following this line of thinking, Bizet's Carmen—a name etymologically linked to *song, charm,* and *law*—may be said to sing about the pleasures of music listening, that is, about the affect of the opera-spectator and its cultural regulation in a manner that both excites and restrains. Conrad returns to this issue again in *A Song of Love and Death* (New York: Poseidon, 1987), 13–14.

8. The French response to Wagner blooms in the 1860s. This makes it contemporary to the burgeoning practice of analyzing operatic music among German musicologists, occasioned, for the most part, by interpretations of Wagner. See Abbate and Parker, *Analyzing Opera,* 6.

9. I have borrowed this term from Philippe Lacoue-Labarthe's *Musica ficta (figures de Wagner)* (Paris: Christian Bourgois, 1991), to which I shall return in the section of this chapter called "The *Carmen* Case." For the time being I would like to examine this effect of Wagner's music in broader and more performance-oriented terms than those of Lacoue-Labarthe.

10. While applauding the new self-consciousness in opera theory about the way in which a nineteenth-century search for unity and organic coherence finds itself allied with Wagner's often politicized self-proclamations on the subject of *musikdrama* theory, the writer of French sensibility cannot help but be nonetheless struck by the subtitle of Abbate's and Parker's exciting volume *Analyzing Opera: Verdi and Wagner.* For, even if the great names are aligned in conflict so as to nurture explorations into the limitations of strict binary oppositions (in this case, the "symphonist" and the "melodist"), the absence of French voices in this "story" of modern operatic analyses nonetheless reveals a complicity not only with disciplinary distinctions but also with the national borders of these distinctions. On the other side of this story is what Jacques Derrida might call the other of this story. Concepts such as text, narrative, discourse, and even Joseph Kerman's "drama," caught between antidisciplinary quotation marks, are ways of discussing signifying behaviors that cross between, deconstruct, or destabilize such distinctions. Until recently, however, these concepts have remained distinctly French. Therefore, echoing Mallarmé's defiance of Wagner some one hundred years ago, we might once again ask if a French imagination of poetic, theoretical bent can now rival a Germanic impetus toward the wholeness of disciplinary vigor.

11. Gustave Flaubert, *Madame Bovary* (Paris: Garnier-Flammarion, 1966), 247–54. All translations from *Madame Bovary* are my own.

12. Flaubert is, of course, not alone in his critique of opera-spectators who do not listen to the music; in Balzac no one listens.

13. This particular passage, in which Emma screams and blends her voice into that of the orchestra, has been used as an image of identification at the

opera by several critics for diverse reasons. In my thinking, however, the loss of self-consciousness associated with the scream is much less significant than the constant oscillation between identification and critical self-awareness. Important discussions of this scene include Herbert Lindenberger's in *Opera: The Extravagant Art* (Ithaca: Cornell Univ. Press, 1984), 159–62. Lindenberger's main point is that operatic scenes in novels allow the persistence of the "traditional high style" within the setting of a "world of lowly things . . . [and of] . . . lowly style" characteristic of the realist novel (166–67). McClary also cites part of this passage in her chapter on *Lucia di Lammermoor*, in *Feminine Endings*, as does Kurt Ringger in *"Lucia di Lammermoor* ou les regrets d'Emma Bovary," in *Littérature et Opéra*, ed. Philippe Berthier and Ringger (Grenoble, Fr.: Presses Universitaires de Grenoble, 1987), 69.

14. On Wagner's project to rewrite the history of opera, see Lindenberger, *Opera*, 60–61; on his piecing together of a German national past, see Carl Dahlhaus on *Tannhaüser* in *Richard Wagner's Music Dramas* (Cambridge: Cambridge Univ. Press, 1979), 21–24.

15. See Harold James, *A German Identity, 1770–1990* (New York: Routledge, Chapman, and Hall, 1989), 10–11.

16. Charles Baudelaire, "Richard Wagner et *Tannhaüser* à Paris," in *L'Art romantique. Oeuvres complètes*, ed. Jacques Crépet (Paris: Louis Conard, 1923), 3:203–8. All translations from the essay are my own. On the question of correspondences in Baudelaire's reading of Wagner, see Richard Sieburth, "The Music of the Future," in Hollier, *New History of French Literature*, 790–92. See also Margaret Miner for further insight into Baudelaire's notion of analogic responses in different brains in "Putting the Emphasis on Music: Baudelaire and the *Lohengrin* Prelude," 389.

17. Stéphane Mallarmé, "Rêverie d'un Poëte français," "Crise de vers," *Oeuvres complètes*, ed. Jean Aubry and Henri Mondor (Paris: Gallimard, 1945), 360–68, 541–46.

18. *Nietzsche contra Wagner*. In *The Portable Nietzsche*, ed. and trans. Walter Kaufmann (New York: Viking Penguin, 1954), 664.

19. Lacoue-Labarthe remarks that Baudelaire's reaction to Wagner, though admiring, is nonetheless a response by a Frenchman (*Musica ficta*, 61).

20. Friedrich Nietzsche, *The Birth of Tragedy and the Case of Wagner*, trans. Walter Kaufmann (New York: Random House, 1967), 158.

21. Nietzsche's interest in the non-European qualities of *Carmen* is related as much to his focus on the politics of "subject-effects" in opera as it is a sign of his complicity with what Susan McClary calls the "violent, egoistic possessiveness" of ethnic and sexual others by the Europeans (*Bizet*, 118).

22. Marco de Marinis defines the class of material objects known as theatri-

cal performances as "all theatrical phenomena where the so-called *presentational* aspect variously prevails over the representational aspect; where *turning inward* (self-reflexivity or self-referentiality) prevails over turning outward; where production (of meaning, reality, etc.) prevails over reproduction (*The Semiotics of Performance*, trans. Aine O'Healy [Bloomington: Indiana Univ. Press, 1993], 48–49).

23. Slavoj Zizek, *The Sublime Object of Ideology* (London: Verso, 1989), 87.

24. It is important to note that, although Bizet's own "political" project may not have been directly opposed to Wagner's, it did offer an alternative form of opera to Jacques Offenbach's political satires designed to question Louis Philippe's "popular" royalism. Lacoue-Labarthe makes this point about Wagner's gesture toward "Restoration" (*Musica ficta*, 47).

25. Georges Bizet, *Lettres (1850–1875)*, ed. Claude Glayman (Paris: Calmann-Lévy, 1989), 207.

26. Charles Gaudier summarizes newspaper reviews of the opening of *Les Pêcheurs* which criticized Bizet's Wagnerian tendencies in the following terms: "une orchestration trop chargée, des harmonies piquantes, et une recherche mal entendue de l'originalité" [an overwrought orchestration, spicy harmonies, and a poorly understood search for originality]. In *Carmen de Bizet: Etude historique et critique, Analyse musicale* (Paris: Librairie Delaplane, 1922). McClary also looks for the "German" in Bizet's *Carmen* (*Bizet*, 22).

27. I am arguing that Bizet uses the comic-opera form in anticipation of what Lacoue-Labarthe calls, in his discussion of Schoenberg's *Sprechgesang*, a "*méditation en acte*" (*Musica ficta*, 223).

28. Bizet, *Carmen. Opéra comique en quatre actes. Livret de Henri Meilhac et Ludovic Halévy d'après le roman de Prosper Mérimée*, ed. Gérard Billaudot (1875; reprint, Paris: Billaudot, 1981), 15. All translations from this original libretto are my own. It is the source for all of the citations of Bizet's *Carmen*, unless otherwise noted.

29. Susan McClary makes the point that in the original form of *Carmen* José prefers speech to song until, because of his emotional intensity, he is forced to express himself musically (*Bizet*, 46, 80).

30. Lawrence Kramer, "Musical Form and Fin-de-Siècle Sexuality," *Music as Cultural Practice, 1800–1900* (Berkeley: Univ. of California Press, 1990), 135–75.

31. Michel Poizat, *L'Opéra ou le cri de l'ange* (Paris: Métaillié, 1986), 70–78.

32. On the question of excess in operatic representation, see Herbert Lindenberger's *Opera: The Extravagant Art* (Ithaca: Cornell Univ. Press, 1984).

33. Jean-Louis Martinoty describes the relevance of the etchings by Davillier and Doré in their *Tour du monde illustré* album (1874) to Bizet's version of the *Carmen* story and its mise-en-scènes (100–106). See also McClary's discus-

sion of many reviewers of the first performance who consider the setting and music of the Parisian "café-concert," or cabaret, transported into the opera (*Bizet*, 52, 75).

34. It is striking in this light that reactions to the opening were all extreme in their praise or criticism of the piece. The largest selection of translated excerpts from the original reviews can be found in Mina Curtiss's book. Winton Dean relies almost exclusively on her translations. According to Eugène Héros's notes for "La Première de *Carmen*" (MS no. RO2604), "le tout Paris y était." In the audience were the reviewers of over twenty-four newspapers, along with theater directors and composers (Duquesnel, Cantin, Offenbach, Weber), performers (Hortense Schneider, Marie Colombrer, Jane Essler), and elegant worldly people (the Rothschilds, the Aguados, the prince of Sagan). This public was well disposed but remained indecisive in its overall appraisal of the show. These notes were eventually published in *Candide* (5 Feb. 1925) on the occasion of the fiftieth anniversary and resetting of *Carmen*.

35. Theodor Adorno, *In Search of Wagner*, trans. Rodney Livingstone (London: NLB, 1981), 100–101. Adorno makes a direct link between Wagner's *Gesamtkunstwerk* and the ideology of national socialism by associating their common tendency to conceal modes of production. Citing a letter of 23 March 1890 from Chamberlain to Cosima Wagner on Liszt's *Dante* symphony, Adorno associates ecstasy with concealment and national politics: "Perform this symphony in a darkened room with a sunken orchestra and show pictures moving past in the background—and you will see how all the Levis and all the cold neighbors of today, whose unfeeling natures give such pain to a poor heart, will all fall into ecstasy" (107).

36. Mina Curtiss (*Bizet*) remains the best and largest resource for the study of the first reviews of the opera, as I have noted, though all are translated, as they are in Winton Dean's *Bizet*. I am grateful to the curators at the Bibliothèque de l'Arsénal for help retrieving the originals.

37. It is also significant to note, in the context of this visual thematics of circles and enclosures, that Peter Brook begins his *La Tragédie de Carmen* with an image of these circles. As Frank Rich describes it in his review of the stage performance: "When we first meet the gypsy temptress Carmen, she tosses tarot cards into a small circle of rope placed on the dirt. When we last see her 80 minutes later she and her outcast soldier lover, Don José, make one final walk around the ring before meeting up with the destiny those cards have dealt. Many other circles come in between—drawn in sand and outlined in rope—but the largest of them all is not seen, only felt: it's the noose that Mr. Brook, through the astonishing power of his art, steadily tightens around the audience's throats"

(qtd. in Peter Brook, *A Theatrical Casebook* [London: Methuen, 1988], 350). For more on Brook's *Carmen*, see 334–52.

38. Clément makes the point that the walls of the arena are the visual counterpart to the division between the stage space and the space of the opera house, as well as, I might add, the division between the sonic and acoustic music every spectator encounters (Clément, *Opéra*, 102). In this performance space emblematically divided between fictive and real enclosures (the arena that is not there and the Salle Favart that is), while José and the orchestra are unable to stop the unbearable sliding of chromaticism characteristic of bohemian energy except through violence and closure, the arena duplicates the Salle Favart by providing a socially sanctioned place in which the ambiguities of law and pleasure can be contained and channeled. And, as Clément ultimately proposes, Carmen's energy continues to resonate between the protocols of fictive and real performance spaces.

39. Stendhal, *Racine et Shakespeare* (Paris: Calmann-Lévy, n.d.), 6.

40. Catherine Clément, *L'Opéra ou la défaite des femmes* (Paris: Bernard Grasset et Fasquelle, 1979). I shall be citing the text in French and bracketing Wing's translation, *Opera, or the Undoing of Women*, because I am interested in discussing the particular style of Clément's presentation. My own modifications are indicated in the text.

Chapter 4: *Carmen:* Choreofilm

1. David Wills makes the association between the four *Carmen* films of 1983–84 and the European Community, but he focuses on Carmen as an adaptation of Margaret Thatcher's relation to the Continent (*"Carmen:* Sound/Effect," 33). Rather than identifying Carmen with any real political figure, as does Wills, I am interested in exploring what Denis Bertrand considers Carmen's migratory or nomadic transcultural qualities in "Les Migrations de Carmen," *Le Français dans le Monde* 181 (Nov.–Dec. 1983): 103–8. Moreover, although Saura's film was a contemporary of Thatcher's government, it was also composed in the context of formal negotiations opened between Spain and the EC members in 1979 and with the original hope, following the *transición* and the election of Felipe Gonzáles, that Spain would enter the EC in 1983. In this light the film seems more specifically related to the very real problems (economic disparity, agricultural concerns, cultural and regional differences) posed by the potential entrance of the poorer Mediterranean members: Spain, Portugal, and Greece. On the history of Spain's relations to the EC, see Urwin, *Community of Europe*, 208–9.

2. I would reiterate my introductory suggestion that Godard's film also concerns itself with a formal *Carmen* in its interspersing, throughout the film narra-

tive, of pensive images of the ocean accompanied by Beethoven's quartets. This, however, is a formal *Carmen* inspired by Bizet's opera rather than by Mérimée's Spain or, as Godard put it in his interviews with the *Cahiers du cinéma: "Carmen, c'est la musique!"*

3. Susan Leigh Foster offers an insightful discussion of Yvonne Rainer's use of narrative in her choreography as a foil that foregrounds the ways in which the dancing body is mapped and coded by cultural and ideological pressures (*Reading Dancing: Bodies and Subjects in Contemporary American Dance* [Berkeley: Univ. of California Press, 1986], 187–88, 259 n. 3).

4. This purer image of European identity is taken up by Frédéric Deval in *Le Flamenco et ses valeurs* (Paris: Aubier, 1989), 12, 23.

5. In "Les migrations de Carmen" Denis Bertrand reads Carmen as a nomadic signifier open to all kinds of new readings (105). Although he also notes that the tale is shaped around a series of oppositions—order and disorder, defiance and fatality, festival and tragedy, etc. (105)—he never attends to the structural and formal oppositions undoubtedly responsible for *Carmen's* continual renewing of the liberation of signifying possibilities in the various doubled forms characteristic of its successive versions.

6. Marvin D'Lugo, *The Films of Carlos Saura: The Practice of Seeing* (Princeton: Princeton Univ. Press, 1991), 8–10, 53.

7. Put otherwise, although D'Lugo cites Christian Metz's admonition that any study of the film apparatus must be informed by both psychoanalytic and sociological inquiries (*Films of Saura*, 10), D'Lugo only considers the sociological imperatives of the cinematic apparatus in Saura's films. I am suggesting, on the other hand, that, as we attend to the transposing of earlier models in the film, we become aware that in its theatricalized encounter of social and psychic pressures, Saura's *Carmen* stages the potential adaptation of cultural identities as well.

8. Susan McClary discusses the ideological force of the orchestral frame of Bizet's opera in *Bizet* (62–66) and *Feminine Endings* (53–79). On Mérimée's use of the frame narrative, see Bowman, "Narrator and Myth," 475–82; Laurence M. Porter, "Subversion of the Narrator in Mérimée's 'La Vénus d'Ille,'" *Nineteenth Century French Studies* 10, nos. 3–4 (1982): 268–77; and Robinson, "Mérimée's *Carmen*," 1–2, 13–14.

9. Claudia Gorbman, *Unheard Melodies: Narrative Film Music* (Bloomington: Indiana Univ. Press, 1987), 11–18.

10. This gesture of self-distinction calls to mind the first film in Saura's dance trilogy, *Blood Wedding*, in which Gades, as Leonardo, is clearly distinguished from the rest of the company.

11. Nietzsche, *Nietzsche contra Wagner*, 666. It is striking, in the context of

Saura's filming of theatrical dance, that Nietzsche associates this "wariness" with the rhythms of dance and places it in vigorous opposition to the effect Wagner creates of swimming and submergence. It is also significant that Gorbman *(Unheard Melodies)* associates "unheard melody" with Wagnerian sound.

12. In *Introduction to the Dance* John Martin uses the concept of "inner mimicry" to account for the way in which participants identify in an imaginary kinesthetic manner with bodies exactly like our own: "though to all outward appearances we shall be sitting quietly in our chairs, we shall nevertheless be dancing synthetically with all our musculature" (qtd. in Foster, *Reading Dancing*, 256–57 n. 76).

13. On the imaginary fantasy of the dancer's body as a mobilized statue, see Pierre Legendre, *La Passion d'être un autre* (Paris: Seuil, 1978), 231–32.

14. *Merce Cunningham, le danseur et la danse,* interview with Jacqueline Lesschaeve (Paris: Pierre Belfond, 1980), 78–79, 82.

15. D'Lugo also considers the dance mirror to be the film's "principal agency of narrative enunciation," but he is most concerned with its ironic function as the "signifier of the spectacle of imposture to which Antonio is bound" *(Films of Saura,* 206). That is, whereas D'Lugo never wavers in his sense that Gades is unable to either live or choreograph anything not already determined by "cultural imposture," I argue that the film focuses on performance and "aliveness" as a way out of the colonized culture and, especially, from the perspective of the film "reader." It does so, I shall argue, by offering only partial scenes and blurred boundaries and by remaining, in the end, unfinished.

16. This ending always works as a sign of the film's formal duplicity but is rarely conceived from this perspective. Rather, everyone seems amazed by it, as if it were revealing something about the imaginary/real components of the film that were not present from the start. See, for example, McClary, *Bizet,* 135–36; and D'Lugo, *Films of Saura,* 212.

17. Karin Pendle, *Eugène Scribe and the French Opera of the Nineteenth Century* (Ann Arbor, Mich.: UMI Research Press, Studies in Musicology, 1979), 339–43.

18. Stanley Brandes, *Metaphors of Masculinity* (Philadelphia: Univ. of Pennsylvania Press, 1980), 58.

19. Marian Smith discusses the use of familiar melodies from opera to aid the dance spectator's narrative sense of performances during the 1830s and '40s in Paris ("Borrowings and Original Music: A Dilemma for the Ballet-Pantomime Composer," *Dance Research* 6, no. 2 [Fall 1988]: 3–29).

20. Conley insists that the appearance of written words in film always supposes, in addition, a highly charged signifying moment (*Film Hieroglyphs* [Minneapolis: Univ. of Minnesota Press, 1991]).

Works Consulted

Abbate, Carolyn. *Unsung Voices: Opera and Musical Narrative in the Nineteenth Century*. Princeton: Princeton Univ. Press, 1991.

———. "Erik's Dream and Tannhäuser's Journey." In *Reading Opera*. Ed. Arthur Groos and Roger Parker, 129–67. Princeton: Princeton Univ. Press, 1988.

Abbate, Carolyn, and Roger Parker. *Analyzing Opera: Verdi and Wagner*. Berkeley: Univ. of California Press, 1989.

Adorno, Theodor. *Aesthetics and Politics*. Ed. and trans. Ronald Taylor. London: Verso, 1977.

———. *In Search of Wagner*. Trans. Rodney Livingstone. London: NLB, 1981.

———. *Philosophy of Modern Music*. Trans. Anne G.Mitchell and Wesley V. Blomster. New York: Seabury Press, 1973.

———. "Fantasia sopra Carmen." *Gesammelte Schriften*. Vol. 16. Ed. Rolf Tiedermann. Frankfurt: Suhrkamp Verlag, 1978.

Anderson, Benedict. *Imagined Communities*. 1983. Reprint. London: Verso, 1993.

Anderson, Laurie. *Stories from the Nerve Bible: A Retrospective, 1972–1992*. New York: HarperCollins, 1994.

Anzieu, Jacques. *Le Moi-peau*. Paris: Bordas, 1985.

Arc. L'Opéra comme théâtre 27 (Dec. 1990).

Armstrong, Nancy. *Desire and Domestic Fiction: A Political History of the Novel*. New York: Oxford Univ. Press, 1987.

Armstrong, Nancy, and Tennenhouse, Leonard. *The Imaginary Puritan: Litera-*

ture, Intellectual Labor, and the Origins of Personal Life. Berkeley: Univ. of California Press, 1992.

Bakhtin, Mikhail Mikhailovich. "Epic and Novel." In *The Dialogic Imagination.* Ed. Michael Holquist. Trans. Caryl Emerson and Michael Holquist, 3–40. Austin: Univ. of Texas Press, 1981.

Barthes, Roland. *Image, Music, Text.* Trans. Stephen Heath. New York: Hill and Wang, 1978.

———. "Le Discours de l'histoire." *Poétique* 49 (Feb. 1982): 12–21.

Batchelor, Jennifer. "From *Aïda* to *Zauberflöte*—The Opera Film." *Screen* 25, no. 3 (May–June 1984): 26–38.

Baudelaire, Charles. *Oeuvres complètes.* 2 vols. Ed. Claude Pichois. Paris: Gallimard, 1975.

———. "Richard Wagner et *Tannhaüser* à Paris." *L'Art romantique. Oeuvres complètes.* Vol 3. Ed. Jacques Crépet. Paris: Louis Conard, 1923.

Baudelaire: actes du colloque de Nice. Paris: Minard, 1968.

Bénédict. "Revue musicale." *Le Figaro,* 3 Mar. 1975.

Benjamin, Walter. *Charles Baudelaire: A Lyric Poet in the Era of High Capitalism.* Trans. Harry Zohn. London: NLB, 1973.

Bernard, Suzanne. *Le Poème en prose de Baudelaire à nos jours.* Paris: Nizet, 1959.

Bersani, Leo. *Baudelaire and Freud.* Berkeley: Univ. of California Press, 1977.

Berthier, Philippe, and Kurt Ringger, eds. *Littérature et opéra. Colloque de Cérisy, 1985.* Grenoble: Presses Universitaires de Grenoble, 1987.

Bertrand, Denis. "Les Migrations de Carmen." *Le Français dans le Monde* 181 (Nov.–Dec. 1983): 103–8.

Bishop, Tom. "I Love You, Moi Non Plus." In *France's Identity Crises.* Ed. Lawrence D. Kritzman. *SubStance* 76–77 (1995): 21–29.

Bizet, Georges. *Carmen. Opéra comique en quatre actes. Livret de Henry Meilhac et Ludovic Halévy d'après le roman de Prosper Mérimée.* Ed. Gérard Billaudot. 1875. Reprint. Paris: Billaudot, 1981.

———. *Carmen: Opera in Four Acts.* New York: G. Schirmer, 1959.

———. *Carmen, Oper in drei Akten von Henri Meilhac und Ludovic Halévy.* Ed. Fritz Oeser. Kassel: Alkor-Edition, 1964.

———. *Lettres (1850–1875).* Ed. Claude Glayman. Paris: Calmann-Lévy, 1989.

Blanchard, Gérard. *Images de la musique de cinéma.* Paris: Edilig, 1984.

Borch-Jacobsen, Mikkel. *Lacan: le maître absolu.* Paris: Flammarion, 1990.

———. *Lacan: The Absolute Master.* Trans. Douglas Brick. Stanford, Calif.: Stanford Univ. Press, 1991.

Borrow, George Henry. *The Zincali, An Account of the Gypsies of Spain. The Works of George Borrow.* Ed. Clement Shorter. Vol. 10. New York: G. Wells, 1923–24.

Bowie, Malcolm. *Freud, Proust and Lacan: Theory as Fiction.* Cambridge: Cambridge Univ. Press, 1987.

Bowman, Frank Paul. "Narrator and Myth in Mérimée's 'Vénus d'Ille.'" *French Forum* 33 (1960): 475–82.

Brandes, Stanley. *Metaphors of Masculinity: Sex and Status in Andalusian Folklore.* Philadelphia: Univ. of Pennsylvania Press, 1980.

Braudel, Fernand. *Ecrits sur l'histoire.* Paris: Seuil, 1969.

Brook, Peter. *A Theatrical Casebook.* London: Methuen, 1988.

Brooks, Peter. *Reading for the Plot: Design and Intention in Narrative.* New York: Vintage Books, Random House, 1985.

Cahiers Eidôlon. Special issue. *Carmen.* 25 (Oct. 1984).

Case, Sue-Ellen. *Performing Feminisms: Feminist Critical Theory and Theater.* Baltimore: Johns Hopkins Univ. Press, 1990.

Célis, Raphäel, ed. *Littérature et musique.* Brussells: Facultés Universitaires Saint-Louis, 1982.

Certeau, Michel de. *L'Ecriture de l'histoire.* Paris: 1975.

Chambers, Ross. *Room for Maneuver: Reading (the) Oppositional (in) Narrative.* Chicago: Univ. of Chicago Press, 1991.

———. *Story and Situation: Narrative Seduction and the Power of Fiction.* Minneapolis: Univ. of Minnesota Press, 1984.

———. "Poetry in the Asiatic Mode, Baudelaire's 'Au Lecteur.'" *Phantom Proxies: Symbolism and the Rhetoric of History. Yale French Studies* 74 (1988): 97–116.

———. "Violence du récit: Boccace, Mérimée, Cortázar." *Canadian Review of Comparative Literature* 13, no. 2 (1986): 159–86.

Chion, Michel. *Le Son au cinéma.* Paris: *Cahiers du Cinéma* / Editions de l'Etoile, 1985.

Clément, Catherine. *L'Opéra ou la défaite des femmes.* Paris: Grasset et Fasquelle, 1979.

———. *Opera, or the Undoing of Women.* Trans. Betsy Wing. Minneapolis: Univ. of Minnesota Press, 1988.

Cogman, P. W. M. "The Narrators of Mérimée's *Carmen.*" *Nottingham French Studies* 27, no. 2 (1988): 1–12.

Collier, Mary Blackwood. *La Carmen essentielle et sa réalisation au spectacle.* Peter Lang, forthcoming.

———. "Carmen: Femme Fatale or Modern Myth?" Paper presented at the Eighteenth Annual Colloquium on Literature and Film, West Virginia University, Sept. 1993.

Combe, Dominique. *Poésie et récit: une rhétorique des genres.* Paris: José Corti, 1989.

Comettant, Jean-Pierre Oscar. "Revue musicale." *Le Siècle*, 15 Mar. 1875.

Conley, Tom. *Film Hieroglyphs: Ruptures in Classical Cinema*. Minneapolis: Univ. of Minnesota Press, 1991.

Conrad, Peter. *Romantic Opera and Literary Form*. Berkeley: Univ. of California Press, 1977.

————. *A Song of Love and Death: The Meaning of Opera*. New York: Poseidon Press, 1987.

Curtiss, Mina. *Bizet and His World*. New York: Knopf, 1958.

Dahlhaus, Carl. *Musikalischer Realismus*. Munich: Piper, 1982.

————. *Richard Wagner's Music Dramas*. Cambridge: Cambridge Univ. Press, 1979.

Dällenbach, Lucien. *Le Récit spéculaire: essai sur la mise en abyme*. Paris: Seuil, 1977.

Dasgupta, Gautam. "Italian Theater in the New Europe: Notes on Santarcangelo dei Teatri XXII." *Performing Arts Journal* 44 (May 1993): 63–70.

Dean, Winton. *Bizet*. London: J. M. Dent, 1975.

De Lauretis, Teresa. *Alice Doesn't: Feminism, Semiotics, Cinema*. Bloomington: Indiana Univ. Press, 1981.

Deleuze, Gilles, and Félix Guattari. *L'Anti-Oedipe: capitalisme et schizophrénie*. Paris: Editions de Minuit, 1975.

————. *Anti-Oedipus*. Trans. Robert Hurley, Mark Seem, and Helen R. Lane. Minneapolis: Univ. of Minnesota Press, 1983.

Derrida, Jacques. *The Other Heading: Reflections on Today's Europe*. Trans. Pascale-Anne Brault and Michael B. Naas. Bloomington: Indiana Univ. Press, 1992.

Deval, Frédéric. *Le Flamenco et ses valeurs*. Paris: Aubier, 1989.

D'Lugo, Marvin. *The Films of Carlos Saura: The Practice of Seeing*. Princeton: Princeton Univ. Press, 1991.

During, Simon, ed. *The Cultural Studies Reader*. London: Routledge, 1993.

Europe 760–61 (Aug.–Sept. 1992).

Flaubert, Gustave. *Madame Bovary*. Paris: Garnier Flammarion, 1966.

Fleshman, Sherrie. "Transitions in Narrative Distancing in the Short Stories of Balzac, Mérimée, and Flaubert." Ph.D. diss., University of Oregon, 1994.

Foster, Susan Leigh. *Reading Dancing: Bodies and Subjects in Contemporary American Dance*. Berkeley: Univ. of California Press, 1986.

Foucault, Michel. *L'Archéologie du savoir*. Paris: Gallimard, 1969.

————. *L'Histoire de la sexualité*. 3 vols. Paris: Gallimard, 1976.

France's Identity Crises. Ed. Lawrence D. Kritzman. *SubStance* 76–77 (1995).

Füglister, Robert L. "Baudelaire et le thème des bohémiens." *Etudes Baudelairiennes II*, 99–143. Neuchâtel, Switz.: La Baconnière, 1971.

Fulcher, Jane F. *The Nation's Image: French Grand Opera as Politicized Art.* Cambridge: Cambridge Univ. Press, 1987.

Furet, François, and Richet, Denis. *La Révolution.* Paris: Réalités Hachette, 1965.

Furman, Nelly. "The Languages of Love in *Carmen.*" In *Reading Opera.* Ed. Arthur Groos and Roger Parker, 168–83. Princeton: Princeton Univ. Press, 1988.

Gaudier, Charles. *Carmen de Bizet: Etude historique et critique, Analyse musicale.* Paris: Librairie Delaplane, 1922.

Gautier, Théophile. *Emaux et Camées.* Paris: Minard, 1968.

———. *Histoire de l'art dramatique en France depuis vingt-cinq ans.* 6 vols. Leipzig: Hetzel, 1858–59.

Genette, Gérard. *Figures I, II, III.* Paris: Seuil, 1966–72.

Godard, Jean-Luc. *Jean-Luc Godard par Jean-Luc Godard.* Ed. Alain Bergala. *Cahiers du Cinéma* / Editions de l'Etoile, 1985.

Gombrich, E. H. *Art and Illusion.* New York: Pantheon, 1956.

Gorbman, Claudia. *Unheard Melodies: Narrative Film Music.* Bloomington: Indiana Univ. Press, 1987.

Gould, Evlyn. "Prosper Mérimée Is Thinking the Revolution." In *The French Revolution of 1789 and Its Impact.* Ed. Gail Schwab and John R. Jeanneney, 135–45. Westport, Conn.: Greenwood Press, 1995.

Guichard, Daniel. "Mérimée, *Carmen* (Chapitre III)." *L'Ecole des Lettres* 77, no. 15 (June 1986): 25–37.

Harrison, Hank. *The Dead Book: A Social History of the Grateful Dead.* New York: Links Books, 1973.

Héros, Eugène. "La Première de *Carmen.*" *Candide,* 5 Feb. 1925. MS no. RO2604.

Hobsbawm, Eric J. *The Age of Empire, 1875–1914.* New York: Vintage Books, 1989.

———. *Nations and Nationalism since 1780: Programme, Myth, Reality.* Cambridge: Cambridge Univ. Press, 1990.

Hollier, Denis, ed. *A New History of French Literature.* Cambridge: Harvard Univ. Press, 1989.

Horrocks, Gillian. "A Semiotic Study of *Carmen.*" *Nottingham French Studies* 25, no. 2 (1986): 60–72.

Hunter, Robert. *A Box of Rain, Lyrics, 1965–1993.* New York: Penguin, 1993.

James, Harold. *A German Identity, 1770–1990.* New York: Routledge, Chapman, and Hall, 1989.

Jameson, Fredric. *Ideologies of Theory.* 2 vols. Minneapolis: Univ. of Minnesota Press, 1988.

————. *The Political Unconscious: Narrative as a Socially Symbolic Act.* Ithaca: Cornell Univ. Press, 1981.

Johnson, Barbara. *Défigurations du langage poétique: la seconde révolution baudelairienne.* Paris: Flammarion, 1979.

Kaufmann, Vincent. *Le Livre et ses adresses (Mallarmé, Ponge, Valéry, Blanchot).* Paris: Méridiens Klincksieck, 1986.

Kerman, Joseph. *Opera as Drama.* New York: Knopf, 1956.

Kivy, Peter. *Osmin's Rage: Philosophical Reflections on Opera, Drama, and Text.* Princeton: Princeton Univ. Press, 1988.

Knight, Arthur and Kit, eds. *Kerouac and the Beats: A Primary Sourcebook.* New York: Paragon House, 1988.

Koestenbaum, Wayne. *The Queen's Throat.* New York: Poseidon Press, 1993.

Kramer, Lawrence. *Music as Cultural Practice, 1800–1900.* Berkeley: Univ. of California Press, 1990.

Kristeva, Julia. *Etrangers à nous-mêmes.* Paris: Gallimard, 1988.

————. *La Révolution du langage poétique: l'avant-garde à la fin du XIXe siècle: Lautréamont et Mallarmé.* Paris: Seuil, 1974.

————. "Women's Time." *Feminist Theory: A Critique of Ideology.* Chicago: Univ. of Chicago Press, 1981.

Lacan, Jacques. *Ecrits.* Paris: Seuil, 1966.

————. *Encore.* Paris: Seuil, 1975.

————. *Le Séminaire, livre XX.* Paris: Seuil, 1975.

Lacoue-Labarthe, Philippe. *Musica ficta (figures de Wagner).* Paris: Christian Bourgois, 1991.

Lafont, Robert. *Nous, peuple européen.* Paris: Editions Kimé, 1991.

Lagenevais, F. de. "Revue musicale." *Revue des Deux Mondes,* 15 Mar. 1875.

Lauzières, Achille de. "Revue musicale." *La Patrie,* 15 Mar. 1875.

Legendre, Pierre. *La Passion d'être un autre.* Paris: Seuil, 1978.

Levin, David J., ed. *Opera through Other Eyes.* Stanford: Stanford Univ. Press, 1994.

Lindenberger, Herbert. *Opera: The Extravagant Art.* Ithaca: Cornell Univ. Press, 1984.

Maclean, Marie. *Narrative as Performance: The Baudelairean Experiment.* London: Routledge, 1988.

Mallarmé, Stéphane. *Oeuvres complètes.* Ed. Jean Aubry and Henri Mondor. Paris: Gallimard, 1945.

Mannoni, Octave. *Clefs pour l'Imaginaire ou l'Autre Scène.* Paris: Seuil, 1969.

Marinis, Marco de. *The Semiotics of Performance.* Trans. Aine O'Healy. Bloomingon: Indiana Univ. Press, 1993.

Martinoty, Jean-Louis. "De la Réalité au réalisme." *L'Avant-Scène Opéra* 26 (Mar.–Apr. 1980): 100–106.

Matteo, and Carola Goya. *The Language of Spanish Dance*. Norman: Univ. of Oklahoma Press, 1990.

McClary, Susan. *Feminine Endings: Music, Gender, and Sexuality*. Minneapolis: Univ. of Minnesota Press, 1991.

———, ed. *Georges Bizet: Carmen*. New York: Cambridge Univ. Press, 1992.

Merce Cunningham, le danseur et la danse. Interview with Jacqueline Lesschaeve. Paris: Pierre Belfond, 1980.

Mérimée, Prosper. *Carmen. Romans et nouvelles*. Ed. Henri Martineau. Paris: Gallimard, 1951.

———. "Lettre sur les voleurs en Espagne." *Revue de Paris* (Aug. 1832).

Miner, Margaret. "Dionysos parmi les bohémiens, un parcours baudelairien." *Europe* 760–61 (Aug.–Sept. 1992): 48–61.

———. "Putting the Emphasis on Music: Baudelaire and the *Lohengrin* Prelude." *Nineteenth-Century French Studies* 21, nos. 3–4 (Spring–Summer 1993): 384–401.

Mitchell, W. J. T. *On Narrative*. Chicago: Univ. of Chicago Press, 1980.

Morin, Edgar. *Penser l'Europe*. Paris: Gallimard, 1987.

Mosse, George L. *Nationalism and Sexuality: Respectability and Abnormal Sexuality in Modern Europe*. New York: H. Fertig, 1985.

Murger, Henry. *Scènes de la vie de Bohême*. Ed. Michel Lévy. 1861. Reprint. Paris: Editions d'Aujourd'hui, 1979.

Nietzsche, Friedrich. *The Birth of Tragedy and the Case of Wagner*. Trans. Walter Kaufmann. New York: Random House, 1967.

———. *Nietzsche contra Wagner*. In *The Portable Nietzsche*. Ed. and trans. Walter Kaufmann, 661–83. New York: Viking Penguin, 1954.

———. "Wagners Kunst ist Krank." *Die Geburt der Tragödie, Der Fall Wagner, Werke* 1–2. Ed. Karl Schlechter. Darmstadt, Ger.: Wissenschaftliche Buchgesellschaft, 1964.

Oeser, Fritz, ed. *Carmen, Oper in drei Akten von Henri Meilhac und Ludovic Halévy*. Kassel, Ger.: Alkor-Edition, 1964.

Ollier, Jacqueline. "Carmen d'hier et d'aujourd'hui." *Corps Ecrit: L'Opéra* 20 (Dec. 1986): 113–22.

Orgel, Stephen. *The Illusion of Power*. Berkeley: Univ. of California Press, 1975.

Orr, Linda. *Headless History: Nineteenth-Century French Historiography of the Revolution*. Ithaca: Cornell Univ. Press, 1990.

———. "The Blind Spot of History: Logography." *Yale French Studies* 73 (1987): 190–214.

———. "The Revenge of Literature: A History of History." *New Literary History* 18 (1986–87): 1–22.

————. "*The Clothing of Clio* by Stephen Bann." *History and Theory* 24, no. 3 (1985): 307–25.

Oswald, François. "Revue musicale." *Le Gaulois*, 3 Mar. 1875.

Parker, Douglas Charles. *Georges Bizet: His Life and Works*. Freeport, Conn.: Books for Libraries Press, 1969.

Pendle, Karin. *Eugène Scribe and the French Opera of the Nineteenth Century*. Ann Arbor: UMI Research Press. Studies in Musicology, 1979.

Phillips, Harvey E. *The Carmen Chronicle: The Making of an Opera*. New York: Stein and Day, 1973.

Pilkington, Anthony E. "Narrator and Supernatural in Mérimée's 'La Vénus d'Ille.'" *Nineteenth Century French Studies* 4, nos. 1–2 (1975–76): 24–30.

Poizat, Michel. *L'Opéra ou le cri de l'ange*. Paris: Métaillié, 1986.

Pomfret, John. "Exodus in Europe." *Washington Post National Weekly Edition*, 2–8 Aug. 1993: 6–7.

Porter, Laurence M. "Subversion of the Narrator in Mérimée's 'La Vénus d'Ille.'" *Nineteenth-Century French Studies* 10, nos. 3–4 (Spring–Summer 1982): 268–77.

Poulet, Georges. *La Poésie éclatée: Baudelaire/Rimbaud*. Paris: Presses Universitaires de France, 1980.

Pushkin, Alexander. *Collected Narrative and Lyrical Poetry*. Trans. Walter Arndt. Ann Arbor: Ardis, 1984.

Ramsland, Marie E. "Inspiration avec un sourire ironique: 'La Vénus d'Ille' de Mérimée." *Essays in French Literature* 23 (Nov. 1986): 19–28.

Reading Opera. Ed. Arthur Groos and Roger Parker. Princeton: Princeton Univ. Press, 1988.

Renan, Ernest. *Oeuvres complètes*. Paris: Calmann-Levy, 1947.

Reyer, Ernst. "Feuilleton." *Journal des Débats* (11 Mar. 1875).

Rimbaud, Arthur. *Complete Works, Selected Letters*. Trans. Wallace Fowlie. Chicago: Univ. of Chicago Press, 1966.

————. *Oeuvres complètes*. Paris: Gallimard, 1951.

Ringger, Kurt. "*Lucia di Lammermoor* ou les regrets d'Emma Bovary," in *Littérature et Opéra*, ed. Philippe Berthier and Kurt Ringger. Grenoble, Fr.: Presses Universitaires de Grenoble, 1987.

Robert, Frédéric. *Georges Bizet*. Paris: Seghers, Musiciens de tous les temps, 1965.

Robinson, Peter. "Mérimée's *Carmen*." *Georges Bizet: Carmen*, 1–14. New York: Cambridge Univ. Press, 1992.

Ross, Kristin. *The Emergence of Social Space: Rimbaud and the Paris Commune*. Minneapolis: Univ. of Minnesota Press, 1988.

Roy, Jean. *Bizet*. Paris: Seuil/Solfège, 1983.

Sand, George. *La Dernière Aldini*. Vie d'artistes, 129–254. Paris: Presses de la Cité, 1992.

Sartre, Jean-Paul. *Baudelaire*. Paris: Gallimard, 1947.

Schlossman, Beryl. *The Orient of Style*. Durham, N.C.: Duke Univ. Press, 1991.

Schmidgall, Gary. *Literature as Opera*. New York: Oxford Univ. Press, 1977.

Schor, Naomi. *George Sand and Idealism*. New York: Columbia Univ. Press, 1993.

Seigel, Jerrold. *Bohemian Paris: Culture, Politics, and the Boundaries of Bourgeois Life, 1830–1930*. New York: Viking Penguin, 1986.

Sieburth, Richard. "Symbolist Poets Publish *La revue wagnérienne:* The Music of the Future." In *A New History of French Literature*. Ed. Denis Hollier, 789–98. Cambridge: Harvard Univ. Press, 1989.

Smith, Marian. "Borrowings and Original Music: A Dilemma for the Ballet-Pantomime Composer." *Dance Research* 6, no. 2 (Fall 1988): 3–29.

Spectacle-Musique I, Opéra/Textes. Musique en jeu 14 (May 1974).

Steinmetz, Jean-Luc. *La Poésie et ses raisons*. Paris: José Corti, 1990.

Stendhal. *Racine et Shakespeare*. Paris: Calmann-Lévy, n.d.

Stewart, Susan. "The State of Cultural Theory and the Future of Literary Form." *Profession* (1993): 12–15.

Tambling, Jeremy. *Opera, Ideology and Film*. New York: St. Martin's Press, 1987.

Terdiman, Richard. *Discourse/Counter-Discourse: The Theory and Practice of Symbolic Resistance in Nineteenth-Century France*. Ithaca: Cornell Univ. Press, 1985.

Thomsen, Christian W. "Peter Brooks 'La Tragédie de Carmen' und Carlos Sauras 'Carmen'-Film. Zwei Experimenten in zeitgenössischer Theater- und Film-Ästhetik." *Studien zur Ästhetik des Gegenwartstheaters* (Winter 1985): 150–69.

Urwin, Derek W. *The Community of Europe: A History of European Integration since 1945*. London: Longman, 1991.

Vattimo, Gianni. *The End of Modernity: Nihilism and Hermeneutics in Postmodern Culture*. Trans. Jon R. Snyder. Baltimore: Johns Hopkins Univ. Press, 1988.

———. *La Fine della modernità*. Milan: Garzanti, 1987.

Velay-Vallantin, Catherine. *L'Histoire des contes*. Paris: Fayard, 1992.

Wallerstein, Immanuel. *Geopolitics and Geoculture*. Cambridge: Cambridge Univ. Press, 1991.

Weill, Georges. *L'Europe du XIXème siècle et l'idée de nationalité*. Paris: Albin Michel, 1938.

Weisstein, Ulrich. *The Essence of Opera*. 1964. Reprint. New York: Norton, 1969.

White, Hayden. *The Content of the Form: Narrative Discourse and Historical Representation*. Baltimore: Johns Hopkins Univ. Press, 1987.

————. *Metahistory: The Historical Imagination in Nineteenth-Century Europe.* Baltimore: Johns Hopkins Univ. Press, 1973.

————. "Figuring the Nature of Times Deceased." Eugene, Oreg.: University of Oregon, 1988.

————. "The Value of Narrativity in the Representation of Reality." "The Narrativization of Real Events." In *On Narrative.* Ed. W. J. T. Mitchell, 1–23. Chicago: Univ. of Chicago Press, 1980.

Wills, David. "*Carmen:* Sound/Effect." *Cinema Journal* 25, no. 4 (1986): 33–43.

Wing, Nathaniel. *The Limits of Narrative: Essays on Baudelaire, Flaubert, Rimbaud, and Mallarmé.* London: Cambridge Univ. Press, 1986.

Winn, James Anderson. *Unsuspected Eloquence.* New Haven, Conn.: Yale Univ. Press, 1981.

Zeldin, Theodore. *The French.* London: Collins, 1983.

Zizek, Slavoj. *The Sublime Object of Ideology.* London: Verso, 1989.

Index

oppositionality *(cont'd)*
in Mérimée, 60, 63–64, 87–88; in
opera, 6–8, 93–94, 98, 107; in
Rimbaud, 42–52
Orientalism, 77, 184n. 11; in Baudelaire, 29–30, 38–41; in Bizet, 91,
125–26; and Bohemia, 23–26, 55–
56, 59; in Rimbaud, 42–51, 193n.
13; in Saura, 162, 171, 202n. 15
Orr, Linda, 19, 61, 183n. 4, 184n. 5
Oswald, François, 116–17
otherness. *See* alterity

pan Europe, 10–13, 97, 181n. 12, 192n.
7; and Gypsies, 26; in Mérimée,
63, 76. *See also* Mazzini, Giuseppe;
nationalism
Parker, Roger, and Abbate, Carolyn,
90, 195n. 6
performance, 1, 2, 177; in Bizet, 66,
114–26; and community, 9–10,
32–33, 102, 157; in Saura, 153–55,
158–60 *(see also* Gypsies); in Wagner, 98–99, 100–101, 123–24. *See
also* dance; flamenco
*Petits poèmes en prose (Le Spleen de
Paris)* (Baudelaire), 30, 34–42, 36,
190n. 39
pleasure. *See jouissance*
Poizat, Michel, 110–12, 140–41, 150,
194n. 3
Pomfret, Jean, 11, 181n. 15
pop culture, 3, 101–2, 144–45; and ideology, 90, 107, 130
postmodernism, 20, 162
Poulet, Georges, 43
Prénom: Carmen (Godard), 1, 13, 152,
182n. 20, 200n. 2
presentational text, 104, 197n. 22; in
Bizet, 115–16; in Saura, 155, 164,
167, 176

print capitalism, 3, 55, 190n. 41. *See
also* nationalism
prose poem, 3, 63; in Baudelaire, 34–
42, 188nn. 27, 31, 189n. 34; in Rimbaud, 42, 44–51
psychoanalysis, 81, 103, 156; and film,
168–69, 201n. 7. *See also* identification; *jouissance*; unconscious, the
Pushkin, Alexander, 2, 31, 179n. 3

realist fiction, 61–62, 65, 71–72, 192n.
8; in film, 160–61, 171; in opera,
195n. 7, 196n. 13
récit, 44, 47, 189n. 35
renewability, 4, 12–13, 16–17, 152–54,
169, 201n. 5; of Baudelaire, 34–35,
36, 186n. 23, 188n. 27; of Bizet,
141–42; of Bohemia, 30–33, 52–59,
91, 186n. 22; of Rimbaud, 43–44,
50–52
rêverie, 95, 99–100. *See also* unconscious, the
*Review of the Two Worlds, The. See
Revue des deux mondes, La*
revolution: failed, 45, 50, 57–58, 163;
of 1968, 18–19, 22, 58 *(see also*
Bohemia); and opera, 92, 98; and
opposition, 56, 57 *(see also* oppositionality); and reminiscence, 26–
27, 67–68. *See also* counterculturalism; French Revolution
Revue des deux mondes, La, 10–11, 16,
61, 125
Reyer, Ernst, 141
Rimbaud, Arthur, 3, 16; and Baudelaire, 42–43, 51, 52; and the Beats,
190n. 40; and Bohemia, 29–31, 54,
59; and the Surrealists, 186n. 21;
and Wagner, 93, 101. Works: "Alchimie du verbe," 45; "Bateau
ivre," 42–44; "Coeur volé," 42;

Library of Congress Cataloging-in-Publication Data

Gould, Evlyn.
    The fate of Carmen / Evlyn Gould.
        p.   cm. — (Parallax)
    Includes bibliographical references and index.
    ISBN 0-8018-5366-4 (hardcover : alk. paper). — ISBN 0-8018-5367-2
(pbk. : alk. paper)
        1. Mérimée, Prosper, 1803–1870. Carmen.   2. Bizet, Georges,
1838–1875. Carmen.   3. Carmen (Motion picture : Emiliano Piedra
Productions)   4. Carmen (Fictitious character)   5. Performing arts—
History—20th century.   I. Title.   II. Series: Parallax
(Baltimore, Md.)
    PQ2362.C33G68   1996
    843'.7—dc20   96-10772
                                                                CIP

Lightning Source UK Ltd.
Milton Keynes UK
UKOW05f0615071113

220574UK00002B/67/A